PROPOSITIONS

to the PhD thesis *Out of Office, a study (*
Vacancy and Transformation as a Mea
by Hilde Remøy

1. The transformation potential of office buildings correlates to the time span of investment perspectives.

2. To prevent structural vacancy, flexible minds will contribute more than adaptable buildings.

3. Good design reduces vacancy risks.

4. High initial investments do not guarantee a longer lifespan.

5. Throwawayism is the biggest threat to a sustainable built environment.

6. The hog cycle in real estate is here to stay.

7. Valuing structurally vacant office buildings by their potential future rent is like assessing the survival potential of an already deceased patient.

8. High valuation of this book leads to lower book-values.

9. 10 birds in the bushes are worth 1 in the hand!

10. Doubt goes with science like belief goes with religion.

These propositions are considered opposable and defendable and as such have been approved by the supervisor prof. ir. H. de Jonge.

STELLINGEN

Bij het proefschrift *Out of Office, a study on the Cause of Office Vacancy and Transformation as a Means to Cope and Prevent* van Hilde Remøy

1. De transformatiepotentie van kantoorgebouwen correleert met de tijdspanne van investeringsperspectieven.

2. Om leegstand te voorkomen doet een flexibele geest meer dan aanpasbare gebouwen.

3. Een goed ontwerp verkleint het risico op leegstand.

4. Hoge investeringen zijn geen garantie voor een lange levensduur.

5. Wegwerpcultuur is de grootste bedreiging voor een duurzame omgeving.

6. De varkenscyclus in vastgoed zal blijven bestaan.

7. Het taxeren van leegstaande kantoorgebouwen op basis van verwachte toekomstige huurinkomsten vertoont een sterke overeenkomst met het schatten van de overlevingskansen van een overleden patiënt.

8. Een hoge waardering voor dit boek leidt tot lagere boekwaarden.

9. Beter 10 vogels in de lucht dan 1 in de hand!

10. Twijfel hoort bij wetenschap zoals geloof bij religie.

Deze stellingen worden opponeerbaar en verdedigbaar geacht en zijn als zodanig goedgekeurd door de promotor prof. ir. H. de Jonge.

Out of Office

Out of Office

A Study on the Cause of Office Vacancy and Transformation as a Means to Cope and Prevent

PROEFSCHRIFT

ter verkrijging van de graad van doctor
aan de Technische Universiteit Delft,
op gezag van de Rector Magnificus prof. ir. K. Ch. A. M. Luyben,
voorzitter van het College voor Promoties,
in het openbaar te verdedigen op
maandag 12 april 2010 om 10:00 uur

door Hilde Therese REMØY
Master of Science in Architecture, Norwegian University of Science and Technology
geboren te Herøy, Noorwegen

Dit proefschrift is goedgekeurd door de promotor
Prof. ir. H. de Jonge

Copromotor
Dr. ir. D.J.M. van der Voordt

Samenstelling promotiecommissie
Rector Magnificus, voorzitter
Prof. ir. Hans de Jonge, Technische Universiteit Delft, promotor
Dr. ir. D.J.M. van der Voordt, Technische Universiteit Delft, copromotor
Prof. dr. M.C. Kuipers, Technische Universiteit Delft
Prof. dr. ir. P.J.V. van Wesemael, Technisch Universiteit Eindhoven
Prof. dr. E. Finch, University of Reading
Prof. dr. S. Hunnes Blakstad, Norwegian University of Science and Technology

ISBN 978-1-60750-520-4

Keywords: Transformation, adaptability, structural vacancy, office buildings, locations and market

Published and distributed by IOS Press under the imprint Delft University Press

Publisher
IOS Press
Nieuwe Hemweg 6b
1013 BG Amsterdam
The Netherlands
tel: +31-20-688 3355
fax: +31-20-687 0019
email: info@iospress.nl
www.iospress.nl
www.dupress.nl

LEGAL NOTICE
The publisher is not responsible for the use which might be made of the following information

PRINTED IN THE NETHERLANDS

Contents

Preface

Cause

Conclusions 222

Preface

During my architectural study in Norway, I got acquainted with the architects love and hate for context. Though architects long for a tabula rasa, architecture cannot as such be experienced without context, but becomes meaningless, and hence, context is needed. This context is the existing built environment; transformed by every new building that is added to or subtracted from it, or by any change in the function, form, technique or economy of existing buildings. Transformation designs, just like the designs of new buildings, all lead to changes in the built environment. My interest for transformations of existing buildings eventually came from this notion. Transformations were an important part of the work, designing transformations of offices into a restaurant, of offices into housing, or the transformation into housing of a school still containing the memories of all the former pupils; they are all examples of functional and formal transformations, and all examples of how existing buildings shape the way we live and work.

Although transformations are an increasingly important part of real estate developments, I was interested in finding out why transformations do not take place more often. It seems quite absurd that so many buildings, such as offices and buildings for manufacturing, are left vacant while new buildings are developed at a high pace, sometimes even next to redundant buildings and often without convincingly higher quality. Does that mean that the existing buildings are functionally obsolete? Or maybe the owner of the building asks too high rents? At least, the location must be good; otherwise new buildings would not be developed there. Or…could new buildings possibly be built for speculation and will these within few years also be redundant? And why then, are redundant offices not sold or renovated or transformed to accommodate new functions?

These were all questions that made me apply for a PhD position at the faculty of architecture at Delft University of Technology. The questions I was so interested in finding an answer to, could be incorporated in research for the department of Real Estate & Housing. Dealing with such practical issues as office buildings, this thesis is intended not only for academics, but also for practitioners dealing with office buildings and the built environment. I hope this book will be a valuable addition to the discussions on office- and urban developments, and that it may inspire new ways of dealing with existing real estate.

Hilde Remøy, Rotterdam, January 2010.

INTRODUCTION

1 Introduction

1.1 Research field

This thesis examines transformation as a way of coping with structural vacancy in office buildings, and to which extent structural vacancy can be prevented in the future. Transformation in this research implies the functional transformation from offices into housing and changes that have to be made in the building structure to accommodate the new function, given that at least the load bearing structure has been kept. Structural vacancy is defined as vacancy of the same square metres of office space over a period of three years or longer, with no perspective on future tenancy.

Developing knowledge about the critical causes of structural vacancy is a fundamental part of this research. These causes will be explored and elaborated upon. The research comprises three partial studies, cause, cope and prevent, focusing on the cause of structural vacancy, if transformation is a possible way of coping with structural vacancy, and to which extent structural vacancy may be prevented or limited in the future. The three partial studies correspond to the three book-parts following this introduction.

This introduction chapter describes the research background and how it has been carried out. First, the research field is described, leading to a problem statement and the formulation of the main research questions. A short description of the research methodology follows, while the methodology is discussed more thoroughly in the subsequent book-parts. Finally, the chapter is concluded by the research design and an outline of the dissertation.

1.1.1 Office buildings, their locations and the commercial office market

Market

Commercial office markets are best described as markets where office space is sold and bought, let and rented, and characterised by the demand and supply of office space. Office markets worldwide grew as a result of growing business and financial services after the Second World War, fuelled by the need for flexible accommodation to support organisational growth and changes. Real estate became popular for investment companies looking for new assets (Kohnstamm and Regterschot 1994), creating a distance between the owner and the occupier perspective of office buildings and introducing the real estate developer and the investor as stakeholders in a commercial office market. In the Netherlands, 65% of the office stock is rental offices (Bak 2008). Within the commercial office market, office organisations choose accommodation based on quantitative and qualitative demands and preferences. Office organisations base their accommodation strategies on expected future demand for office space, compared to their current supply. By determining the future match of demand and supply, a plan for realising the supply needed in the future can be drawn, see Figure 1 (De Jonge et al. 2008).

The commercial office market may also be described by this model, though office space is then supplied by investors and demanded by the user

Designing an Accommodation Strategy (DAS model)

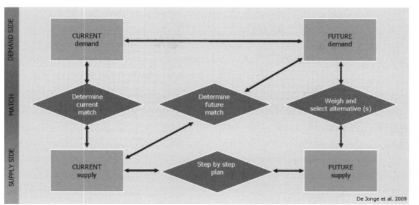

Figure 1 "Designing an accommodation strategy" (DAS model)

organisation. In the commercial real estate market there is no direct pursue for a match between demand and supply, though indirectly, a match is equal to a balanced and well functioning office market. Furthermore, real estate developers and investors recognise the advantages of a balanced office market and develop office space to achieve a best possible fit. When discussing the office market, this thesis focuses on the commercial office market.

Location

The office location has developed as specific part of the city during the 20th century. In the first years of the industrial revolution, office buildings were constructed near the industrial locations, or they were, like the earlier banks, governmental offices and stock-exchanges, located in the city centres, mixed with retail, culture and housing (Bluestone 1991). The ideology of the modern movement implied a functional separation of industry, offices, housing, retail and culture with infrastructure used to connect and separate the different functions. This ideology originated in ideas about creating a better life for the working class, separating housing from hazardous (industrial) activities and governing the workers' right to an eight hour day, but was developed further to comprise all urban functions. The functionalist ideals were leading in a period of large urban growth and are still dominating the lay-out of our cities, although our ideas about living and working are changing (Florida 2004). Transitions from the industrial to the information economy take place in cities throughout the world and impose changes in the built environment. Significant examples of urban transitions are the Docklands in London and the Bicocca in Milan, developed on former industrial sites that after years of urban growth had changed from fringe locations to central urban locations (Edwards 1992; Bastianello 1995). Newer monofunctional office locations were located on city fringes as well, and are still rather isolated. These locations accommodate a large part of the existing office supply.

13

Figure 2 Office building for Swiss Re, more commonly referred to as the "Gherkin", completed in 2003, and the Uffizi in Florence, completed in 1581

Building

As office buildings have changed significantly during the last 500 years, it is reasonable to discuss these changes and study how they relate to the preferences of office organisations and the way office buildings are used. The office building type as we know it today, represented by buildings like the "Gherkin" (Figure 2) has gone through quite some development from the first office building recognised as such by architecture historians: the Uffizi in Florence from 1581. Though buildings like this, accommodating offices for governments, banks and stock exchanges, existed already in medieval times, the Uffizi represents a building type that would be in use until the beginning of the 20th century. Specialised office buildings were not common until the industrial revolution, when development of mass production techniques and clustering of work in factories led to the need for coordination and administration. Office buildings were needed for this administrative revolution. The development of the office building type was led by the US, with Europe following and copying the American development (Frampton 1992; Duffy 1998; Van Meel 2000; Kohn and Katz 2002). The first office buildings were developed to accommodate the administration of industrial firms and were mostly constructed for an owner-user. As office employment grew; firms rather invested money in their core business than in their buildings; flexibility was needed and office buildings were standardised to meet the demands of standard office organisations. However, recent studies showed that office organisations have different demand profiles and therefore demand different types of offices (Worthington 1998; Van Meel 2000; Atelier V and Motivaction 2005; Gillen 2008). The standard office may not fit all office organisations. Additionally, due to technological progress, outsourcing of office work, demographic and cultural changes, the accommodation needs of office organisations change, influencing the functional lifespan of office buildings.

1.1.2 Transformation

As stated by Brand (1994) buildings are processes, not completed products. Still, buildings are static, or immobile, and accommodation strategies are necessarily directed towards a specified future match. The future fitness of use of a building is assessed at certain points in time both in corporate real estate management and in real estate management, and may lead to decisions of selling, demolishing, adapting or transforming a building in order to achieve a new match between demand and supply.

Transformation is a possible development when a building is structurally vacant and is assessed to be functionally obsolete while its technical lifespan is not ended. As a result of functional obsolescence, the building does not yield any financial benefit to its owner and is therefore also considered financially obsolete.

In literature (Nutt et al. 1976; Salway 1987; Baum 1993; Blakstad 2001), several forms of obsolescence are discussed:

- Aesthetic (visual) obsolescence, resulting from outdated appearance
- Functional obsolescence, resulting from changing ways of working
- Legal obsolescence, resulting from new legal standards
- Social obsolescence, resulting from image issues and increasing demands by occupiers
- Tenure obsolescence, resulting from disagreements between landlord and occupier
- Structural (physical) obsolescence, by Baum referred to as deterioration
- Financial obsolescence, resulting from misbalance between costs and benefits
- Environmental obsolescence, resulting from environmental changes (fine dust etc.)
- Locational obsolescence, resulting from functional obsolescence and image issues of the location
- Site obsolescence, resulting from misbalance between site value and building value

In this study, mainly functional, technical and financial obsolescence are discussed, as parallels to functional, technical and financial lifespans. Functional obsolescence in this study is seen as real and relative; covering also for aesthetic, legal and social obsolescence. Though the relationship between aesthetic and functional obsolescence can be discussed, they both occur as results of user dissatisfaction, just like social obsolescence. Legal obsolescence on the other hand, results from new legal standards. However, legal obsolescence is related to the functionality of the building, hence it is also comprised as functional obsolescence. Structural obsolescence is in this study referred to as technical obsolescence. Tenure obsolescence is not discussed further here, as mainly the relationship between physical characteristics and user preferences are studied. Environmental, locational and site obsolescence are not mentioned in this study. Site obsolescence should, according to definition, lead to demolition and new construction on the site. Environmental and locational obsolescence are implicitly incorporated in this study, and could be used to describe buildings that are structurally vacant because of the characteristics of their locations.

Adaptation or transformation is feasible if the building is functionally, technically and financially fit for new use, and if possible within the existing legal framework (Blakstad 2001; Heijer 2003). The buildings future value is determined by its value to the user; meaning the value in use by means of supporting the user's main activity, and its value to the owner, determined by the return on investment and therefore partly determined by the buildings (potential) value in use to the user (Douglas 2006). Next to financial motives, transformation may be triggered by a monumental status of the building or by specific historical, cultural or architectural values (Latham 2000; Back et al. 2004; Douglas 2006; Zijlstra 2006).

1.1.3 Preventing structural vacancy: Transformability

There are different approaches to prevent or limit structural vacancy in the future. Transformation is not only a possible way of coping with structural vacancy, but as a development strategy high transformation potential can also be a way of preventing or limiting structural vacancy. Preventing structural vacancy by this approach means that the adaptability and transformability of the building is optimised. Buildings functional adaptability or capacity to change has been studied intensively since the 1960s by groups like SAR (Stiching Architecten Research or in English: Foundation for Architectural Research) that was initiated by Habraken, following his book on adaptability in housing (Habraken 1972).

The aims of adaptability research have changed, from focusing on adaptability as a means of democratising the production of mass-housing to the current focus on functional change, temporal use and time-based architecture (Habraken 1972; Leupen et al. 2005). Adaptability has mainly been studied as an architectural concept, focusing on adaptability as a means of facilitating changes in the use and management phase of a building. In this research, extending buildings lifespan and thereby contributing to a more sustainable built environment is the reason to suggest adaptability and transformability as a means of preventing structural vacancy.

1.2 Problem statement

The high structural vacancy in the Dutch office market was the reason to start this research in 2005. The main objective was residential transformation of structurally vacant office buildings. Structural vacancy is seen as a problem and transformation as a possibility for coping with the structural vacancy in office buildings. However, only by knowing the cause of structural vacancy, its occurrence may be prevented, or may at least be limited in the future. Consequently, the working title of this dissertation has been "Structural vacancy of office buildings: Cause, Cope, Prevent".

By the end of 2007, the Dutch office market comprised approximately 45 million square metres office space (GLA[1]), of which 6 million square metres were vacant. As older buildings are left for preferred new buildings, the vacancy concentrates in the older stock and structural vacancy occurs. Estimates (DTZ 2007; Dynamis 2007) consider between 1 and 2 million square metres structurally vacant, sustaining the suggestion of a stratification of the real estate market where old buildings on decaying locations are deprived or even prospectless in the office market.

Structural vacancy is first of all a societal problem of economic and social decay. Uncertainty and social insecurity are visualised through vandalism and graffiti, break-ins and illegal occupancy. Though an investor may spread the risk of structural vacancy by building a diverse portfolio and only has to face building depreciation when selling, he also suffers a lack of income. Additionally,

---

1 The numbers are rough, as there is no total overview of the office building stock. Numbers are based on real estate agents databases and Bak (2008) and comprise buildings larger than 500 square metres within municipalities with a stock of more than 10000 square metres.

high vacancy hits building investors indirectly because of its negative influence on the market, though investors still tend to see the problem as somebody else's problem (Remøy and Van der Voordt 2007).

Transformation into housing is one of the possible ways to cope with structurally vacant office buildings, together with renovation and upgrading, consolidation, redevelopment, or demolition and new construction. An investor who is active in the office market is likely to choose consolidation or renovation and upgrading, but he can also choose to sell the building to a housing developer for residential transformation. Theoretically, if the net present value for transformation is higher than for consolidation, the building should be transformed. However, there are several obstacles for transformation as a way of coping with structural vacancy. The alleged high value of the structurally vacant building is the first obstacle, and is followed by the locations low potential for accommodating housing, the limited legal and financial feasibility of transformation, little knowledge and specific risks that are related to transformation projects and processes.

A concept for limiting future structural vacancy may be found by combining the knowledge about the cause of structural vacancy and transformation as a way of coping with it. Based hereupon, this dissertation responds to the goals described in 1.3, aiming at answering the main research questions.

1.3   Research goals and main research questions

The aim of this research is to develop and present knowledge on whether structural vacancy in existing office buildings can be coped with by transformation and to which extent it can be prevented in future buildings. Knowledge and insight in the critical causes of structural vacancy is fundamental for this research. These causes will be explored and elaborated upon. A conceptual framework will be developed and presented for building transformation as a means of coping with structural vacancy and as a way of preventing future structural vacancy. The following questions will focus on the cause of structural vacancy of office buildings, and how to cope with and prevent the problems related to structural vacancy:

1.   What are the causes of structural vacancy; which role do market conditions play and which part can be ascribed to location and building characteristics?

2.   Can building transformation be used to cope with structural vacancy? Compared to other alternatives, such as consolidation, redevelopment or adaptation; to which extent is building transformation a feasible way of coping with structural vacancy?

3.   To which extent can structural vacancy in new developments be prevented? Can structural vacancy be limited through the development of adaptable or transformable office buildings?

1.4 Research methodology

1.4.1 Research approach

Although the outline of this book suggests a chronological research from cause to cope to prevent, doing research and writing a dissertation is an iterative process. Developing a theoretical framework, testing this through literature studies and empirical studies and redefining the theory were done during the time span of four years within which this research was performed. This research comprises three

	Market	Location	Building
Cause			
Cope			
Prevent			

Table 1: The research structure is explained by this matrix that can be filled in by answering the main research questions.

main research themes, each requesting a different research strategy and the use of different research methods and tactics. Though the three themes could have been presented as three different studies, part of the results that are presented would then be left out: the whole is more than the sum of its parts. Hence, the research structure (Table 1) was an important part of the research strategy. This research can be described by 9 focal fields that were apparent in an early stage and that describe the structure of this research as a matrix of related partial studies.

1.4.2 Research perspective

The research as a whole is built up as a multiple phased research design; the three partial studies are defined separately and chronologically findings are used as input in the next partial study. As a whole and within each part, combined research strategies are applied; deductive as well as inductive methods are used. There are practical reasons for triangulation by combining strategies, as each research method has its strengths and weaknesses on all levels, from research perspective to research strategy and tactics, and since no method is without flaws (Patton 2002). The research perspective of this thesis is interpretive. From this point of view, triangulation by combining research strategies and tactics is a way of dealing with natural biases. The interpretive perspective implies that though a study may be conducted objectively, a research will never be value-free; the researcher's background will influence the social construction of reality (Miles and Huberman 1994; Groat and Wang 2002).

1.4.3 Research strategy

Literature reviews and theoretical framework

Literature reviews were used to develop a theoretical framework and generate hypotheses that are later tested based on empirical research in the first part, Cause. In part two and three of this dissertation, Cope and Prevent, literature review is used to broaden and connect existing studies (Groat and Wang 2002) and thereby

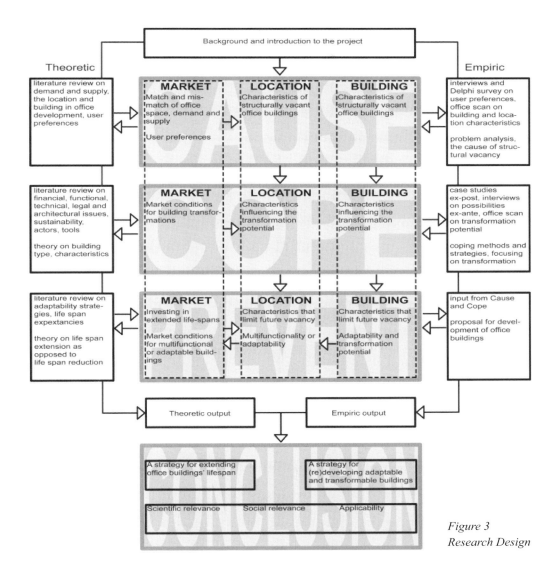

Theoretic   Empiric

Background and introduction to the project

literature review on demand and supply, the location and building in office development, user preferences

interviews and Delphi survey on user preferences, office scan on building and location characteristics

problem analysis, the cause of structural vacancy

MARKET
Match and mis-match of office space, demand and supply

User preferences

LOCATION
Characteristics of structurally vacant office buildings

BUILDING
Characteristics of structurally vacant office buildings

CAUSE

literature review on financial, functional, technical, legal and architectural issues, sustainability, actors, tools

theory on building type, characteristics

MARKET
Market conditions for building transfor-mations

LOCATION
Characteristics influencing the transformation potential

BUILDING
Characteristics influencing the transformation potential

COPE

case studies ex-post, interviews on possibilities ex-ante, office scan on transformation potential

coping methods and strategies, focusing on transformation

literature review on adaptability strate-gies, life span expectancies

theory on life span extension as opposed to life span reduction

MARKET
Investing in extended life-spans

Market conditions for multifunctional or adaptable build-ings

LOCATION
Characteristics that limit future vacancy

Multifunctionality or adaptability

BUILDING
Characteristics that limit future vacancy

Adaptability and transformation potential

PREVENT

input from Cause and Cope

proposal for devel-opment of office buildings

Theoretic output   Empiric output

A strategy for extending office buildings' lifespan

A strategy for (re)developing adaptable and transformable buildings

Scientific relevance   Social relevance   Applicability

CONCLUSION

Figure 3
Research Design

developing a theoretical framework. In Prevent this framework is further developed by deductions based on the empirical material from the two first parts, cause and cope. The literature reviews and development of the theoretical framework are discussed subsequently in the three chapters cause, cope and prevent.

Empirical studies, qualitative and quantitative methods

In the three parts, different research methods were used. Quantitative research methods are used to analyse large numbers of data to generate descriptive statistics and in order to make predictive statements about the relationship between characteristics and behaviour, as done by regression analyses. Qualitative research methods on the other hand, are used because they are suitable for analysing smaller amounts of data that contain detailed information, and because of the possibility they provide for understanding and explaining specific behaviours and processes.

1.4.4   Association with current and previous research

At the Delft University of Technology, the first studies on transformation as a means of coping with structurally vacant office buildings were conducted in the 'nineties. These studies were carried out by students and supervised by Van der Voordt and Geraedts. Subsequently, Van der Voordt and Geraedts continued the research, publishing a tool to determine the vacancy risk of office buildings (Geraedts and Van der Voordt 2003, 2007) and a tool to explore a buildings transformation potential (Geraedts and Van der Voordt 2003; 2007). In 2007, a book was published in Dutch on transformation of office buildings, focusing on examples, instruments, actors and other themes. The book was edited by Van der Voordt, Geraedts, Remøy and Oudijk (Van der Voordt et al. 2007). Part 1 of this research, Cause, is closely related to the PhD thesis of Philip Koppels (forthcoming, 2010), focusing on the correlation between physical characteristics of offices (building and location) and the office rent level. The empiric data collection for this part of the research was conducted in collaboration with Koppels, and several articles have been written based hereupon (Koppels et al. 2007; Remøy et al. 2007; Remøy et al. 2008; Koppels et al. 2009; Koppels et al. 2009; Remøy et al. 2009; Remøy et al. 2009).

1.4.5   Research design and outline

The thesis outline and research design describe the structure of the PhD research (Figure 3). The three themes of the research; cause, cope and prevent, are studied in the three main parts of this book. Subchapters describe aspects considering market, location and building for each of these themes. After the three main parts the research is concluded and ends with a reflection on the scientific and social relevance of this research and the relevance and applicability for practice.

CAUSE

Cause

Vacancy of office buildings is caused by a mismatch between demand and supply of office space. If the office market is unbalanced, the vacancy may rise substantially and lead to structural vacancy. If office space is continuously added to such a market, the structural vacancy will continue to increase. A mismatch in demand and supply is quantitative: there's simply an oversupply of office space in the market. However, a mismatch in demand and supply of office space is also a mismatch in the quality of the office space. Within an office market that is geographically limited, office users' preferences relate to the physical characteristics of a property's location and building characteristics. This section concentrates on revealing which location and building characteristics are preferred by office users and if structurally vacant office buildings share location and building characteristics that may possibly explain vacancy. The physical characteristics of structurally vacant office buildings are revealed.

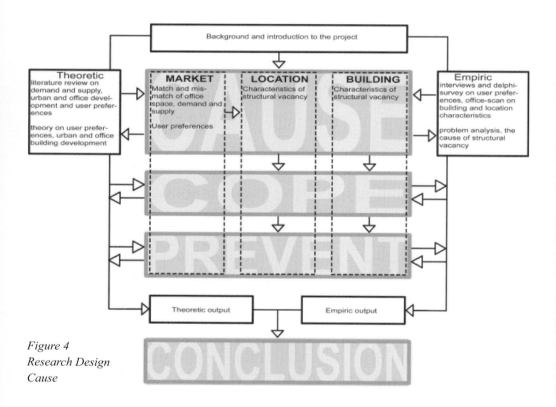

Figure 4
Research Design
Cause

2   Research Design Cause

In an unbalanced office market with a high vacancy level, the office users' preferences for specific location and building characteristics determine which buildings are rented out and which buildings remain vacant. Office users move within one office market, (re)locating to office buildings that fit their choice of a market segment, and that fit their preferences for locations and buildings that are described by specific characteristics.

Most studies on office users' preferences are stated preferences studies, most commonly based on interviews with CEO's or facility managers of office organisations. In this research, combined strategies are applied. Through a literature review, push and pull factors of office accommodation are studied, and by applying a Delphi-survey (stated preferences) office users preferences are revealed. The "Office Scan" reveals the physical characteristics of structurally vacant office buildings and locations and thereby tests the findings from the Delphi study. Using mixed methods is a way of triangulation or validating the findings of one study by applying a different study of the same phenomenon (Groat and Wang 2002; Patton 2002; Johnson and Onwuegbuzie 2004). In this research the literature review and the two empiric studies are of different weight, play different roles and are conducted as different phases of the research. This kind of research is often referred to as a multiple-phase design or a sequential design. According to Groat and Wang, it has its specific strengths and weaknesses, its strength being that each strategy can be presented fully and distinctly, while its weaknesses lie in the potential lack of connection and coherence between the different parts of the research. This potential pitfall is not specific only to this part of the research – Cause – but is also recognised to be one of the possible dangers of this whole research, as part 2 – Cope – builds forth on Cause, while finally part 3 – Prevent – again uses the results of both part 1 and 2. However, knowing the risks of the research design is the first step that needs to be taken to avoid the pitfalls and enhance its strengths. According to the aims of the research, the sequential design was found to be appropriate to this part of the research, which is specifically designed as a sequential exploratory design, where an exploratory qualitative study is followed by a quantitative validating or hypothesis testing study (Greene and Caracelli 1997; Sandelowski 2000; Hanson et al. 2005). The two empiric studies play significant different roles in the research. Though the first and exploratory empiric part would generate its own significant results, the power of the results may be disputed, whereas the second and quantitative study validates and empowers the first study by statistically significant results. On the other hand, the second and quantitative study could be conducted based on the literature review, without being preceded by the first empiric study. However, even if the results would be found significant, the choice of the research variables could imply an intrinsic research error. Again, the advantages of triangulation by using different research methods are apparent.

In the first empiric part of the research, the Delphi survey, location and building characteristics were defined based on the literature review of user preferences (Louw 1996; Korteweg 2002; Rodenburg 2005). The validity and importance of the predefined characteristics were tested and possible new characteristics were sought after. Six location characteristics and 15 building characteristics were defined. In the second part, the Office Scan, the results from the first part were tested, based on a study of 200 office buildings in Amsterdam. The study implies a quantitative study of location and building characteristics, studying the buildings' performance and structural vacancy level compared to the appearance of specific location- and building characteristics. In the remainder of this chapter, the methodology and techniques of the three parts will be described.

Both empiric data collections used were conducted to give input to this thesis and to the thesis of Koppels, with contribution from both researchers. The data collection was not restricted as result of the co-operation, on the contrary in some cases collected material was or seemed superfluous to one or the other thesis. However, the synergy effects of the joint effort prevailed over the possible negative effects. The analysis of the first study, the Delphi-survey, was also conducted as a joint effort. The results of this analysis were used as input for the Office scan, the second study, and were reported in two conference proceedings (Koppels et al. 2007; Remøy et al. 2007).

2.1 Literature review

Literature reviews may play different roles in a research; it may be used to identify research questions, to focus on the topic of inquiry or to broaden and connect existing knowledge, to understand the background of the research question, and to understand the origin of an idea and the current conceptual landscape in which this idea is embedded. In this study, the literature review was used to focus on the topic as well as for developing a context or setting a scene for the empiric part of the study (Groat and Wang 2002).

The context of this study is set by market conditions that impact the demand and supply of office space in the office market, conditions that are studied by means of the literature review. Henceforward, the market conditions resulting in vacancy and eventually structural vacancy are also studied by means of literature review. Additionally, some interviews were held, though these had the character of sustaining and completing the information already collected by the literature review. As this study focuses on revealing the location and building characteristics that are associated with structural vacancy, the literature review was also used to identify characteristics that are found to be of importance in existing studies on the same theme, thereby broadening and connecting existing knowledge and creating a point of departure for the empiric studies.

2.2 The Delphi Method

The Delphi-method was developed to predict long-range trends in science and technology. It has been extended to applications in policy formations and decision making and has become a widely used tool for validating and aiding forecasting and decision making in a variety of disciplines. In the field of real estate, the method has been sporadically used; see for example Green and Price (2000), Dewulf and de Jonge (1994). The Delphi method has been used with a variety of methodological interpretations and "modifications" (Powell 2003). Because of this "flexibility" it was criticised for lacking methodological rigour (Delbecq et al. 1975; Hasson et al. 2000; Okoli and Pawlowski 2004). Consequently research guidelines were developed and extended to increase the methods credibility. It is considered a useful technique for tapping and combining individual judgements in order to address a lack of agreement or an incomplete state of knowledge (Delbecq et al. 1975). In this study the Delphi ranking approach is applied. This approach has also been used in the management field to form group consensus about the relative importance of issues.

2.2.1 Technique

The Delphi technique is essentially a series of sequential questionnaires or "rounds", interrupted by controlled feedback, seeking to gain the most reliable consensus of opinion of a group of experts. Key elements of Delphi are to provide feedback to the panel members about their individual contributions of information and knowledge, assessment of the group judgement or view, the opportunity for individuals to revise their view and anonymity of the individual responses (Linstone and Turoff 1975). A possible approach to the first part of the study could have been through a stated preferences study among office user organisations (questionnaires, vignettes, and enquiries). There are several reasons for choosing another approach: office users only consider their choice of office space at the moment of relocations, which is not on a frequent base. Second, there's a considerable chance that only interested organisations would respond to the enquiry, so the result would not be representative for office organisations in general. Third, stated preferences are considered less valid; the respondent answers are biased towards a wanted situation, not towards a realistic situation.

A Delphi-approach on the other hand, has several advantages, as recognised by Okoli and Pawlowski (2004) and Hasson (2000). First, the expert panel consists of experts who deal with office space preferences on a daily basis and they would answer the questions more appropriately. Second, a panel of experts is more appropriate than any individual expert's answers: the study gains validity through inter-subjectivity. Third, when compared to other high-performing group decision methods, Delphi has the advantage that it does not require experts to meet physically. Fourth, the requirements for the size of the Delphi panel are modest since it does not depend on statistical power but rather on group dynamics for arriving consensus among experts: in this case 18 experts were involved. Fifth, the Delphi-study is flexible, the interviews with experts allow for the collection of richer data, informing further research. Additionally, the Delphi method might be used for further construct validation through asking the experts to react on the researcher's interpretation of the indicators or characteristics chosen for the study. Finally, non-response is typically very low in Delphi surveys since participation is mostly assured personally by the researchers, as it was in this study.

Several considerations should be taken into account to ensure the credibility of Delphi findings. First, the appropriateness of the Delphi method to address a specific subject should be defined (Fink et al. 1991). Second, clear guidelines should exist for the ranking procedure and for the number of objects to be used in subsequent rounds (Schmidt 1997). Third, the data collection procedures and format of the feedback to the panel members should be considered (Fink et al.

Figure 5
Panellists
ranking location
and building
characteristics
using cards.

1991). Fourth, a rigorous procedure should be used to identify and select relevant experts (Delbecq et al. 1975). Fifth, pre-defined criteria should be formulated for the identification of a justifiable consensus levels; and how many rounds are appropriate (Fink et al. 1991; Schmidt 1997). Finally, the researchers should make good use of available statistical techniques to support their conclusions.

2.2.2 Data collection

Commonly, a Delphi approach consists of two to four rounds of questions. The number of rounds depends on whether the research started uninformed with open questions or with a list of issues, the time available, and considerations of sample fatigue (Hasson et al. 2000). Typically, the first round is uninformed and consists of open questions. The open structure of the first round allows participants to elaborate on the topic investigated (Rowe 1994) and is believed to increase the richness of the data collected. The aim of the first round is to identify issues to be addressed in the subsequent rounds (Powell 2003). In this study though, the object of study has been extensively described in literature, from which in total fifteen building characteristics and six location characteristics were identified. Existing knowledge, limited time and possible sample fatigue, suggested a two round structure. In the first round interviews were held with each individual panellist. During the first part of the interview the experts were asked to rank the location and building characteristics according to the importance for the preference of a tenant. During the ranking process, the interaction between the panellist and the researcher was kept to a minimum. However, the panellists were encouraged to state their motivation for the provided rank. The second part of the interview consisted of semi-structured questions, allowing for validation of the provided list of characteristics and addition of characteristics. By structuring the interview in two parts, the benefits of an open, unstructured first round were incorporated in a two-round Delphi procedure. To ascertain the collective opinion, descriptive and inferential statistics were used. The second round was conducted by e-mail. By means of a short report the experts were informed about the ranking range of the characteristics and the average panel ranking, compared to their own ranking. This allowed the panellists to relate their own responses to the groups' responses. Subsequently, the panellists were asked to revise their ranking to obtain a higher degree of consensus.

The questionnaires and the ranking procedure were tested in two pilot rounds with fellow researchers as panel members. Pilot testing of questionnaires is said to be optional and may improve the feasibility of administration (Jairath and Weinstein 1994). The test rounds served to test the ranking procedure, to assess the number of characteristics that could be included in the survey, and to determine if the description of characteristics was consistent and evident. As a result, several changes were made in the procedure: the description of the context, characteristic descriptions and ranking instructions were extended, and two office user profiles were added. In the first test round, the panel members commented that ranking of the building- and location characteristics according to the general preference of tenants was difficult; office user preferences differ according to the organisation type. To cope with this predicament, two office user profiles were applied, based on profiles defined by Atelier V (Atelier V and Motivaction 2005), the two profiles are described in Table 2. These were used next to the previously used general profile. Atelier V recognises seven profiles; the selection of the two profiles was based on the proportion of users in the Amsterdam office market that fit these profiles, determined by means of transaction statistics. Henceforth, a second pilot round was performed satisfactorily; no further adjustments were made. The second pilot was performed with "fresh" panel members to reduce errors from possible learning effects.

Urban Specialists	Status sensitive professionals
Urban specialists depend on the urban surroundings wherein they operate. The urban environment inspires and alerts; their core business is dynamic. The organisations are small to middle sized service providers, who consider content more important than creativity. Urban specialists comprise (graphical) design firms, PR bureaus, consultants, real estate advisors and lawyers. The image and reputation of the organisation are important factors, but not as to gain a higher status.	Status sensitive professionals represent office organisations that already have a reputation and a renowned name. Often these organisations are large multinationals or big service providers. The firms name is a brand, a recognised trade name. The office buildings where these organisations are housed, do not have to enhance the firms' status, but should confirm it. Status sensitive professionals are considered conservative and risk avoiding.

Table 2 The office space user profiles used in this study as defined by Atelier V

2.2.3   The panel

There are two key aspects to consider in the composition of the expert panel; size and the qualifications of experts. The number of panel members may vary, for example Reid (1988) notes panel sizes ranging from 10 to 1685 while other recommend the number of participants to vary according to the scope of the problem and resources available (Delbecq et al. 1975; Fink et al. 1991; Hasson et al. 2000). Literature recommends a Delphi panel size ranging from 10 to 18 experts (Okoli and Pawlowski 2004). Some state that the more participants the better, since with increasing numbers of experts the reliability of a composite judgement increases. However, Delphi does not require the expert panel to be a representative sample for statistical purposes. Significance is based on the qualities of the expert panel (Powell 2003), and group dynamics (Okoli and Pawlowski 2004). To a great extent the credibility of the Delphi research findings depend on a careful selection of experts.

Selection of the appropriate experts is of critical importance for the Delphi method. An expert was previously defined as "informed individual" (McKenna 1994), as "specialist" in their field (Goodman 1987) or someone who has knowledge about a specific subject (Davidson 1997; Lemmer 1998; Green 1999). The vagueness of the term "expert" amplifies the importance of a structured and transparent approach for selecting the relevant experts. Heterogeneous expert panels, characterised by members with various backgrounds and points of view are believed to produce more reliable answers than homogeneous groups (Delbecq et al. 1975; Rowe 1994), due to the consideration of different perspectives and a wider range of alternatives. Okoli and Pawlowski (2004) have developed guidelines, based on those developed by Delbecq et.al (1975), for the selection of experts. They strongly recommend the use of a knowledge resource nomination worksheet (KRNW) to structure the selection of experts. The purpose of the KRNW is to help categorise the experts before actually identifying them and to prevent that important classes of experts are disregarded (Okoli and Pawlowski 2004). In this study, the experts should have significant knowledge about the users' selection criteria for office space. The panel members were selected from three disciplines; academics, practitioners and government officials (Table 3). Within the group of practitioners different subgroups were recognised; architects, real estate developers, facility advisors, real estate agents (brokers) and property investors. The selection criteria differed for the three disciplines.

Academics were selected based on their publications about office user preferences in the Dutch context. Practitioners were selected based on user orientation, market share and local Amsterdam office market knowledge. Relevant firms were identified for each subgroup, contacted through personal networks, and were asked to propose the most appropriate person within the firm to be a member of the expert panel. Government officials were selected based on relevant work experience and publications. Apart from the participants associated with the Delft University of technology, 14 organisations were asked to participate in the panel. All agreed to participate. Three organisations provided two experts from different departments.

Table 3: The expert panel composition

Disciplines	Number of experts
Acadamics	5
Architects	1
Real estate developers	1
Facility advisors	2
Real estate agents	5
Property investors	2
Goverment officials	2
Total number of experts	18

2.3 The Office Scan

Based on the results from the Delphi survey, the next phase in the two-phase research design was set up. The rankings of the Delphi survey concluded on 6 location characteristics and 15 building characteristics that are important to office organisations searching for new accommodation. The characteristics that were ranked in the Delphi study are applied in the office scan; studying the revealed preferences of office users in the Amsterdam market. The characteristics that were studied in the Delphi survey comprise several aspects that are measured separately in the office scan before they are combined again into one characteristic. For instance, layout flexibility comprises the square metres of a standard floor, the possibility for subdividing the floor into separate units, the distance between columns, the adaptability of the interior walls, the free floor height and the type of ICT infrastructure.

200 office buildings in Amsterdam were studied, and structural vacancy is registered in 106 of these. Structural vacancy is seen as the strongest indicator that office space is not preferred by the office users. The conditions for incorporating specific buildings in the study were clear; the user preferences should be measurable, so in buildings selected for the study either structural vacancy is registered, or at least one transaction has taken place in the building since 2001.

Following the conclusions of former research (Walen 1988; Dinteren 1989; Louw 1996; Korteweg 2002), the most preferred office buildings were expected to have sufficient parking places, have a good exterior appearance and contribute to the recognisability of its users. Also, the location of the building should have a high status and should be well accessible by car. Studies by DiPasquale (1996) and Dunse (2001) warns us about the importance of submarkets within office markets, and in a pre-study for the office scan the existence of submarkets within the Amsterdam market were revealed, defined geographically and by rent-level. The existence of submarkets within the Amsterdam office market suggests a hierarchy of location and building characteristics, according to which the influence of the location characteristics are subordinate to the spatially defined market, and the influence of building characteristics are again subordinate to the location, a mechanism that is also argued for by the expert panel in the Delphi survey (Remøy et al. 2007). In former studies the accessibility by car and public transportation within the different Amsterdam submarkets was analysed, revealing that the accessibility within all submarkets is sufficient without displaying big differences. According to this, it is also possible to explain why, in the Delphi-survey, accessibility is recognised as important to the user preference, but is not used to explain vacancy.

2.3.1 Technique

The Office Scan is a series of quantitative analyses using regression techniques. Regressions are typically useful for revealing the correlation between two variables (Hosmer and Lemeshow 2000; Field 2005). In real estate financial research, regression analyses are often used to establish hedonic models (Wheaton 1997; Colwell et al. 1998; Dunse and Jones 1998). Most examples of hedonic models in real estate research consider the relationship between specific characteristics and the rent level of the analysed property (Wheaton 1997; Dunse and Jones 1998) and in some studies the relationship between specific characteristics and the value of the sale transactions (Colwell et al. 1998). Structural vacancy (vacancy of the same square metres of office space over a period of three years or longer, with no perspective on future tenancy) may be seen as an extreme property value, arguing from a Willingness-To-Pay point of view. From this point of view, the value of a property is defined by the property's fitness of use to the specific user, again influencing the amount that a potential user is willing to pay for renting (part of) the property. If there is no potential user who is willing to pay, the property remains vacant.

Hedonic real estate models are based on the assumption that a property can be described by its specific physical or hedonic characteristics and that the contributory value of each characteristic can be estimated, something that makes the method suspicious to some researchers in the field of architecture, the built environment and real estate management. However, in this study logistic regressions are used (paragraph 7.6), since most of the variables studied are categorical data. Rather than focusing on the contribution of each characteristic to structural vacancy, this research aims at establishing a typological description of structurally vacant office buildings, comparable to the descriptions of building typologies or taxonomies in the field of architecture. In an ideal research world, a building would be 100% structurally vacant or 100% rented out. However, few buildings are 100% structurally vacant. In the sample, 106 buildings have some level of structural vacancy, and 66 buildings have at least 30% structural vacancy. Assuming that a property's physical characteristics are indeed causally related to the structural vacancy, the structural vacancy level at which this is no more true needs exploration. According to Field, (2005) the critical value may be approximated by performing several regressions using the structural vacancy as outcome variable, testing several levels using logistic regressions and comparing the outcomes to the results of linear regressions. In this study, the choice of levels to study was also determined by the available data, and finally a regression model was developed using structural vacancy as output variable, and a second model using a vacancy level of 30% or higher as output variable.

According to market data (DTZ 2009; Dynamis 2009) and former studies (Remøy and De Jonge 2007; Remøy et al. 2008), specific characteristics like year of construction are shown to correlate to structural vacancy. However, "year of construction" also correlates to location characteristics like type of location, distance to railway stations and image of the location, and also to several building characteristics. Possible correlations are studied and reported. The characteristics that are studied are defined in the Delphi study, then validated in the Office Scan and are thereafter used for describing structurally vacant office buildings typologically.

2.3.2   Data collection

Data were retrieved by different methods and different sources. First, different existing databases were consulted. The transaction and supply databases of DTZ (DTZ Zadelhoff is one of the main real estate advisors and brokers in the Netherlands) were used. These databases are updated yearly and date back to 1994. The databases include transactions and supply reported by the larger Dutch real estate brokers. Several other real estate brokers also produce and maintain such databases and the differences between them are small. The data from DTZ database though seem more complete than other databases that were also considered for use. The data on the total office building stock were acquired from a database by Bak on the Amsterdam office building stock, see e.g. Bak (2006; Bak 2008). This database also dates back to 1994, something that made it possible to calculate levels of vacancy and structural vacancy over a longer period of time. Both databases register properties by address, city quarter, neighbourhood, and finally by coordinates, making it possible to link the databases to analysis tools such as Arc-GIS. Digital maps were acquired from the Municipality of Amsterdam. Information about location characteristics, such as distances to highway accesses, train stations, squares and green areas were obtained from the Netherlands Institute for Spatial Research (RPB).

Based on the transaction and supply database of DTZ, properties were selected for the Office Scan. 200 buildings were selected, based on specific prerequisites: Firstly, the buildings should be listed in the transaction database one or more times since 2001, or the building should be registered with some level of structural vacancy by the end of 2007. Secondly, the building should originally be constructed for offices. This point is important for part two of the study, Cope. Thirdly, the buildings should be situated within the borders of Amsterdam like defined by real estate brokers. In this way the market conditions are kept as context for the study, making it possible to focus on the location and building characteristics.

The owners or managers of the selected properties were contacted to gather information about the physical characteristics of location and building that were defined in the Delphi survey. However, many hours were spent to trace the owners of specific properties and finally only few owners were willing to cooperate. In accordance with the investors who did contribute to this study, a specific description of each office building was left out. To collect the data needed for the analyses, the subsequent procedure was followed: The location characteristics and the building characteristics assessable in the exterior were obtained by visiting the properties, while the buildings interior characteristics and characteristics described by metric measurements were acquired by studying the construction drawings of the buildings, available at the drawing archives at the Municipality of Amsterdam. The data were collected following and filling in a predefined protocol in order to ascertain a complete data collection and a similar registration of the data. Most collected data consider objective facts. However, some characteristics consider subjective assessments of the experienced quality of location and building. These assessments were performed during the visits to the locations and buildings, though photographs were made to enable a comparison of the assessed properties and a tuning of the assessed values.

The assessment team consisted of 4 student-assistants and the PhD candidates Hilde Remøy and Philip Koppels. The on-location assessments and the studies of the construction drawings at the municipality of Amsterdam were mainly conducted by the student-assistants, two working on the location assessments and two working on the drawing assessments. The first assessments were conducted with the whole team, in order to inform, improve and align the assessment method. During the data collection period, the correctness of the assessments was checked regularly.

3 Theoretical framework: The commercial office market.

The commercial office market could best be described as three separate markets; the office space market, the development market, and the asset market. The basic market forces joining the three are the demand and supply of office space. In the space market, office users (office organisations) see office space as a means of production. Organisation size, type and way of working determine the users' preference for office space with certain physical characteristics, weighted by their willingness to pay. In the development market, based on the property market value, potential profits and risks of new development decide whether new developments will be started. Finally, in the asset market, office space is traded and sold from one actor to another, the price being defined by the demand and supply of offices and the expected future financial value of the asset. A significant difference with other financial assets is the influence of location and building characteristics on the property's price. Though this basic description of the office market applies worldwide; local, regional, national and superregional markets have their specificities that make comparison of the markets problematic. Geography, national and regional politics and policies influence the markets, as do of course also demographics, economic rise and fall, technology and technological progress, and financial market developments, including the level of the interest rates, see *Figure 6*. In this research, the market dynamics related to the demand and supply, match and mismatch of office space and the changes of these are seen as causes of structural vacancy (Table 4). Based on literature reviews, this chapter will describe these market forces in order to develop a theoretical framework of the forces at play. Within this framework, the preferences of office users for specific location and building characteristics will be revealed, and the relation between these characteristics and structural vacancy will be discussed.

Table 4 Market, location and building are the 3 topics considered within the 3 themes of this research, Cause, Cope, Prevent. The topics comprise several aspects.

	Cause	Cope	Prevent
Market	Supply and demand, match and mismatch		
Location	Characteristics, user preferences		
Building	Characteristics, user preferences		

3.1 Market dynamics

In a balanced office market, the quantitative demand and supply of office space will not differ significantly. In economic upswing, the market will show signs of scarcity, while during a recession some excess vacancy will be seen (Keeris 2007). Vacancy as a result of this match and mismatch is a natural phenomenon and equals 3% - 8% of the total supply of the office market (Wheaton 1999; Tse and Webb 2003). In an unbalanced market however, the vacancy rises substantially, caused by a significant mismatch between the demand and supply of office space. In markets with continuous high levels of vacancy, structural vacancy can occur.

The occurrence of structural vacancy means that some office buildings are preferred to others; office users move from one building to another within an office market of abundance. Structural vacancy occurs when oversupply becomes structural as a result of increasing supply and constant demand, or opposite; as a result of constant supply and decreasing demand. Office users' preferences for a specific office space are based on the property's building and location characteristics. Locating or relocating an organisation, office users first consider market characteristics: When the choice is made for a specific geographic market and a specific market segment, building and location characteristics finally decide which property is preferred. This research focuses on office users' preferences for specific building and location characteristics, or more specific – the relationship between structural vacancy and specific location and building characteristics in an unbalanced market. Though on a high level market segments and spatial definitions determine users' preferences for locating an office organisation, the market conditions are also regarded as the context within which the physical characteristics of location and building preferences.

3.2 Effect of economic changes

Macro-economic changes have an effect on the employment market that again is a determinant of the demand of office space. In a balanced office market, economic growth will increase the employment and thereby increase the demand for office space (Wheaton 1999), quantitatively or qualitatively. Changes in the supply of office space on the other hand, are results of development costs and expected future revenues (Brounen and Eichholtz 2004). *Figure 6* shows the conceptual model of the office markets dynamics used in this study.

The model shows the balance between demand and supply of office space, described qualitatively by location and building characteristics. Quantitatively, the demand is described by the employment market (number of employees) and the square metre usage per employee. The supply is described by the available building stock, square metres in construction and the planning capacity. Mismatch between the demand and supply, qualitatively or quantitatively, results in scarcity of office space or, as in the current market situation, a surplus of office space, resulting in structural vacancy.

Economic growth causes growth in the employment market that again causes growth in the office space demand. The study by Brounen and Eicholtz (2004) also indicates a significant relationship between lagged employment growth and new supply of office space. However, it also warns against the effect a shrinking labour force will have on this relationship, as the growth of the labour force (positive or negative) and not of the employment growth will drive office space demand. Other factors may also disturb the relationship. Demographic changes may be caught up by more women working, by increasing the legal pension age, by actively looking for qualified personnel abroad, the so-called knowledge migrants, by within country migration, or by an increase in the number of square metres office space per employee. The actual trend however, is a decrease of the amount of office space per employee. With the number of "distant workers" increasing (CBS 2006) an increasing number of companies work with flexible work spaces, in many cases another term for desk sharing or less work-places than employees within the organisation.

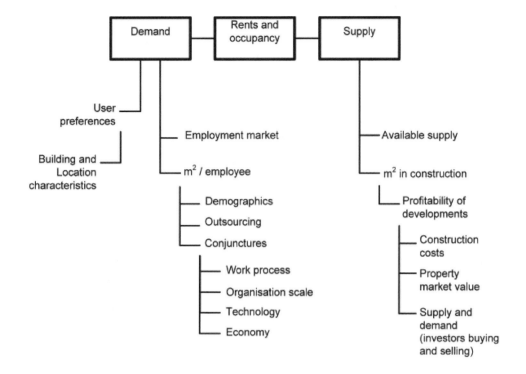

Figure 6
Demand and
supply of office
space

On the supply side, Brounen and Eicholtz's study showed the relationship between lagged employment growth and new supply of office space. This phenomenon is well known in the office market and is referred to as the "hog cycle". The growth of the office space supply shows a cyclic behaviour that lags 2-3 years behind of the economic cycles and the office space demand, registered as office space absorption. This lag is caused mainly by the production time of real estate, as the real estate cycle can be said to be initiated by office organisations signalling the need for new accommodation, followed by the design and development phase of real estate and finally the completion of an office building.

However, this idea of supply following the demand is derived from an ideal perception of the real estate market. Real estate developers and investors engaged in the development of office space are driven by the expected revenues of office developments and investments versus the costs of the development and operation. While the costs are directly linked to interest rates, the availability of qualified employees and the prices of land and material, the possible future revenues are not simply dependant of the quantity of the existing supply. If the interest rates are low, the costs of the development of new real estate are low, and speculation in development of real estate arises. Accordingly, an oversupply of office space is generated, and based on office users preference for certain building- and location characteristics, a market arises where new buildings drive out older buildings and where the relative ageing of office buildings happens at an increasing pace.

3.3 Spatial market definitions

Office markets are typically geographically defined and limited and to a great extent also related to place and the meaning of place, definitions that are again bound both by culture, history and economy (Norberg-Schulz 1980; Harvey 1989; Jameson 1999; Augé 2000; Sassen 2002). Typical examples of place that also define geographical markets are national capitals or main cities, to which different conditions apply than to neighbouring satellite-towns or even national second markets. However, in a study of the British real estate market, a system of interrelated submarkets was described; referring to spill-over between local markets was found to exist as nearby markets are to a certain degree complementary and offer substitution to a specific geographical market (Mouzakis and Henneberry 2008). Within geographical defined markets, submarkets can exist, limited by geographical, historic and cultural borders. A well-known example is Manhattan in New York, with the Lower Manhattan as a specific submarket. Already since the 17th century functioning as a centre for business and administration, the area is spatially limited by the borders of the island to the west, south and east, and by Chamber Street and the landing of the Brooklyn Bridge in the north (Figure 7). Its historic and cultural development has caused the concentration of financial services in this area, further separating it from bordering submarkets that accommodate different kinds of occupiers. The existence of submarkets was also verified by Fuerst (2007), who found that the rent determining variables of adjacent Manhattan submarkets were differing significantly. His findings were sustained by Stevensons study of the dynamics of the London office market, concluding that the intrinsic characteristics of a submarket differ from the surrounding submarkets because of discontinuations and different types of tenants (2007).

Figure 7 Lower Manhattan, New York City. Source: www. flikcr.com

3.4 The Netherlands

The Dutch office market has been characterised by growth since the nineteen fifties, corrected by cyclic movements. This growth was also seen in the growth of rental offices, a long term trend. In 1994, the percentage of rental offices was 56% of the total stock of office buildings, while in 2007; this percentage had risen to 62% (Bak 2008). The office market growth is flattening out; although the development of new office buildings is still ongoing and the supply is growing, the demand of office space is more or less constant. Renting organisations feel less attached to their office buildings than owner-users. Office work changes, organisations wish to be flexible, rental agreements become shorter and the rent difference between new buildings and existing buildings is small.

During the nineteen-seventies and -eighties, the Dutch office market experienced its first post-war crises, with high levels of vacancy and structural vacancy. However, the economic upswing caused by the expansion of the IT and internet services sector absorbed all vacancy in few years, until the bubble burst in 2001. After the dramatic rise in office space vacancy from 2001 to 2005, the amount of office space in use has stabilised. Since new office space is still being added and existing office space is not taken off the market, there's a surplus of office space on the market. At the same time, organisations and work processes are becoming more dynamic, rental agreements become shorter and since the price difference between renting new buildings and existing buildings is also small, organisations move to new buildings. In the past decade, a replacement market has developed (Soeter and Koppels 2006; Remøy 2007). There is no quantitative demand for additions and new buildings to take the place of older buildings.

Existing buildings and locations are ageing. An increasing part of the supply is obsolete and will be difficult to rent out, even in the case of an economic upswing. According to DTZ, in The Netherlands 1 million m² of office space is prospectless. Dynamis, the largest Dutch commercial real estate broker cooperation, considers 500 000 m² as prospectless, and adds 1,5 million m² as deteriorated (DTZ 2006; Dynamis 2006). The buildings are outdated and are located on decaying, monofunctional locations. The vacancy problem is mainly considered a location problem. Among the problematic locations are the office- and industrial parks from the 1980s, next to highways or ring roads and badly accessible by public transport. The development of these locations is explainable in the perspective of the eighties. Accessibility by car was the most important location characteristic, as shown in surveys of the Amsterdam office market by Korteweg in 1988 and 1991 (Korteweg 2002). The market showed an economic upswing, there was political support for urban extensions and the city centres were blocked for commercial developments. Mono-functional office parks were developed which 25 years later are functionally and economically obsolete.

Although from a user perspective the function of office space is to accommodate the activities of office organisations, this view is different from the view of the real estate investors. Investments are driven by the possible future revenues, which are found to be present in the current replacement market (Keeris and Koppels 2006). Despite that the vacancy in the office market is high, the investment market for A1 locations is expected to have a stable and positive development in 2008, with a positive growth of the rental incomes and stable initial yields (Property.nl 2008). Though some municipalities are restricting the possibilities for development of office space without a designated user, the users that are found for new developments in most cases already rent space within or nearby the new development. In these cases, offices are developed for the replacement market; office users move from their existing accommodation to new developed offices.

Supply and Market absorption Offices

x 1000 m² lettable floor area

Total supply

Total absorption
Net absorption

New supply
New completed construction

years

Source: Vastgoedmarkt/PropertyNL/DTZ/Bak (2008).
Elaborated by TU Delft, Building Economics.

Figure 8 Office space demand and supply. The office space supply cycle lags behind on the office space demand cycle.

Within the Netherlands the differences between the local markets are huge. At the end of 2008, the average vacancy in the Netherlands was 12%. The highest vacancy could be found in the satellite towns of the larger cities in the west of the country (the Randstad) and in Amsterdam, while the smaller cities and conurbations in the east and south of the country have a much lower vacancy rate, together with the remaining three cities in the Randstad: The Hague, Rotterdam and Utrecht that all have a lower registered vacancy than the Dutch average. The differences are found both in the supply and the demand; The Hague has a stable office market with a high level of governmental offices, enhancing the stability of office space absorption, while the high office space vacancy in Rotterdam during the last economic slump in the 1980s has caused a conservative view on revenues from new developments.

Amsterdam is by far the largest Dutch office market with 5.7 million square metres gross lettable floor area, whereas the size of the second and third Dutch markets; The Hague and Rotterdam, are estimated to be 3.8 and 3.2 million square metres (www.cbs.nl). However, the estimates are considerably different; Boer Hartog Hooft estimates the Amsterdam office stock at 6.5 million square metres (BHH 2008), and CB Richard Ellis and Jones Lang LaSalle reports 6.9 million square metres (Bak 2008). The office rental prices also differ significantly between the cities and regions. While the top rents in Amsterdam are above 300 euro/ m2, the top rents in Rotterdam and Den Haag approximate 200 euro/ m2.

3.5 Amsterdam

Amsterdam has been the main city and main office market since the seventeenth century when the Dutch East India Company (VOC) had its base in Amsterdam, at that time with offices connected to homes or warehouses. Commercial and financial services still play an important role in the Amsterdam office market with 34% of the office space occupancy, compared a Dutch average of 21% (CBS 2006). The importance of these segments in Amsterdam is stable through time (Jennen and Brounen 2006).

The Amsterdam office market is geographically limited as shown in Figure 9. In some studies, the nearby markets of Amstelveen, Diemen and Hoofdorp are incorporated in what is then referred to as the Greater Amsterdam office market. However, administrative, historic and cultural differences together with geographical limitations are important for the spatial understanding of a market and have for this study led to the chosen limitations. The Amsterdam office market can further be divided into submarkets as shown in the figure. This subdivision is derived from DTZ Zadelhoff.

Figure 9 The geographic definition of the Amsterdam office market (photo:Google Earth)

The most recent economic cycle had a significant effect on the Amsterdam office market; as the economic expansion started in 1997 and went on until its climax in 2001, the demand for office space was rising explosively. The lagged development of office space followed, and was finally leading to just as explosive vacancy numbers, first seen in 2004 (DTZ 2006). Since 2005, the vacancy numbers have been more or less stable, and in 2008 15.3% of the Amsterdam office stock was vacant. While the economic growth has stagnated, and with it the growth of office employment, the development and construction of new office buildings has been continued. The vacancy in the Amsterdam office market is caused by the continuous development of new office buildings, not by office-unemployment and economic slump. The construction of new office space is encouraged by the municipality, who is developing and exploiting land in different parts of the city by leasehold; since 2000 focusing on the development on the Zuidas in Amsterdam South and on the IJ, the riverbanks north of the centre. Additionally, also the office area in South East is being expanded, and new office space is also added to the Western part of the city. The municipality's yearly revenues from land leasehold increased from less than 20 million euro in 1996 to close to 60 millions in 2006 (OGA 2006).

3.6 Relations and parallels to national and international markets

The study of the Amsterdam office market is to every extent a case study of the dynamics within one specific office market. However, the similarities of market mechanisms and market developments in different markets are apparent when reviewing literature of research on different markets and cities (see 3.1). Describing different office markets by their characteristics in a typological way could contribute to reveal further similarities between markets. In this way, findings from studies on specific markets like the Amsterdam office market can, to a certain extent, be generalised.

3.7 Summary and conclusions

The office market is defined as the sale and purchase or letting and renting of office space. Its basic market forces are the demand and supply of office space. The demand and supply of office space relates to the quantity and quality of office space within specific geographical limits. Within these spatially bound markets, office organisations search for office space that fits their organisation, defined by market segment, location and building characteristics that enables the organisation to perform their core business.

Amsterdam is the largest geographically defined office market in the Netherlands, and is significantly larger than the second office market, The Hague. The dynamics that were found in the studies of other cities are also at play in the Amsterdam office market. Office organisations locate their businesses within this spatially defined office market, choosing accommodation first by market segment, then by location and building characteristics. The location and building characteristics and the office users' demand have developed in the course of time; along with economic, technological and cultural changes.

The supply of office space, also qualitatively described by building and location characteristics, has grown and changed as well. Following high expectations for future economic and employment growth and the possibilities for inexpensive financing, new offices were developed at a high pace during the last 20 years. Though the vacancy of office space has been increasing, new developments have been and are still popular with office users, making it interesting for developers to continue the production of office space, even in a saturated market. In the following chapter, the historical development of office locations and buildings will be described, resulting in the current office locations and buildings.

4 Theoretical framework: the office building and location

Office buildings and their locations have emerged and developed in the urban setting only since the end of the 19th century. Until the industrial revolution offices were mainly found as workspaces connected to houses, workshops or early factories. In the beginning of the 20th century, as the office building was still a young building type, urban plans and architecture were developed according to the utopian principles of that time, based on ideas of health and social security and promising sufficient space, sun and air for the cities' key functions: housing, work and recreation. The architecture and urban design of our buildings and cities are still based on the principles of this unique period of history. However, these principles no longer apply to our way of living or to the way corporations and their employees (wish to) work, and so office buildings and locations that are developed according to these principles and that are not potentially transformable start to deteriorate and will become obsolete in an ever increasing pace. This chapter considers the historic development of the office building and location until today and sketches the frames within which office locations and buildings today are being developed.

4.1 The emergence of offices and the industrial revolution

The history and origin of office work and office buildings is described by several authors who studied the typology of (office) buildings or the configuration of office space (Pevsner 1976; Duffy and Powell 1997; Veldhoen 1998; Van Meel 2000; Kohn and Katz 2002). Though banks, stock-exchanges and governmental buildings existed already in the middle ages, specialised office buildings were not invented until the industrial revolution, when the development of mass production techniques and larger scale factories led to the need for coordination and administration, and also the scale of the administration became too big to be performed from home. Office buildings were needed for this administrative revolution, and work was separated from living. The first specialised office buildings were based on the older types, used by bankers, dealers and notaries. The Uffizi (Giorgio Vasari, 1581) in Florence is a famous example (Figure 10), preceding one of the first Dutch examples, the city hall on Dam Square (1665). The work in this office was performed in huge halls at long tables, an office type that was used until the twentieth century's writing rooms.

Figure 10
The Uffizi in Florence (1650), an early specific office building.

At the beginning of the twentieth century office work changed dramatically. In the factories, progress was made in efficient production of goods. Work processes were split into a series of processes, partly performed by machines, partly by workers; people are seen as part of the machinery. Based on the routine

Figure 11 The Rookery building (Burnham and Root 1888). A transitional structure in modern architecture evolution, employing both masonry wall-bearing and skeletal frame construction techniques. (Bluestone, 1991)

work in the factories, Frederick Taylor developed a vision on administrative work that would be followed worldwide. Hierarchy, rationality, work division, precision and supervision became central themes. Offices were grand halls with factory-like lines of small desks, the 'white collar factories'.

The first modern office buildings were developed in England and the United States, though the most eminent development of office buildings during the next century would concentrate in the United States (Pevsner 1976). In the Netherlands, two of the listed monuments of this time are the White House in Rotterdam (1897) and the office building of the Dutch Trading Company in Amsterdam (1920), De Bazel. During the industrial revolution, office buildings were situated near the industrial locations, or they were, like the earlier banks, governmental offices and stock-exchanges, situated in the inner cities, mixed with retail, culture and housing (Bluestone 1991). The size of the office buildings though was considerable, and buildings such as the office building of the Dutch Trading Company were way out of scale when compared to its urban context. During the twenties and thirties, office buildings were also developed near or in combination with infrastructural works.

At the same time, steel (first cast iron) structures were introduced to the construction industry, making it possible to develop larger structural spans. By using this relatively light and compact material, less space was needed for the structure and more floors could be stacked on top of each other. At the same time, technical developments, such as the development of the safety elevator, took place. High-rise without elevators would be impossible. The development of high-rises in New York and Chicago signified the office building development in the early 20th century. From then on, developments in office buildings followed the economical growth cycles (Kohn and Katz 2002).

After the Second World War strong economic growth led to the expansion of the service sector and the arising of the service economy. In the US, artificial lighting and mechanical ventilation led to the development of deeper office buildings. The US was leading within the area of office architecture. Europe was following the developments in the US but the scale of the buildings was not applied here. The deep open floors did not answer to the European office culture. European architects were not really interested in the lay-out of offices, but the formal language of American modernism to a great extent determined the exterior appearance of office buildings. The facade structure was given much attention. Studies were carried out on the grid of the facade structure and the possibility for flexible interior divisions of floor plans in spaces of different size. The curtain wall had its break through and Le Corbusiers Domino plan was applied.

The ideological ideas of the sixties also influenced architecture; architects started concerning more about work processes and the interior of the workspace instead of just designing the facade, the envelope. The rejection of hierarchical mindsets and the focus on communication and human relations led to the development of the office landscape, introduced to Europe by the German consultancy firm 'Quickborner Team'. The office landscape was for many organisations too radical, and in the Netherlands, architects experimented with new lay-outs and variants of the office landscape, resulting in the team office, of which Herman Hertzbergers building for Centraal Beheer is the most significant (Figure 12). From the nineteen fifties onwards the initiation of the service economy started influencing the construction of office buildings, though until the sixties, office buildings were mostly contracted and owned by the user of the building. In the sixties, the growth of the service economy exploded and the office market emerged as a new phenomenon. From then on, office buildings were developed for tenancy (Kohnstamm and Regterschot 1994) in a growing market, leading up to the current situation with 64% of the square metres of office space in the Netherlands being rental offices (Bak 2005).

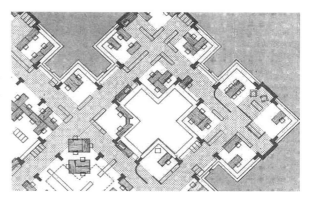

*Figure 12
Example of a
'Team Office',
the office
building for
"Centraal
Beheer" in
Apeldoorn
by Herman
Hertzberger
(Hertzberger,
1991)*

In the seventies, the increase of rental offices led to standardisation of the structure and the interior of office buildings. The energy crisis in 1973 brought up more interest for climatic control. Insulated facades and double glazing were introduced, combined with not operable windows. The Dutch building decree was altered and required more daylight access in office buildings. The office landscapes lost popularity. Employees complained about the internal climate, lack of privacy and outside view. Office landscapes clashed with the European office culture. Especially in Northern Europe office buildings were narrow because of the preferred office lay-out: cellular offices along a corridor.

From 1985 onwards most employees worked with a computer. More computers and other technical apparatus required new cabling, cooling and more attention to the indoor climate. The buildings were narrow. All workplaces were near the facade and computers were served by a cable stalk in the facade. The ideas about office work have changed. With mobile phones, laptops, internet and e-mail the employee has become less dependant of the office building. Shared or flexible workspace has become normal. At the same time, more people work at home or at different places during the week. Office buildings are standardised according

43

Figure 13
Dutch poster
announcing
the 1935 CIAM
exhibition and
conference on
architecture
and urbanism,
focusing on
the functional
segregation
of housing,
working, traffic
and leisure and
the place of these
functions in the
modern city (NAI
archives).

to a main structural grid of 7.2m and a facade grid of 1.8m. Multiple floor types are used and experiments on integrating installations in the floors are conducted.

Although the office building type originated in administrative buildings from the middle age, during its development its characteristics developed and became specific, and the office building type can be recognised as a separate building type. Until the industrial revolution, offices had much in common with housing, and the use of buildings could easily be adapted. From the industrial revolution onwards, the specificities of the office building type started to develop. Mass production of building materials made construction cheaper and led to modular building systems, prefabrication and standardisation. Another force to the increasing standardisation was the economic growth and the changing role of the office user; office users went from owning their own office buildings to being tenants. Office buildings are developed and standardised to accommodate office organisations. With a surplus of office buildings on the market, some buildings become structurally vacant, redundant and obsolescent.

4.2 Functionalism and functional zoning of locations

The fast industrial developments that took place in the late 19th century led to urbanisation, increased population and building density in the cities. The health of citizens was threatened. In the Netherlands, the Dutch housing act was approved in 1901, a law that established certain demands to the quality of housing, and prohibited people from living in shacks, basements and other dwellings that were a threat to the public health. Plans for new neighbourhoods were drawn in urban extension areas (Ibelings 1999; Bakker et al. 2002). New architectural ideals were visualised; by being spacious and letting in sunlight and air the buildings would contribute to the health of their inhabitants. The new ideals were in great contrast to the former architectural styles. Architects were fascinated by machines and so houses were built as 'living-machines', the exterior expressing the explicit function of the interior. The most far-reaching ideas of the modern movement were presented in the 'Charter of Athens', a report on the 1933 CIAM (Congrès Internationaux d'Architecture Moderne) meeting in Athens, though not published until 1943 (Frampton 1992). Their ideas were radical and foresaw the complete demolition of historic cities; comprehensive redevelopment was seen as the only possible solution for dealing with obsolete historic legacy, like in Le Corbusier's Plan Voisin for Paris (Le Corbusier 1986), see Figure 14. Industry, offices and housing were neatly divided and connected by infrastructure and recreation zones, at the same time letting more light, space and air into the urban fabric. Van Eesteren and van Lohuizens plan for the extension of Amsterdam (1934) was developed according to these principles and is described as one of the best examples of functionalistic urban planning (Ibelings 1999).

In Europe, including the Netherlands, the ideas of the modern movement, though developed in the 1930's, were not introduced in the urban development until after the Second World War, when large scale reconstructions and large scale extensions of the existing urban fabric was needed after years with little construction activities. The functionalists' ideas of large scale, single function areas, consisting of industrial mass-produced buildings fit very well with the ideas of politicians, engineers and developers at that time, interested in an effective reconstruction of the damaged areas. In most Dutch cities which had not been bombed during the war, the post-war developments were extensions to the existing cities, also comprising the first office areas, and were developed near the urban centres.

Figure 14 Plan Voisin - Le Corbusier suggestion to redevelop Paris (NAI archives)

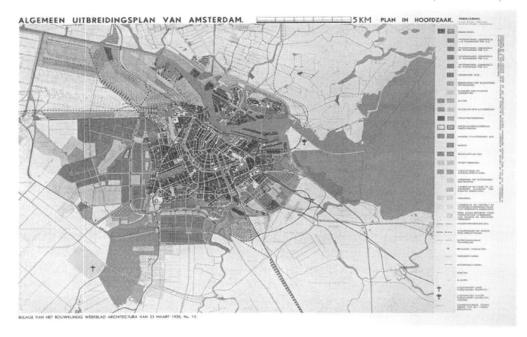

ALGEMEEN UITBREIDINGSPLAN VAN AMSTERDAM. 5 KM PLAN IN HOOFDZAAK.

Figure 15: Plan for extension of Amsterdam by van Eesteren, 1935 (NAI archives)

The functionalist scheme has been applied to the urban design, development and architecture up till now. The effect that functionalist urbanism has had on cities can be experienced everywhere in the Netherlands. In housing areas, during day time the streets and parking lots are vacant, while in the office areas or office parks, all employees leave their work at five in the afternoon by car and leave a ghost-town behind. The city centres are crowded on weekends and almost deserted in day-time on week-days. This functional division of the urban

45

areas leads to traffic congestion as everyone is commuting. The source of the ideas of strict functional divisions and zoning plans were the polluting industrial areas and the unhygienic housing situations of the nineteenth century, but the modern factories have long ago been moved out of the cities because of economic reasons, and the need for functional zoning does not seem evident any more. Large-scale urban areas are still developed following the functionalists urban ideas, albeit according to Harvey the implementation of the modern movement's ideas need to be seen as part of the political and economical climate of the post-war urbanisation (Harvey 1989).

4.3   The city and the creative class

One of the arguments of the modern movement was functional segregation to provide for the health and security of the working class. The functional zoning would not only literally provide distance between the factory smoke and the workers' homes, but also figuratively in the sense of separating work from free-time and recreation, something that was welcome to the working class who had until then had few rights and for whom recreation was something new. Already in the sixties though, Jacobs and others warned against the comprehensive urban redevelopment so offensive to the same working class, and so disruptive to small firms and organisations, not economically viable though socially desirable and adding up to the liveability of urban areas (Jacobs 1961). Jacobs' critic also comprised the continuous employment of rigid zoning plans. The industrial city was dominated and developed by the industrial sector and the administration of it, but the post-industrial city is a centre providing services for itself and for industry that moved to other areas or to other regions or countries, and so in the post-industrial city the functional zoning is not any more functional; the idea itself has become outdated (Tiesdell et al. 1996). According to Florida (2004), the new large working class is the creative class. While the offices of the post-war years were classified as white collar factories, the office workers of the 21st century are highly skilled and working more or less independently. Florida further describes the creative class as consisting of knowledge workers and employees or independents working in the traditional creative industries such as architecture, (graphical) design, arts and crafts, but also comprising university personnel and employees at software or internet development companies. The creative class employees mostly have flexible working hours, and are often able to perform their work from home, just as well as from behind their desk at the company they work for. These employees don't work 8 hours a day and have no need for a separation between their working environment and the place where they live.

4.4 Summary and conclusions

The current office building has been developed in the course of time from the fore-runners of the renaissance until today's highly efficient and standardised offices. While offices used to be designed for a specific client with a less specific function in mind, new offices are designed for a specific function. As the use of office space slightly changes, the buildings become functionally obsolete. Also the locations of offices have changed, from being located in the centre of the cities, to the specific office locations on the urban fringes and near highways. The separation of locations for housing, working and recreating was an idea based on improving the public health of the cities. In post-war planning, offices were defined as a specific function and zoning plans assigned specific zones to monofunctional office locations. Office work is changing and though office buildings and interiors are becoming more like housing, monofuntional locations near the highway are still being developed. Current office employees are not pleased with this environment and the inner city and mixed use locations are (re)gaining popularity as office locations. Accordingly, office buildings in monofunctional locations become obsolete and structurally vacant.

5 Theoretical framework: mismatch, vacancy and structural vacancy

Mismatch of demand and supply of office space on market, location or building level cause an oversupply of office buildings. Ups and downs are common in the office market and a certain level of vacancy is regarded one of the characteristics of a balanced market, and is referred to as natural vacancy. However, vacancy rates increasing for too many years in a row or going above the 8% that are normally considered the upper limit of natural vacancy are signals that the market is not functioning well. Also, if the vacancy rate stays high for several years in a row, a part of the vacancy may have developed into structural vacancy. In this chapter, mismatch, vacancy and structural vacancy on the levels of market, location and building are further described. The causes of structural vacancy are studied through literature review, leading up to a formulation of propositions on the causes of structural vacancy. The propositions will be tested in the chapters 6 and 7.

5.1 National scale

Since 2001 the mismatch between demand and supply of office space has risen to unprecedented levels. In 2007 the office space vacancy on Dutch national level was more than 6 million m² GLA[2], 13% percent of the office space in the Netherlands. Of these 6 million m², real estate agents defined 2 million m² as deprived and unsuited for new rentals of which again 500 000 m² were defined as prospectless (Dynamis 2007). Structural vacancy of a specific building can be dealt with once it is recognised as a problem by the actors involved in management or use of the specific buildings. The active stakeholders are building owners and investors. Municipalities on all levels are the active stakeholders representing societal interests.

This thesis is based on the assumption that physical building- and location characteristics affect the performance of an office building, and whether or not that building is structurally vacant. Some office locations are preferred above others, on local and regional level. Parts of a city are already competing markets but especially bigger firms select a location on a regional; national or even international level. For this reason, I choose to base this research on the study of one specific region. The Amsterdam region not only has the largest office market in the Netherlands, but is also the Dutch regional market that has got the highest rent levels and the highest vacancy rates.

5.2 Location scale

There are several reasons why some locations within the Amsterdam office market are less popular than others. For instance bad accessibility by public transport or car and bad parking possibilities have been mentioned by several studies (Hessels 1992; Louw 1996; Korteweg 2002; Rodenburg 2005). Another factor may be the negative image of the area created by a poor spatial and visual quality. Agglomeration or clustering factors, such as other similar firms moving

---

2 GLA means influence Gross Lettable floor-Area; in the following, m² will refer to m² GLA.

out, lack of facilities and a concentration of ageing premises are also important. Finally, urban zoning and planning policy play an important role. Municipality plans for changing the use of the area can also have consequences for prospects on future development possibilities and thus trigger vacancy. According to market analyses, Monofunctional areas are more probable to experience vacancy (DTZ 2006; BHH 2008), as these are depending solely on one market. Structural vacancy in monofunctional locations will also have a larger impact on the location, as it will soon look deserted. Therefore, monofunctional urban districts deteriorate due to negative market developments in a certain branch. Based on the foregoing, a hypothesis comprising five location characteristics states the expectations of the relationship between location characteristics and structural vacancy:

Structurally vacant office buildings
- are located in monofunctional office locations with insufficient facilities
- are located on fragmented locations and are not part of a business cluster
- are not well accessible by car and public transport
- are located in unsafe locations
- are located on low-status locations

5.3 Building scale

Reasons why organisations prefer some buildings above others when (re)locating may be the image or identity of a building. According to previous studies (Baum 1993; Baum and McElhinney 1997; Korteweg 2002), buildings with a bad spatial-visual quality, building decay and shabbiness or evidence of vandalism will not be chosen. A poor condition or bad technical quality of (parts of) the building or out-of-date or malfunctioning of its installations has been mentioned in several studies as a reason for organisations to leave a building (push factors), not so much as a reason for not moving to a building (pull factors) (Baum 1993). Organisations change and at some points, the changes cannot be facilitated within the current office building and relocating will be necessary. However, several studies have focused on pull-factors attracting office users to specific locations and buildings. Studies by Korteweg (2002) together with market surveys (Venema and Twijnstra Gudde 2004; NVB 2006), show that the buildings status, exterior appearance and interior flexibility have a positive effect on user preferences. Based hereupon, a hypothesis comprising four building characteristics states the expectations of the relationship between characteristics describing the buildings appearance and structural vacancy.

Structurally vacant office buildings
- lack inherent identity
- hinder expression of the organisations' identity
- have a low quality of interior finishes
- provide insufficient facilities

5.4 Building life span and obsolescence

The office user preference for specific locations or buildings changes in the course of time, while the location and building characteristics are more or less static. Typically, one important objective for choosing an office location is now parking possibilities and accessibility by car, while 50 years ago, proximity to customers and employees was far more important (Louw 1996). Building preferences also change due to the revolutions in office work and organisational forms during the last fifty years; Work is more informal and individual, organisations less hierarchical, office hours flexible. As a result, recent office buildings include informal work and meeting spaces while 50 years ago the office building was monotonous in its spatial layout (Van Meel 2000). But buildings are by nature static. Buildings are not good at adapting (Brand 1994).

According to the lifecycle perspective on buildings, the building is seen as a cyclical process (Figure 16). During the initial phases (initiative, briefing, design and construction processes) the building is created. During the cyclical lifespan use and operation alternate with adaptations. At certain stages the building will reach a situation where its future usability and value will have to be assessed, and obsolescence may occur. This can happen because of the buildings technical or functional characteristics (technical or functional obsolescence) or because the costs of use exceeds the benefits of occupation (economical obsolescence). At this point, the building can face major adaptation or its life span may be ended: The building may be demolished (Blakstad 2001; Vijverberg 2001; Heijer 2003).

There is a mismatch between the technical and the functional life span of a building. The main structure of a building is designed according to the Dutch building decree, with rules on safety, health, usability, energy use and environment. The main structure of a building can be expected to serve its use for at least eighty years. The functional lifespan of a building can be exterminated through technological progress, causing changes in the user's requirements, influencing both the layout and the facilities offered in new buildings (Baum 1993; Blakstad 2001). In fact, a building can be functionally outdated already after its first lease-period. When the buildings functional lifespan is ended, the building is functionally obsolete. If the buildings technical lifespan is not concurrently ended, there is a mismatch between the buildings technical and functional lifespan. This structural vacancy finally also ends the economic life span of a building. Accordingly, a hypothesis comprising five building characteristics describes the expected relationship between characteristics describing the match between the buildings functional and technical lifespan and structural vacancy.

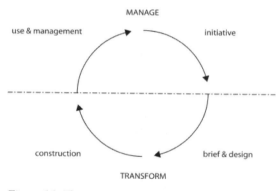

Figure 16: The life cycle of buildings

Structurally vacant office buildings
- are functionally obsolete (inefficient and inflexible)
- are in technical decay
- provide insufficient climatic and workplace comfort
- generate too high energy costs
- have insufficient parking facilities

5.5 Summary and conclusions

Structural vacancy is an increasing threat to the functioning of the Dutch office market. In a market based on growth, office buildings are developed continuously, though the current market situation with a more or less constant amount of office space in use leaves an increasing number of office buildings vacant. As an effect of a replacement market, older buildings are left for preferred new buildings, and the vacancy concentrates in the older stock and structural vacancy occurs. When discussing the office market it is not viable to speak of an international or national office market; the specific local markets and market segments should be considered. This study focuses on the Amsterdam, the biggest office market in the Netherlands. In Amsterdam, as much as 18%, or 1.2 million square metres of office space is vacant, of which a considerate amount is structurally vacant.

In this market, structural vacancy concentrates in buildings with specific physical characteristics. These characteristics describe office buildings that are less preferred by office users than other office buildings. Literature on building quality assessment tools and office user preferences studies, discuss several physical characteristics that describe office buildings and locations and that are considered by office users searching for new office space (Stichting REN 1992; Louw 1996; Korteweg 2002; Venema and Twijnstra Gudde 2004; Rodenburg 2005; NVB 2006).

As user preferences change in the course of time and as new office buildings are continuously added to the market, buildings become functionally obsolete or relatively functionally obsolete: As new office buildings are offered that fit the user better, older buildings are left behind. The mismatch between office buildings' functional lifespan and their technical lifespan causes structural vacancy of office buildings, and finally the end of office buildings' economic lifespan.

6   Delphi study - Office user preferences

The contemporary labour market is stressed, partly because of a lack of qualified, highly educated employees. Employees are not only satisfied with a compatible salary, but consider attractive secondary employment agreements as well. Workplace environment play an ever bigger role (Florida 2004; Rodenburg 2005). Highly educated employees prefer to work in urban well serviced areas rather than in monotonous office parks; the workplace environment should be dynamic, and accessibility by car has become less important. Surroundings that offer the opportunity to have coffee with friends or colleagues during the lunch break or with possibilities for shopping and interaction with other people are highly valued. 'Soft' factors as appearance, ambience and status have become just as important as the 'hard' factors such as accessibility and workplace environment.

Location- and building- characteristics influence organisations' choice of accommodation. There are several kinds of studies on office user preferences, studying push and pull factors, or evaluating variations of supply and demand. The criteria that office users apply when searching for a certain building (pull factors) are different from the criteria for leaving the building (push factors). This research focuses on the criteria that office organisations apply when searching for new office space, and as the term "office user" in literature is used to describe the organisation, it will also be used like that in this chapter. Studying pull-factors was a deliberate choice as these can be related to the actual transactions taking place and the contractual rent for the office space. Vacant office buildings on the other hand remain vacant because no other organisations choose to relocate to those buildings. Organisations act dynamically while buildings are more static, changes are slowly taking place. It is natural for organisations to move from time to time, for instance when an organisation grows and needs more space than available in the current building. Hence, it is more interesting to find out why organisations do not relocate to a certain kind of building than to find out which buildings they leave behind.

6.1   Existing literature and instruments

Based on the literature that is discussed in the following paragraph, 21 building and location characteristics were defined that might affect the location and building preferences of office users (re)locating their organisation. The literature review considered building quality assessment tools and office user preference studies. Only the physical location and building characteristics are considered in this study, and only location characteristics that may vary within the boundaries of one spatially defined market are considered.

Quality, depreciation and property performance

Baum (1991; 1993; 1997) studied the influence of building quality on the utility for the occupier and the investor, seeing quality as the reverse side of depreciation. Noting that though all buildings deteriorate and become obsolete as they age not all buildings deteriorate with the same speed, Baum studied the depreciation rate of office buildings to prove that the relationship between quality and depreciation is stronger than the relationship between age and depreciation. In his research, Baum used building design characteristics as defined by Healey and Baker (1987) who had ranked the characteristics in order of importance to the occupier as follows:

- Internal environmental control
- Heating system
- Improved car parking (relative to surroundings)
- Quality of internal finishes
- Security
- Provision for cable trunkings
- Toilet facilities
- Entrance hall
- Lift performance/availability
- Kitchen/catering facilities
- External appearance of building

Baum recognised the list as incomplete for describing all building design characteristics, and for his revealed preferences study of 125 office buildings in London, characteristics describing flexible flooring and high quality internal environmental services were added. Internal specifications (Interior appearance), configuration (lay-out), external appearance and physical deterioration were found to be the most explaining characteristics in Baums study.

Office buildings and location

In his PhD thesis, "Office buildings and location; a geographical investigation of the role of accommodation in office location decisions", Louw (1996) summarised and confirmed the results of several studies on the characteristics that work as pull-factors for office users, and did not find new characteristics. In addition to Korteweg he cites van Dinteren (1989) and Walen (1988) who both recognise market factors like 'direct availability of office space' as a pull-factor. Since this characteristic is not physical, it is not comprised in the set of characteristics used for this study. Louw's thesis focuses on the role of the building as a pull factor to organisations considering relocation of their offices. As such, Louw sees the accommodation as hierarchical subordinate to the location; something was also constituted in the theoretical framework of this research. Louw further discusses "the chicken or the egg" dilemma of whether the location of office buildings is decided by the office users, or by the developers and investors. The view is argued that since most office organisations are tenants, they search for available office space, and do not consider having a building developed on a location of their choice. However, investors and developers develop office buildings for profit, therefore taking into account the location preferences of office organisations as a development condition.

Obsolescence of office buildings: problem or challenge?

In his dissertation, "Obsolescence of office buildings; problem or challenge?", Korteweg (2002) reveals both building characteristics and location characteristics that are important for office users relocating within the Amsterdam region. The office users that were interviewed were not specifically described by user-profiles or type of organisation; all office organisations relocating within Amsterdam in

1988 and 1991 were incorporated in the survey. The characteristics are summarised in Table 5 and were based on the surveys in 1988 and 1991, where office users were asked which characteristics they thought important when searching for new office space. The table shows characteristics of different types. Korteweg reveals the importance of the characteristics, not of the value of the characteristics. Kortewegs research is interesting to this research since it also considers the relation between office users and their preference for specific location and building characteristics within a specific spatially defined market, and the relation between the users preferences and obsolescence and vacancy of office buildings.

Building characteristics	Location characteristics
Size	Accessibility by car
Flexibility	Proximity to highway/ ring road
Extension possibilities	Parking facilities
Single tenancy	Accessibility by Public transport
Recognisable	Proximity to train station
Status	Proximity to city centre
Aesthetics	Proximity of other offices (clustering)
Height	Proximity of shops
Rent/price	Proximity of cafés and restaurants
Service- and energy costs	Proximity of clients
ICT- facilities	Proximity of airport
Security	Status of the surroundings
Air-conditioning	Visibility from highway

Measuring benefits of multifunctional land use

In her PhD thesis, Rodenburg (2005) considered the valuation of multifunctional land use by different groups of actors. Real estate investors were asked to rate location characteristics by their effect on the rent price per square metre office space. The characteristics were ranked according to importance as follows: accessibility by car, image of the area, geographical location, accessibility by public transport, proximity to Schiphol airport, quality of real estate, labour market, business cluster, multi-functionality, high-visible location, presence of clients, and presence of suppliers. Employees at the South Axis in Amsterdam were then asked to give their view on multifunctionality using an indirect Willingness to pay study (Rodenburg 2006). The study showed that employees were willing to contribute financially to multifunctional design of their working environment.

NVB, Twijnstra Gudde

In a national market-survey Twijnstra Gudde revealed the main pull factors in the selection of office accommodation (Venema and Twijnstra Gudde 2004). The tenants were asked to rate each location and building characteristic according to their perceived importance from 1 (not important) to 10 (very important). A similar survey was conducted by NVB, in this study 800 office space users were asked to rate both location and building characteristics, using the same 1-10 scale as used by Twijnstra Gudde (NVB 2006).

	Twijnstra Gudde 2004	NVB 2006	
Location characteristics	Importance	Importance	
Accessibility by car	8.3	8.4	
Accessibility by public transport	7.6	7.5	
Highly visible location	-	5.4	
Image of the area	7.7	8.4	
Employment market	6.4	6.6	
Parking	8.3	8.4	
Presence of clients	6.1	6.0	
Proximity of shops	5.6	5.4	
Proximity to city centre	5.3	-	
Building characteristics			
Climate control	7.7	6.8	
Energy/service costs	7.5	7.0	
Exterior appearance	7.3	7.2	
Facilities	6.6	6.2	
ICT-facilities	8.3	7.9	
Interior finishing	7.5	7.3	
Layout flexibility	7.6	7.3	

Table 6 Office users' preferences of location and building characteristics (NVB, 2006; Venema and Twijnstra Gudde, 2004)

Real Estate Norm (REN)

The Real Estate Norm (Stichting REN 1992) is a method for communication and review of the choice of office buildings and locations. The REN handles several concepts of location and building built on detailed characteristics. The norm was created by the "Real Estate Norm Netherlands Foundation" through panels that consisted of experts involved in the act of initiative, design and development, and management of office buildings. In the REN numerous location and building characteristics are included, and a variety of indicators are employed to measure the characteristics comprised. Except for location and building characteristics, REN also recognises the characteristics of the site. In this research, the characteristics of the plot are credited either to the location or to the building. The concepts defined by REN (Table 7) have been assessed and applied in more recent research, such as in the study for a Vacancy Risk Meter by Geraedts and Van der Voordt (2003,

Location	Site	Building
Surroundings	Visual	Flexibility
Accessibility	Accessibility	Main entrance
Facilities	Parking	Logistics
Public safety	Extensibility / landscaping	Communication
Potential new personnel	Safety	Technical state
Housing new personnel	Obstructions	Energy use
	Soil pollution	Security
	Laws and rules	Free height of floors
	Prices	Privacy of workplace
		Interior climate
		Sanitary

Table 7: Location, plot and building factors as recognised by REN (1992)

2007). The Vacancy Risk Meter is a tool developed to define the lower end of the office market. The tool considers both location and building characteristics, and is defining the absence of pull factors such as described by the REN to have an impact on a property's vacancy risk. Both tools were developed for quantitative assessments of offices.

6.2 Identification of characteristics for this study

From the literature review, office users' preferences for specific location and building characteristics (pull factors) when (re)locating their organisation were recognised. Both organisational and spatial contexts were defined to frame the study; only characteristics that are not constant within the spatial boundaries of the Amsterdam office market are included; regional differences are not an issue in this study. Based on the literature discussed above, the following 15 building characteristics (Table 8) and 6 location characteristics (Table 9) were recognised as influential on office user preferences.

6.3 Analysis and results

The aim of this study is to test the relative importance of predefined building- and location- characteristics for office user preferences when relocating their organisation, within the Amsterdam area. Since the homogenous office user does not exist, it is unlikely that all office users would ascribe the same significance for each location and building characteristics. Therefore, the Delphi panel members were asked to make separate rankings for two office user profiles that were chosen because of their share on the Amsterdam office market; namely the Urban Specialists and the Status Sensitive Professionals (Atelier V and Motivaction 2005). A third profile, "the general office user" profile was included and used as a reference for the two specific profiles. The Delphi panel gave their judgement in two rounds; the second round was applied to inform the panellists about the opinion of the panel, providing the panellists with the opportunity to reconsider their judgement to strengthen the consensus within the panel.

Kendall W

Before the panel was interviewed, the required degree of consensus for the ranking to be credible was defined. The consensus of the panel can be described by the Kendall's W or Kendall coefficient of concordance W, which measures the degree of association among k sets of rankings. In this study the degree of association among the rankings of building characteristics, and among the rankings of location characteristics of the 18 experts was measured. Kendall's W has a value between 0 and 1. According to Schmidt (1997), as a rule of thumb, a Kendall's W of 0,7 or higher can be interpreted as 'strong agreement' or as high confidence in ranks (Table 10: Interpretation of the Kendall coefficient of concordance W (Schmidt, 1997).

Building characteristics	Description / indicators
Bike parking	Availability and capacity of bike parking facilities
Building facilities	Availability and level of facilities in the building; i.e. restaurant, shops, bank, conference rooms and unit facilities like pantries
Building period	Year of completion
Car parking	Availability, capacity and quality of car parking facilities
Comfort	The building's comfort level defined by type and operability of ventilation or air-conditioning, operable windows, daylight, availability and type of sun shade
Commodities logistic	Quality of internal commodities logistics and separation from routing
Energy performance	Energy costs/ m2 GLA
Exterior appearance	Aesthetics, recognisability of the building, entrance visibility, quality and finish of the exterior
Interior appearance	Aesthetics, size, spatiality and facility level of the entrance, quality and finish of the interior
Layout flexibility	Distance between columns, removability of interior walls, floor surface and flexibility of the ICT facilities
User recognisability	By signs, company logo on the facade, single tenancy or own entrance
Routing	Quality of the internal routing, capacity and usability of elevators and staircases
Security	Availability and type of security facilities per building or unit
Space efficiency	The realisable amount of workplaces per m2 GLA
Technical state	The technical state and maintenance level of exterior and interior

Table 8 Fifteen identified building characteristics to be studied, sorted alphabetically

Location characteristics	Description / indicators
Accessibility by car	Defined by distance and travel time to nearest highway access
Accessibility by public transport	Defined by the proximity and frequency of public transport services
Clustering	Density of related and service organisations in the area
Facilities	The availability and level of facilities in the area, i.e. shops, restaurants
Safety	The social safety of the area at day and night time
Status	Defined by location type, spatial quality, presence of nuisances like wind, stench, noise, obsolescence or vacancy

Table 9 Indentified Location characteristics to be studied, sorted alphabetically

Kendall's W	Interpretation	Confidence in Ranks
.10	Very week agreement	None
.30	Weak agreement	Low
.50	Moderate agreement	Fair
.70	Strong agreement	High
.90	Unusually strong agreement	Very high
W = 1	Complete agreement	Very high

Table 10: Interpretation of the Kendall coefficient of concordance W (Schmidt, 1997)

6.3.1 Building

In the first round, each panellist assigned a ranking number to each building characteristic from 1 to 15; the characteristic considered the foremost important for the users' preferences received the highest rank, rank 1. The mean rank and the median rank of each characteristic was calculated and used to construct a panel ranking (Table 11). The mean rank and the highest and lowest rank assigned were reported to the panellists. The panellists were then given the opportunity to compare their own ranking with the average panel ranking and were asked if they would like to revise their ranking. In the second round, the panel ranking of each characteristic was calculated again, using the mean rank and the median rank.

After the first round, the Kendall W was calculated for all three defined profiles. The Kendall W for the Urban Specialist profile was 0.54, and showed a moderate agreement within the panel. For the Status Sensitive Professionals the Kendall W of the building characteristics was already 0.65, close to the 0.7 that signifies a strong agreement. Not surprisingly, the Kendall W for the general profile was lower than the other two profiles. The expert-panel, just like the test-panel, was reluctant to rank the profile of the general office user, since both market theories and academic papers decline the existence of the general office user. Still, the Kendall W for the general profile, showed a moderate agreement on the building characteristics (0,49)

After the second round of polling, the Kendall W indicated a moderate agreement (0.64) for the Urban Specialists profile and a strong agreement (0.74) for the Status Sensitive Professionals. Again, the ranking of the general office user profile showed less consensus with a Kendall W of 0.62. After the second round, there was a moderate to strong agreement within the panels ranking of the building characteristics, and consequently the polling was stopped.

Top four

From the first to the second round, minor changes in ranking appeared for all three profiles (Table 11). The four top ranked characteristics in the first round stayed the most important in the Urban Specialists profile and in the general profile, while for the Status Sensitive Professionals profile the first six characteristics stayed the same. However, the Kendall W for all profiles changed significantly. Comparing the three profiles to each other the similarities are noteworthy, as the two highest ranked characteristics were the same for all three profiles; car parking and exterior appearance were considered the first and second most important characteristics for user preference. Car parking is related to the accessibility to the building for both employees and visitors. Exterior appearance relates to the aesthetic quality of the building. For the two specific profiles, recognisability is ranked third, while for the general profile it is ranked seventh. It is reasonable to assume that the importance ascribed to the recognisability of the user is related to the type of organisation.

The characteristics ranked four to ten shows small differences in ranking between the two specific profiles. Interestingly, the characteristics ranked four to eight are the same for both characteristics, all describing the functional quality of the office building interior. Technical state and building period were ranked ninth and tenth for the two specific profiles, and several panellists commented upon the interference of these two characteristics with other characteristics of appearance and functionality as a reason for why they were ranked so low.

Lower five

The five building characteristics considered least important by all the panellists, were the same through both rounds, and were also the same for the two specific profiles, the general profile showing a small divergence. The five characteristics mentioned were security, bike parking, routing, energy performance and commodity logistics. In the open part of the interviews from the first round, panel members explained why these characteristics were ranked low: Security and bike parking were mentioned as two characteristics that are easily altered, also for tenants. Energy performance was recognised by the panel as an important issue, but normally only considered by facility managers and not by the decision makers. A major part of the panel considered routing (people) and commodity logistics (of goods and garbage) to be characteristics that are assumed by tenants to be well taken care of by the owner of the building and that the state of these characteristics will be acceptable.

6.3.2 Location

Next to the building characteristics, the expert panel was asked to rank six location characteristics from the most important (rank 1) to the least important (rank 6). The same procedure was followed as for ranking the building characteristics; after the first interview and the ranking of the characteristics, the panellists had the opportunity to revise their opinion for the second round. After the first round, the Kendall W was calculated, and for all three profiles the Kendall W of the location characteristics was much lower than for the building characteristics. The Kendall W for the Urban Specialists profile was (very) weak; 0.28 (see Table 12). For the "status sensitive professionals" profile, the Kendall W of the location characteristics was higher; 0.47 - close to a moderate agreement. Strangely, the Kendall W of the general profile was higher than for the Urban Specialists profile: 0.42.

After the second round, the Kendall W was calculated again. The change in Kendall W between the two rounds was much lower than for building characteristics. Only the general profile revealed significant convergence of opinion. After the second round, the Kendall W's for the ranking of the Urban Specialists profile, the Status Sensitive Professionals and the general profile were respectively 0.35, 0.53 and 0.50. After the second round there was a weak to moderate agreement within the panel, and the confidence within ranks was low

Table 11: Comparison of the rankings of building characteristics from the first and second round

Urban Specialists Ranking	Round 1	Round 2	Change	Status sensitive professionals Ranking	Round 1	Round 2	Change	General profile Ranking	Round 1	Round 2	Change
Car Parking	1	1	=	Car Parking	1	1	=	Car Parking	1	1	=
Exterior appearance	2	2	=	Exterior appearance	2	2	=	Exterior appearance	2	2	=
User recognisability	3	3	=	User recognisability	3	3	=	Space efficiency	3	3	=
Layout flexibility	4	4	=	Space efficiency	4	4	=	Layout flexibility	4	4	=
Space efficiency	6	5	↑	Interior appearance	5	5	=	Interior appearance	6	5	↑
Interior appearance	5	6	↓	Layout flexibility	6	6	=	Comfort	7	6	↑
Comfort	7	7	=	Comfort	8	7	↑	User recognisability	5	7	↓
Building facilities	8	8	=	Building facilities	9	8	↑	Technical state	8	8	=
Technical state	9	9	=	Building period	7	9	↓	Building facilities	9	9	=
Building period	10	10	=	Technical state	10	10	=	Security	10	10	=
Security	11	11	=	Security	11	11	=	Building period	11	11	=
Routing	12	12	=	Routing	13	12	↑	Energy performance	12	12	=
Energy performance	13	13	=	Energy performance	12	13	↓	Routing	13	13	=
Bike parking	14	14	=	Bike parking	14	14	=	Bike parking	14	14	=
Commodity logistics	15	15	=	Commodity logistics	15	15	=	Commodity logistics	15	15	=
Kendall's W*	0.54	0.64	0.10		0.65	0.76	0.11		0.49	0.62	0.13

Table 12 Comparison of the location characteristics rankings from the first and second round

Urban Specialists Ranking	Round 1	Round 2	Change	Status sensitive professionals Ranking	Round 1	Round 2	Change	General profile Ranking	Round 1	Round 2	Change
Accessibility by car	1	1	=	Accessibility by car	2	1	↑	Accessibility by car	1	1	=
Status	2	2	=	Status	1	2	↓	Status	2	2	=
Facilities	3	3	=	Accessibility by public transport	3	3	=	Accessibility by public transport	3	3	=
Business cluster	4	4	=	Business cluster	4	4	=	Facilities	4	4	=
Accessibility by public transport	5	5	=	Facilities	5	5	=	Safety	6	5	↑
Safety	6	6	=	Safety	6	6	=	Business cluster	5	6	↓
Kendall's W*	0.28	0.35	0.07		0.47	0.53	0.06		0.42	0.50	0.09

to fair. New rounds of polling were considered. However, the small change in consensus from the first to the second round signalled that more rounds would not be of added value, and so the polling was stopped. In ranking the location characteristics, little changed from the first to the second round (Table 12). The ranking of the Urban Specialists profile remained unchanged. Accessibility by car was found the most important in both rounds, as it was for the general profile. For the Status sensitive Professionals profile, accessibility by car was ranked first in the second round. Status was ranked second for all three profiles in the second round.

The low Kendall W's showed that the confidence within ranking of the location characteristics was low, and so the rankings should be interpreted cautiously. Accessibility by car was considered the most important characteristic for all three profiles, and the divergence of opinion among the panellists on this characteristic was low. The status characteristics on the other hand, revealed a high divergence of opinion. The panellists commented upon the interdependency of some location characteristics with building characteristics. For instance, if the location has a high facility level, the necessity of facilities in the building will be lower. Also interdependencies between different location characteristics were signalled as a high facility level and good public transport will have positive effect on the social safety.

6.3.3   Checking validity of rankings

Interpreting the rankings of the Delphi panel, there was a significant difference between the agreement of practitioners and academics and government officials. The judgements of the academics and government officials were removed from the data sets, the new data set contained the 11 rankings of the practitioners, still sufficient for a Delphi panel ranking, and new calculations were made. The rankings did not change. The Kendall W for the second round however, rose to 0.77, 0.79 and 0.86 for the building characteristics! For the location characteristics, the Kendall W of the general profile and the "status sensitive professionals" profile rose to 0,55 and 0,56, while for the "urban specialist" profile the Kendall W remained low, at 0,38.

6.3.4   The characteristics of vacant office buildings

"Vacant buildings are ugly and have no parking facilities"

The study shows that accessibility by car and status of the location are the two most important location characteristics for the preference of (all) office users searching for new rental offices, while parking and the appearance of the exterior are recognised as the two most important building characteristics.

In the open second part of the interviews, the experts were asked if the same characteristics as were ranked influencing the office users' preference for specific locations and buildings could also explain vacancy of certain buildings. On location level, low status of the location and low level of facilities in the surroundings were mentioned as the most important reasons, while on building level, an unattractive appearance of the exterior was mentioned as the most important characteristic, specially mentioning buildings constructed between 1970 and 1985. Furthermore, less parking places than the surrounding properties as the second most important characteristic. The explanation was that before searching for new office space, organisations first scan the supply. Repellent buildings on unattractive locations are the first to be discarded. A second filter applied to the available supply will filter out badly accessible locations and buildings with fewer parking spaces than the surrounding properties.

6.4 Summary and Conclusions

The Delphi survey is a stated preferences method, in this case conducted with a panel of experts on office user preferences. It has been used to reveal office users preferences for specific location and building characteristics when acquiring new office space (pull factors), focusing on office users in the Amsterdam office market. Two user profiles were recognised, The Urban Specialist and the Status Sensitive Professional, based on a market report from Atelier V (Atelier V and Motivaction 2005). The Delphi panel was asked to consider both profiles and an additional third general profile when ranking location and building characteristics that they consider important to the three different office user profiles. After two rounds of polling, the Delphi expert panel stated accessibility by car and status to be the most important location characteristics, and also that car parking and exterior appearance are the most important building characteristics. The results were not revolutionary, but rather confirmed the results from earlier studies. However, some characteristics are seen to become more important than in former studies; the facilities characteristic has become more important, something that was also found by Rodenburg (2005), and also the clustering characteristic seems more important than it was for instance in the studies by Korteweg (2002).

The first polling round was conducted as a series of interviews, asking the panellists to rank the location and building characteristics, using cards that were presented to them at the beginning of the interviews, each card describing one characteristic. Next to the ranking, these interviews also consisted of an open second part where the experts were asked which characteristics if any specific; they thought could explain vacancy of certain buildings. On location level, low status of the location and low level of facilities in the surroundings were mentioned as the most important reasons, while on building level, an unattractive appearance of the exterior was mentioned as the most important characteristic, and less parking places than the surrounding properties as the second most important characteristic. The explanation was that before searching for new office space, organisations first scan the supply. Repellent buildings on unappealing locations are the first to be discarded. A second filter applied to the available supply will filter out badly accessible locations and buildings with fewer parking spaces than the surrounding properties.

The Delphi method that was applied here relies on a heterogeneous panel for the power of its conclusions. The validity of the panel was tested by checking the outcome towards the outcome of half of the panel, clustered into a more homogeneous group. The results of this test confirmed the results of the Delphi study; the same results were obtained with a homogeneous panel, though with a higher confidence within ranking.

The hypotheses that were developed from the literature study were tested in the Delphi study, resulting in an intermediary conclusion. The conclusion is formulated as a new hypothesis comprising several partial hypotheses. This hypothesis will be tested in the next chapter, the Office Scan:
Structurally vacant office buildings
- were constructed between 1970 and 1985
- are not well accessible by car and public transport
- are located in unsafe locations
- are located in locations with insufficient facilities
- are located on low-status locations
- are located on monofunctional office locations
- have a low quality of exterior appearance
- hinder expression of the organisations' identity
- are functionally obsolete (inefficient and inflexible)
- have a low quality of interior finishes and routing
- are in technical decay
- provide insufficient climatic and workplace comfort
- generate too high energy costs
- provide insufficient facilities
- have insufficient parking facilities
- lack security measures

Not all the partial hypotheses can be tested by the Office Scan. The data considering expression of the organisations identity could not be retrieved. In the Delphi survey it was measured by the possibility of placing the users name, logo or commercial message on the facade. This variable was not further considered because of its direct association to the building being in use. In the Office Scan the "routing" variable was tested as presence and quality of stairs and elevators and together with the variable "quality of corridors and public space" it was comprised in the "interior appearance" variable.

Furthermore, the partial hypothesis about security, energy costs and facilities in the building were not tested. These data could be retrieved using vignettes, inquiring the employees of office buildings in use, or by inquiries with property managers. As the office scan only considers revealed preferences, these characteristics were not included.

7 The Office Scan

In the preceding chapter, 6 location characteristics and 15 building characteristics were revealed that, according to experts on office organisation accommodation, have a positive effect on the office users' preferences for a specific location and building, within a specific market context. In this chapter, 200 office buildings within the Amsterdam office market are studied and analysed to reveal which location and building characteristics – if any –are significantly associated with structural vacancy. In the United States and the United Kingdom hedonic pricing models are well known and frequently used for studies regarding the influence of physical characteristics on the rental price or sale transactions of real estate properties (DiPasquale 1996; Colwell et al. 1998; Hendershott et al. 1999; Quigley 1999; Wheaton 1999; Fuerst 2007). Research on the value, pricing and vacancy of office space has a longer tradition in these two countries, especially in the United States, than in other European countries. Though studying international literature and specifically literature from these two countries, so far no equivalent studies were found considering the level of structural vacancy of office buildings as a dependent value. Eventually, this research considers 2 models with the dichotomous outcome variables structural vacancy or not, and more or less than 30% structural vacancy. This study is based on the presupposition that structurally vacant office buildings lack qualities that preferred office buildings have, and therefore structural vacancy can be seen as a measurement of user preferences.

7.1 Methodology of data analyses

Logistic regression analyses are used to predict one variable from another variable or from a set of other variables (Hosmer and Lemeshow 2000; Field 2005). These analyses are suitable for studying the combined effect of several independent variables on a dependent variable, though in a combined model, variables impinge on each other and illegitimate associations can be observed, for instance as a result of multicollinearity. Therefore, before running the analyses, the variables were studied one by one, mainly to already take notice of possible strong predictive power of any of the variables, and to discard of independent variables that had no predictive effect on the dependent variable. These analyses were conducted using simple regressions, cross-tabs and bar-charts. Henceforward, the independent variables were tested for interdependent correlations. In the following, variables are discussed that were found to be associated with structural vacancy or structural vacancy at the 30% level. Other variables that were also tested are mentioned in the list of studied variables (Appendix 2). In this study logistic regressions were used, predicting the odds of a specific level of structural vacancy given certain location- and building characteristics. Two models were developed using two different levels of structural vacancy as dichotomous predicted variables. One model used structural vacancy or not, and the other model considered < 30% or > 30% structural vacancy. Variables representing location and building characteristics were the predictors in both models.

Right page:
Figure 17
Sample of office buildings in Amsterdam with structural vacancy

7.2 200 office buildings and locations

The 200 office buildings that were studied are spread out over several locations
in Amsterdam (Figure 18) and were selected randomly from the transaction and
supply databases of DTZ, each database providing approximately half of the
sample. The number of office buildings studied in each location is proportional
to the actual number of office buildings in that location. Within the central canal-
district offices are located in buildings that were originally designed and developed
for other purposes. These buildings are not part of the research sample. Constructed
as houses and warehouses, not only the building characteristics and building
typology differ from the studied office buildings, but also their transformation
potential will differ. The transformation potential of these buildings is mainly
determined by legal aspects of listed buildings and zoning laws. Additionally, the

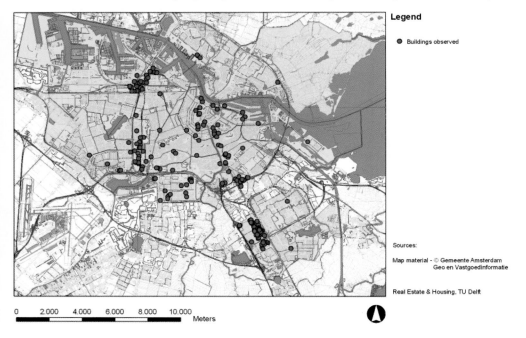

*Figure 18 The
location of the
200 buildings
studied in the
office scan*

scale of these historic buildings is small and neither the buildings nor the available
supply contained by these buildings is retrievable in office market statistics.

   The construction years of the studied buildings differ and herewith the
buildings represent different zeitgeists and architectural styles. Parallel to and to
a certain extent correlating with the different architectural styles and typologies
represented by the studied office buildings, the office locations have changed in the
course of time, and the studied buildings are located in different types of locations,
characterised by their relationship to the urban context, scale of the location,
functional mix, and accessibility.

   The Office Scan is a revealed preferences study confirming or
disqualifying the results of the stated preferences study referred to as the Delphi
Survey. Office users' preference for specific office locations and buildings is based

Location	m2 structurally vacant	Available supply	% structurally vacant	
1 Centre	105,000	1323,000	7.9%	*Table 13*
2 Westpoort	145,800	947,000	15.4%	*Structural*
3 Westerpark	2,000	80,000	2.5%	*vacancy spread*
4 Oud West	2,600	80,000	3.2%	*over the different*
5 Zeeburg	7,100	102,000	7.0%	*locations within*
6 Bos en Lommer	78,000	226,000	34.5%	*Amsterdam*
7 Baarsjes	3,000	49,000	6.2%	*(data retrieved*
8 Amsterdam North	4,700	138,000	3.4%	*from the supply*
9 Geuzenveld/ Slotermeer	14,400	49,000	29.4%	*database of DTZ*
10 Osdorp	12,600	54,000	23.3%	*Zadelhoff, 2007)*
11 Slotervaart	69,700	502,000	13.9%	
12 South East	203,500	1,219,000	16.7%	
13 East / Watergraafsmeer	28,600	482,000	5.9%	
14 Oud-zuid	19,200	512,000	3.8%	
15 Zuideramstel	83,100	769,000	10.8%	
Total Amsterdam	779,300	6532,000	11.9%	

on a preference for a specific geographical market and market segment, followed by a preference for location and building that can be described by its physical characteristics. In concordance with the Delphi study, the location and building aspects that were defined and studied in the survey are also studied in the Office Scan. The studied aspects (Appendix 2) are comprised in a hypothesis stating the relationship between location- and building characteristics and structural vacancy. The hypothesis originally comprised 20 sub-theses, of which 6 were discharged after the Delphi survey (6.4). In the following subchapters this hypothesis and sub-hypotheses are tested.

The structural vacancy in Amsterdam is spread over numerous buildings, some 100% vacant though most buildings have a far lower level of structural vacancy. 106 of the 200 studied office buildings had some level of structural vacancy on the date used for the data collection, the 31st of December 2007. These buildings are again proportionally scattered across Amsterdam and also according to the year of construction and type of location the sample is proportional to the total numbers of the Amsterdam office market.

Though the vacancy has been rising also during the last years, the buildings studied had a registered level of vacancy in the years of 2005, 2006 and 2007. The following figure (Figure 19) shows the total numbers and spread of buildings with structural vacancy throughout Amsterdam, including the buildings in the studied sample. Structural vacancy is concentrating in some locations, like Amsterdam South East and Amsterdam Westpoort. Though if expressed as percentages (*Figure 20*) areas like Bos en Lommer and Osdorp have the highest levels of structural vacancy, these locations don't have a large stock of office buildings. Amsterdam South East and Amsterdam Westpoort on the other hand, together with the city centre, have the highest amounts of office space and also the highest amounts of structurally vacant office space.

Amsterdam South East is a monofunctional office location developed in the 1980s, as part of an area with specific functional zones for retail and leisure, distribution and offices, separated by the railway from the already existing housing location in the Bijlmermeer area. 17% of the total amount of 1.2 million square metres office space in the location is structurally vacant, and in some of the sub-locations the structural vacancy is as high as 45%. Still, new buildings are being developed in this location.

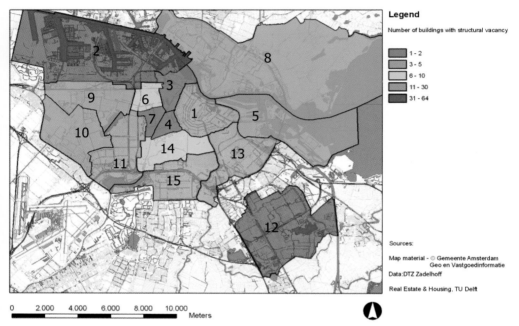

Figure 19
Number of
buildings with
structural
vacancy per
location
(numbered areas
correspond to
numbers in table
13)

Amsterdam Westpoort comprises the two sub-locations Teleport and Sloterdijk and is another area with a large amount of buildings with structural vacancy, also developed as a large scale office location from the eighties onwards. While the Teleport location is characterised by its harbour activities, industry, logistics and offices, the Sloterdijk location is a monofunctional office area with Sloterdijk railway station in the centre. 16% of the approximately 1 million square metres of office space is vacant. Also in this location new developments take place.

The highest structural vacancy levels are found in Slotervaart and in Bos en Lommer, areas with few office buildings. Bos en Lommer has 220000 square metres of office space; 35% is structurally vacant. These areas were developed in the 1950s and 1960s and are large scale office buildings originally developed for owner-occupiers, though most of these occupiers have now moved to other buildings and locations. Also the areas surrounding the Westas/Riekerpolder and the Zuidas/Buitenveldert, locations on the ring-road, have vacancy levels above 10%. The locations near the Westas were developed in the 1950s and 1960s, while the locations near the Zuidas were first developed between 1960 and 1980 as small scale developments before being redeveloped, extended and intensified after 2000 in Amsterdams newest development plan. The structural vacancy in the Zuidas area is concentrated in older office buildings that were built as part of the 1960s development near Buitenveldert.

Finally, the city centre, though its vacancy level is only 8%, comprises a large total amount of structurally vacant office space. Next to South East, the city centre has the most office space with approximately 1.2 million square metres. Though Amsterdam has a historical city centre with numerous historical office

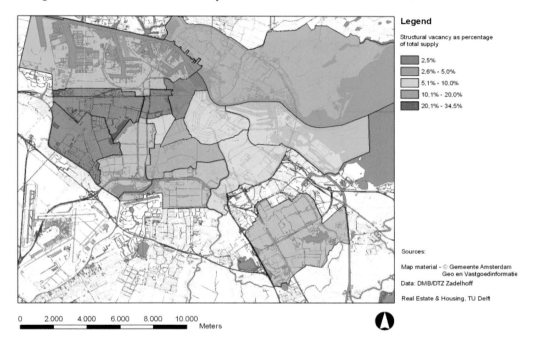

buildings, the centre also has several newer office buildings, developed from the nineteen-sixties onward. The areas north and east of the city centre have few offices and also a low level of structural vacancy.

Figure 20 Percentage of structural vacancy of the total m2 of office space in each location

7.3 Structural vacancy and specific physical characteristics

The association between structural vacancy and location and building characteristics is studied by correlation analyses and visualised by using graphical charts. After these initial studies, regression analyses are conducted. Regression analyses not only makes it possible to draw a picture of the correlation between specific physical building and location characteristics and structural vacancy, but are used to predict the value of one variable from another variable or a set of variables. Logistic regressions are used to model the relationship between a dichotomous outcome variable and a set of independent variables, also called covariates or predictors. Working with a dichotomous outcome variable makes logistic regressions more stable with a smaller number of cases than is needed for a stable linear regression model. In this research, the independent variables in the logistic regression model were used to predict the odds of structural vacancy at a given level. Two models were developed, one with the outcome variable structural vacancy/no structural vacancy, and the other model with the outcome variable >30% structural vacancy/<30% structural vacancy. In the sample of 200 office buildings, 106 had some level of structural vacancy. 56 buildings in the sample had a structural vacancy level higher than 30%.

Next to the location and building characteristics, office buildings can be described by some basic variables. These describe the buildings address and physical coordinates, and also the construction year, renovation year, number of square metres available and the level of structural vacancy, and asking rent. Before analysing the specific location and building characteristics, the effects of the basic characteristic 'Year of Construction' are studied.

Year of Construction

The year of construction is a variable that is significantly correlated to structural vacancy, both when studying this variable as a continuous scale variable and as a dummy variable (Figure 21). The year of construction does not as such describe the actual building but correlates strongly to several building variables that again describe building characteristics. These correlations are first studied to reveal what the variable tells. Flexibility and efficiency of the lay-out, appearance and quality of the interior finish, and comfort are all characteristics described by variables that correlate with the year of construction. Variables that describe the exterior of office buildings and that correlate with the year of construction are type of material and the quality of the facade and the building being a landmark. Also basic building variables like building size and height correlate with the year of construction, as does, not surprisingly, the variable 'year of renovation'. Newer buildings are not yet renovated while older buildings were maybe renovated several times. Only the last renovation is considered as a variable in this research. That the year of construction correlates with so many of the building characteristics is not surprising, as also the theoretical framework of this research shows the changing ideas of architecture and urbanism and the change in building types in the course of time.

Variables describing the building site, such as the quality of the public space, a mix with other functions and the implementation of parking on the site, are also correlating with the year of construction. The year of construction also correlates strongly to a series of location variables; distance to highway, level of services in or near the location, and the amount of other functions in the location. It is noteworthy that the distance to the highway is the only distance variable that correlates with the year of construction; as neither the distance to a station nor to other public transportation shows a significant relationship. The notion of correlations between the year of construction and location characteristics is explainable from the urban development of the city of Amsterdam and its office market, as locations have been laid out successively and since ideas and ideals have changed in the course of time (Jolles et al. 2003; Hoek et al. 2007). In paragraph 7.7 the specific building and location characteristics of office buildings constructed

Structural Vacancy at the 30% level x Year of construction			Year of construction categories				
			<1965	65-79	80-94	>1995	total
Structural Vacancy	<30%	Count	22	20	51	60	153
		Adjusted Residual	2.5	.4	-3.9	2.1	
	>=30%	Count	1	6	35	13	55
		Adjusted Residual	-2.5	-.4	3.9	-2.1	
	Total	Count	23	26	86	73	208

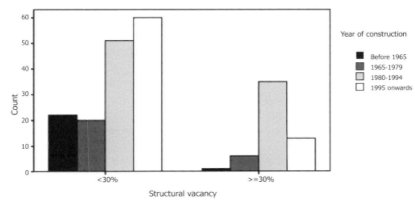

Figure 21 Crosstabs showing the correlation between structural vacancy at the 30% level and year of construction of office buildings. Office buildings constructed before 1965 have lower odds for structural vacancy at the 30% level than other office buildings.

between 1985 and 1995 will be described more thoroughly. A part of the hypothesis that was kept after the Delphi survey stated the following relationship between Year of Construction and structural vacancy:

Structurally vacant office buildings were constructed between 1970 and 1985.

A part of the hypothesis that was kept after the Delphi survey can already be discarded. Figure 21 shows that construction year is a variable that correlates significantly with structural vacancy. Few buildings constructed between 1970 and 1985 have a structural vacancy level of 30% or more. The hypothesis is discarded based on the initial studies of the variable and based on the office scan the association between structural vacancy and construction year is concluded:

Most structurally vacant office buildings were constructed between 1980 and 1995.

7.4   Location characteristics and structural vacancy

Again to make the hypothesis derived from the Delphi survey testable, the location variables and building variables were tested separately. The location variables together describe the five characteristics that were included in the hypothesis on location and structural vacancy: Accessibility by car, accessibility by public transport, facility level, safety and status. The variables were tested in several sequences, with the aim of finally revealing which variables and characteristics increase the odds of structural vacancy in office buildings.

The level of structural vacancy in office buildings differed between the defined locations, as also shown in Figure 19 and *Figure 20*. Describing the locations by some of the location characteristics, the differences could be retrieved just by eyeballing. Some observations of the main location characteristics:

Most locations are well accessible by car, though some are better accessible from the highway than other locations. Accessibility by car is measured as distance in minutes driving from the highway. The city centre is typically less well accessible by car than the other locations.

Most locations are well accessible by train (public transport), though the type of railway station differs. Within the locations there are some differences. Accessibility by public transport is measured in distance from the railway station in metres. For instance, some buildings in South-East are located next to the Bijlmeer station, while other buildings in this location are more than 1 kilometre removed from it. The location is served by bus-lines, but no tram.

The facility level and the mix of functions seem to differ significantly between the locations. In the city centre offices are mixed with housing, retail and leisure, while in South east, Zuidas and Westpoort there are relatively few facilities and little housing. In the Zuidas housing will be added to the program.

Data on the safety of a location are retrieved from the Amsterdam safety-index and is not measured in the Office Scan. The perceived safety relates to the social security of a location and whether or not it is inhabited 24 hours a day. The perceived safety is the highest in the city centre, while objectively measured by number of incidents, the centre is actually the least safe location in Amsterdam (Amsterdam 2003).

The status of the area is retrieved by a combination of variables as well. Quality and ageing of the buildings and public space (including parks) in the location, visibility of the location or the presence of landmarks or historical buildings, and the presence and type of other functions in the location. The City Centre and Zuidas are different examples of high status locations: The City centre because of its historic urban fabric, listed monuments and mix of functions, the Zuidas because it has no industry or distribution business, the main function is offices, it is visible from the highway, the public space and most buildings are new and equipped with high quality materials. The location is contrasted by other locations like again South-East or the smaller locations west to the city centre.

In the following paragraphs, the buildings were analysed by their location variables, studying which location variables increase the odds of structural vacancy. The variables were tested one by one to study possible correlations between the variable and structural vacancy at the levels of >0 and >30%. The variables that correlated positively or negatively at a significance level of 0.25 to the dichotomous variables structural vacancy or >30%structural vacancy were used in the logistic regression.

Finally, a combination of 24 variables was found that together predict the odds of structural vacancy with a correctness of 81%. Using only the four most significant variables the correctness of the prediction was 71.8%. These variables considered accessibility by train and car, parking and the year of construction of the building. Since year of construction of the building is a basic variable, this variable was taken into account also when regarding the location. Parking was seen as a characteristic belonging to the building, since it is mostly arranged per property, though the characteristic relates to the accessibility characteristics. The following series of maps show the location differences between the sample of structurally vacant office buildings and sample of the total stock.

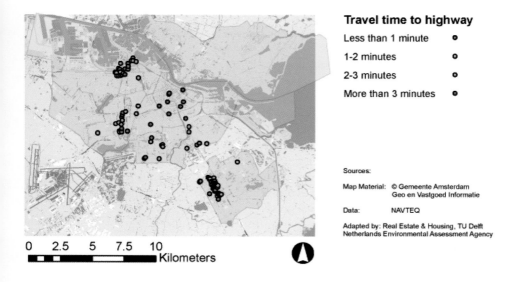

Figure 22 Travel time to the highway from structurally vacant office buildings in the sample.

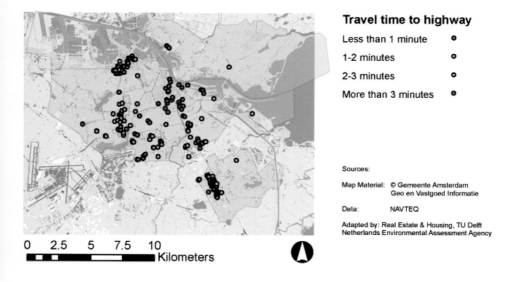

Figure 23 Travel time to the highway from all office buildings in the sample.

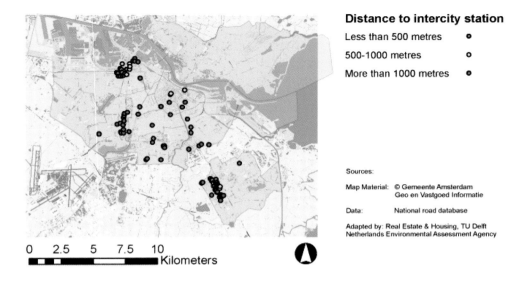

Figure 24 Distance to the intercity station from structurally vacant office buildings in the sample.

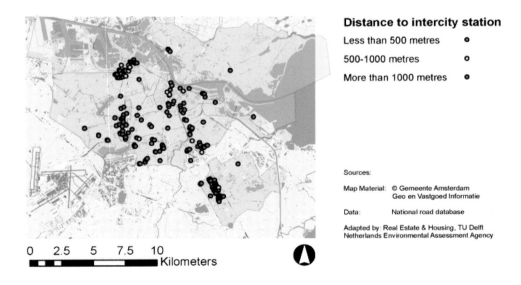

Figure 25 Distance to the intercity station from all office buildings in the sample.

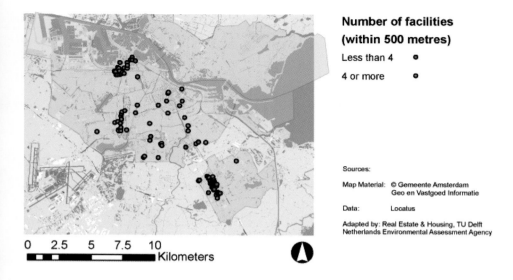

Figure 26 Facilities within 500 metres from structurally vacant office buildings in the sample.

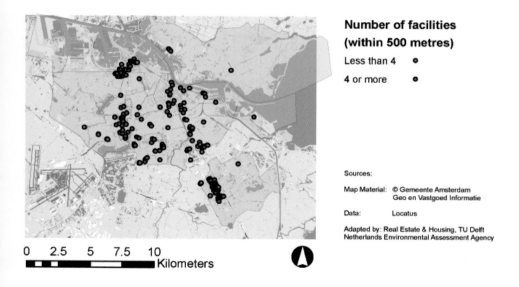

Figure 27 Facilities within 500 metres from all office buildings in the sample.

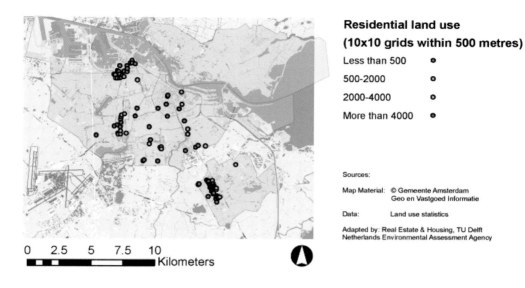

Sources:

Map Material: © Gemeente Amsterdam
                Geo en Vastgoed Informatie

Data: Land use statistics

Adapted by: Real Estate & Housing, TU Delft
Netherlands Environmental Assessment Agency

Figure 28 Housing units within 500 metres from structurally vacant office buildings in the sample.

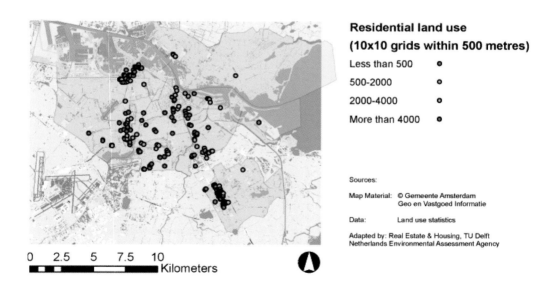

Sources:

Map Material: © Gemeente Amsterdam
                Geo en Vastgoed Informatie

Data: Land use statistics

Adapted by: Real Estate & Housing, TU Delft
Netherlands Environmental Assessment Agency

Figure 29 Housing units within 500 metres from all office buildings in the sample.

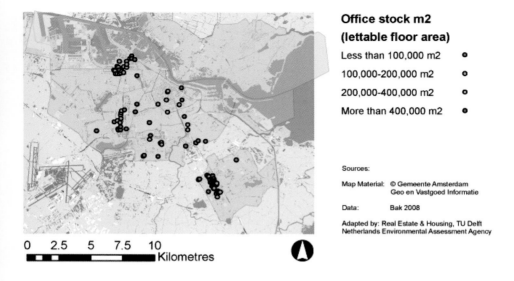

Figure 30 Square metres office space within 500 metres from structurally vacant office buildings in the sample.

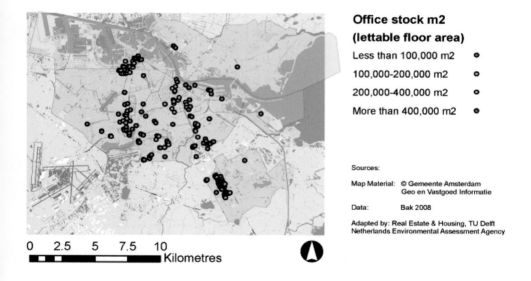

Figure 31 Square metres office space within 500 metres from all office buildings in the sample.

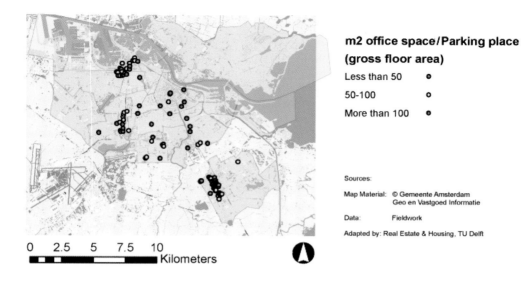

Figure 32 Parking places/m² office space for structurally vacant office buildings in the sample.

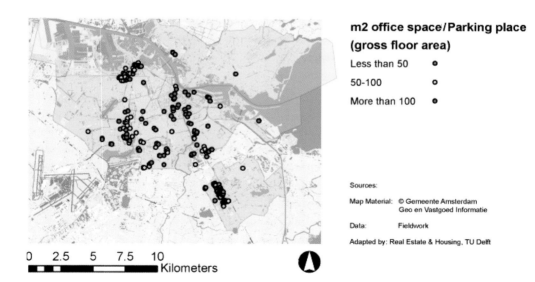

Figure 33 Parking places/m² office space for all office buildings in the sample.

7.4.1 Accessibility by car

Accessibility by car is an important variable in the logistic regression. Using the scale-variable of travel time from the building to the nearest highway exit, the odds of structural vacancy at a level of 30% or more decreased as the building was located further from the highway! This result was not expected, and because the association between distance to the highway and structural vacancy was also not linear, further tests were conducted with this variable defined as dummy-variables. These tests showed that buildings that were located closer to the highway exit than a 2 minutes drive had increased odds of structural vacancy; while buildings located more than 2 minutes drive from the highway had lower odds of structural vacancy.

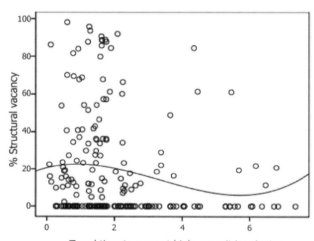

Figure 34 the Y-axis shows the level of structural vacancy in percentages, the X-level shows the distance to the nearest highway-exit.

In buildings located further away than 2 minutes, the structural vacancy was significantly lower. The results of the correlation analysis were not expected and not easily explained. In former research (Louw 1996; Korteweg 2002) and in the Delphi study, accessibility by car was found to be the most important characteristic describing the quality of a location. However, before claiming to have revealed breaking news about the association between structural vacancy and accessibility by car, the variable accessibility by car was tested to look for explanations by building characteristics and other location characteristics. For instance, accessibility by car was found to work as a proxy for other characteristics that are typically related to locations near highways, such as industrial and distribution areas.

The correlation between accessibility from the highway and other location characteristics was studied, and a correlation at the 0.01 level was found between accessibility and the level of facilities in the location. According to these analyses, office buildings well accessible from the highway are often located in industrial or distribution locations with few or no facilities within 500 metres. Office buildings with this combination of characteristics more often than other office buildings have a structural vacancy level of 30% or higher. The variable 'accessibility by car' was used as input in the multi-variable regressions. If in these analyses other variables would explain the high level of structural vacancy in office buildings near the highway, the variable would not be important for the analysis, or the value of the variable would be corrected.

Structural Vacancy x Distance to highway exit							
			Distance to highway exit in minutes				
			< 1	1-2	2-3	> 3	total
Structural Vacancy	no	Count	21	36	18	29	104
		Adjusted Residual	-1.7	-1.4	.6	3.0	
	yes	Count	32	46	15	12	105
		Adjusted Residual	1.7	1.4	-.6	-3.0	
	Total	Count	53	82	33	41	209

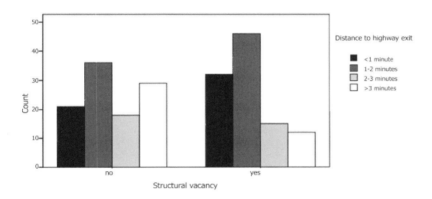

Figure 35 Crosstabs showing the correlation between structural vacancy at the 30% level and year of construction of office buildings.

Industrial and distribution location x Distance to highway exit							
			Distance to highway exit in minutes				
			< 1	1-2	2-3	> 3	total
Industrial and distribution location	no	Count	25	28	29	35	117
		Adjusted Residual	-1.5	-5.1	4.0	4.2	
	yes	Count	28	54	4	6	92
		Adjusted Residual	1.5	5.1	-4.0	-4.2	
	Total	Count	53	82	33	41	209

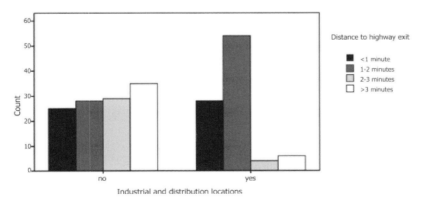

Figure 36 Crosstabs showing the correlation between structural vacancy at the 30% level and year of construction of office buildings.

7.4.2 Accessibility by public transport

*Figure 37
Crosstabs
showing the
correlation
between
structural
vacancy and
distance to IC
station.*

Structural Vacancy x Distance to IC station

			Distance to IC station in metres			
			< 500	500-1000	> 1000	total
Structural Vacancy	no	Count	16	12	76	104
		Adjusted Residual	-1.0	-2.9	3.2	
	yes	Count	22	29	54	105
		Adjusted Residual	1.0	2.9	-3.2	
Total		Count	38	41	130	209

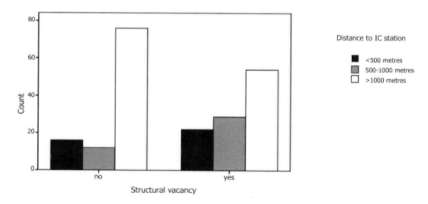

Accessibility by public transport is defined by several variables in the logistic regression; the distances to the nearest railway station, InterCity station and tram and metro stops in metres. The distance to the nearest bus-stop was tested but did not correlate with structural vacancy. If the distance to the nearest InterCity station, metro- or tram stop increases, the odds of structural vacancy increases. However, the correlation with structural vacancy was not found to be linear for any of the variables. Studying the variable distance to nearest InterCity station by cross-tabulation and using a bar chart, its relationship to structural vacancy became clearer. Looking at buildings with structural vacancy, it became clear that there is a positive correlation between structural vacancy and the distance to nearest InterCity station. However, if looking at the buildings that were not structurally vacant, a high number of office buildings located further than 1000 metres away from an InterCity station were found. Studying the maps (Figure 24, Figure 25), these office buildings appear to be located on locations in or near the city centre. Furthermore, the maps show clustering of structural vacancy near the railway stations Amsterdam Sloterdijk and Amsterdam Bijlmer ArenA. These buildings cause a high level of structural vacancy in office buildings located closer to the InterCity station than 500 metres. The variables distance to the nearest InterCity station, metro- or tram stop were all applied to the multi-variable analyses.

7.4.3 Facilities

Structural Vacancy at the 30% level x facilities within 500 metres					
			facilities within 500 metres		
			< 4	>= 4	total
Structural Vacancy	no	Count	42	111	153
		Adjusted Residual	-3.1	3.1	
	yes	Count	28	28	56
		Adjusted Residual	3.1	-3.1	
	Total	Count	70	139	209

Figure 38 Crosstabs showing the correlation between structural vacancy and the presence of 4 or more facilities within 500 metres.

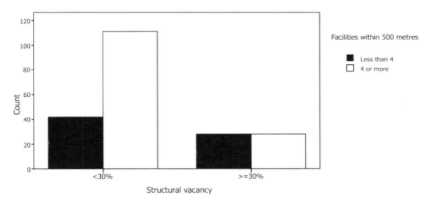

The amount of facilities in a location correlates significantly to structural vacancy. In the sample, if 4 or more shops and restaurants were located within 500 metres, 26% of the buildings had a structural vacancy level of 30% or more. If there were less or none of these facilities in the area, the percentage increased to 43%. The correlation between a 30% level of structural vacancy and a restaurant or café within 50 metres from the building was also tested. Here, if a restaurant or café is located within 50 metres from the building, 23% of the buildings have a structural vacancy level of 30% or more. If there are none, the percentage increases to 31%. The presence of facilities within 500 metres from the building was found to be of higher importance than a café next door, but in the regression analyses both variables were used.

The logistic regression model showed that the presence of shops and restaurants within 500 metres around the building decreases the odds of structural vacancy at the level of 30%, and if removed from the total model the models fit would decrease. The amount of shops and restaurants in the location expresses its urbanity and liveliness. Locations with few or no facilities tend to be places where people are not encouraged to spend time outdoors. Facilities like restaurants and bars also tend to have opening hours that extend those of offices, production and shops, and contribute to a 24/7 use of the location.

7.4.4 Status

Figure 39
Crosstabs
showing the
correlation
between
structural
vacancy and
littering in the
location.

Structural Vacancy x Litter in location

			Litter in location			
			none	some	substantial	total
Structural Vacancy	no	Count	11	89	8	108
		Adjusted Residual	.2	.8	-1.2	
	yes	Count	10	83	13	106
		Adjusted Residual	-.2	-.8	1.2	
	Total	Count	21	172	21	214

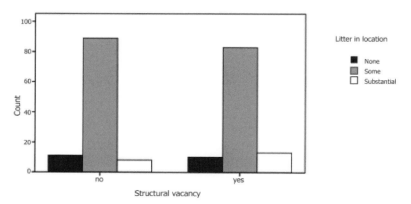

Next to accessibility by car, status was found the second most important location characteristic in the Delphi survey. The status of a location is described by several variables. Some of these are variables describing building characteristics; i.e. recognisability, quality of the facade materials and the technical state of the facade. These characteristics correlate strongly to the year of construction of the building; hence year of construction was also studied as a variable influencing the status of the building. The building characteristics were combined in a meta-variable that described the quality of buildings in the location. Furthermore, variables describing the public space were seen as part of the characteristic defining the status of a location. These are variables like the level of littering and graffiti in on the site and the quality of the street furniture on or adjacent to the site. The type of activities taking place in the location also contributes to the status of the location. The number of office buildings, the amount of square metres of office buildings, and the employment in industry and logistic distributions in the area are variables that are measured.

7.5 Building characteristics and structural vacancy

After the Delphi survey, the hypothesis about the relationship between the building characteristics and structural vacancy was refined to 9 partial hypotheses. These describe the 10 characteristics efficiency, flexibility, exterior appearance, recognisability, interior quality, technical quality, comfort, energy costs, internal facilities or services, and parking. Again, the variables were tested in several sequences, in order to obtain not only the best predicting model but the most reliable model. The 10 characteristics were, like the location characteristics, subdivided into variables that together describe the characteristic. The variables were tested for correlations with structural vacancy by using cross tabulations and bar charts, and finally regressions were conducted per variable to study the influence of the variable on structural vacancy at the 30% level.

7.5.1   Interior quality

Office buildings are rarely let fully furnished; rather the work-floors are delivered as "basic" as possible, so the actual appearance of office buildings interior is decided by the tenant. The variables that describe the buildings interior quality and that show interesting correlations to structural vacancy are floor size, height and spatiality of the entrance, and the standard free floor heights. The ratio of elevators per square metre lettable floor space, and the availability of a central staircase and possible use of escape stairs as secondary stairs were also studied but showed no correlation to structural vacancy. The square metres dedicated to sanitary facilities per floor, is the last interior quality-variable that was measured. This variable reflects the general quality of the interior and the net/gross ratio of usable area vs. rented area. The last variable showed slight correlation with structural vacancy, but was less interesting than the variables discussed in the following.

The space ratio of the entrance is defined by the REN norm (Stichting REN 1992) as one of the variables that describes the quality of a buildings interior. The space ratio is defined as the entrance surface divided by the entrance height. The figure above shows that if the space ratio is between 8 and 15 fewer buildings are structurally vacant at the 30% level than if the variable has another value. For an entrance of 50 square metres, a space ratio between 8 and 15 means that the height of the entrance is between 3.3 metres and 6.3 metres, describing in that case an entrance with a ceiling height between normal floor height and double. On the other hand, low entrances or entrances with a floor height relatively low compared to the floor size of the entrance, as well as high entrances, relatively high compared to the floor surface, show significant correlations with structural vacancy.

The floor height of office buildings is another important aspect of the quality of the interior. The free floor height, or usable height, is in the Netherlands defined by the building decree (VROM 2003) to be at least 2.6 metres. This term applies for new constructions, while older buildings may still have a free floor height lower than 2.6 metres, though few examples are registered within the research sample. The most commonly used free floor height is between 2.6 and 2.8 metres. The variation between 2.6 metres and 2.8 metres does not necessarily mean that the total floor height (including the construction) is higher; it is given by the total height minus the construction height, minus the height needed for installations. A correlation was found between structural vacancy and office buildings with a free floor height between 2.6 and 2.8 metres, although the relationship was not significant. Structural vacancy at the 30% level correlated negatively to a free floor height higher than 2.8 metres.

*Figure 40
Crosstabs
showing the
correlation
between
structural
vacancy at the
30% level and
entrance
spatiality.*

Structural Vacancy at the 30% level x Entrance spatiality						
					Entrance	spatiality
			<8	>=8, <15	>=15	total
Structural Vacancy	<30%	Count	22	42	94	158
		Adjusted Residual	-.4	2.2	-1.6	
	>=30%	Count	9	7	40	56
		Adjusted Residual	.4	-2.2	1.6	
	Total	Count	31	49	134	214

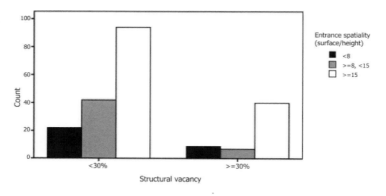

*Figure 41
Crosstabs
showing the
correlation
between
structural
vacancy at the
30% level and
free floor height.*

Structural Vacancy at the 30% level x Free Floor height						
					Free Floor	height
			<2.6 m	>=2.6, <2.8 m	>=2.6m	total
Structural Vacancy	<30%	Count	4	116	38	158
		Adjusted Residual	-.4	-1.3	1.5	
	>=30%	Count	2	46	8	56
		Adjusted Residual	.4	1.3	-1.5	
	Total	Count	6	162	46	214

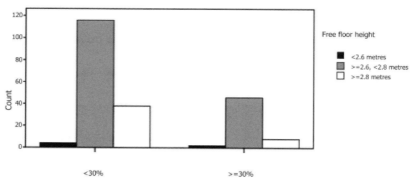

7.5.2 Efficiency and flexibility of the floor plan

Structural Vacancy at the 30% level x Distance between columns						
			Distance between columns			
			>= 8 m	6-8 m	<= 6 m	total
Structural Vacancy	<30%	Count	28	86	44	158
		Adjusted Residual	1.9	-2.5	1.2	
	>=30%	Count	4	41	11	56
		Adjusted Residual	-1.9	2.5	-1.2	
	Total	Count	32	127	55	214

Figure 42 Crosstabs showing the correlation between structural vacancy and distance between columns.

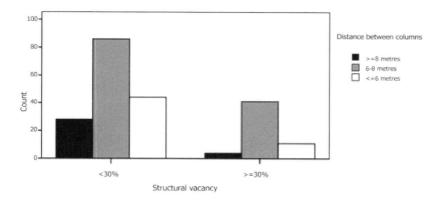

The efficiency and flexibility of the floor plan are two characteristics that together decide the functioning or possibly the malfunctioning and functional obsolescence of a building. These characteristics were defined by the size of a standard floor, the distances between columns (bay width) in both directions, and the measurements of the facade grid. First, the variables were tested for correlations. This analysis showed that a decrease in the measurements of the structural grid, defined by the distance between columns, correlated to structural vacancy at the 30% level. Running a logistic regression analysis on these variables against 30% structural vacancy revealed that if the distance between the columns is 8 metres or more, the odds of structural vacancy at the 30% level will decrease. The relationship between the facade grid and structural vacancy tells the same story; the odds of structural vacancy at the 30% levels increase if the measurements of the facade grid increase. A large distance between the columns and a small scale facade grid both increase the flexibility of the floor plan, showing that decrease of flexibility will increase the odds of structural vacancy at the 30% level.

Next to being a measurement for the flexibility in use of the office building, the measurements of the structure is one of the important measures to determine the transformation potential of office buildings. Small distances between columns and low ceiling height decrease a buildings transformation potential. A wide facade grid complicates the placing of interior walls for e.g. a housing or hotel function.

7.5.3 Exterior appearance and recognisability

Figure 43
Crosstabs
showing the
correlation
between
structural
vacancy at the
30% level and
facade material.

Structural Vacancy at the 30% level x Facade material

			stone	glass	metal	bricks	comp	total
						Facade material		
Structural Vacancy	<30%	Count	30	16	29	52	31	158
		Adjusted Residual	.2	-3.0	.1	1.1	1.2	
	>=30%	Count	10	15	10	14	7	56
		Adjusted Residual	-.2	3.0	.0	-1.1	-1.2	
	Total	Count	40	31	39	66	38	214

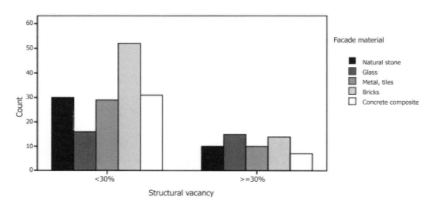

In the Delphi survey the panellists stated that structurally vacant office buildings are ugly buildings from the nineteen seventies and eighties with curtain walls of prefab concrete. Since "ugly buildings" is a rather subjective term, other variables were sought for interpreting the external appearance of the building as a characteristic. The variables that define the external appearance of the building are building height, whether the building is a landmark, a listed monument or a building with specific architectural expression, the facade materials and the technical state of the facade. These are the same variables that define the buildings recognisability, though in this category, landmark, high-rise and specific architectural expression are the most important variables. The variables facade material and technical quality of the facade both correlated to structural vacancy at the 30% level if the facade material was glass or natural stone, and if the technical quality of the facade was low. As ageing of building facades is closely related to the year of construction of the building, a combined variable was included in the logistic regression models. In the models, the combined variable was found to be a more significant predictor than the facade material variable. Additionally, if the building was a landmark or a high-rise, this correlated negatively to structural vacancy at the 30% level. However, few buildings were found in the category landmark or high-rise!

7.5.4 Comfort

Structural Vacancy at the 30% level x Daylight admittance							Figure 44

			Daylight admittance				
			>=70%	50-70%	<50%	total
Structural Vacancy	<30%	Count	11	39	108	158
		Adjusted Residual	1.4	.0	-.7	
	>=30%	Count	1	14	41	56
		Adjusted Residual	-1.4	.0	.7	
	Total	Count	12	53	149	214

Figure 44 Crosstabs showing the correlation between structural vacancy at the 30% level and daylight admittance.

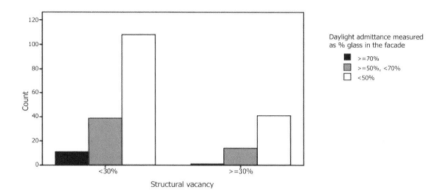

Daylight admittance measured as % glass in the facade
■ >=70%
▨ >=50%, <70%
☐ <50%

The characteristic comfort indicates the climatic comfort of the work place. The experience of climatic comfort is known to depend on whether or not facilities are available for controlling the indoor climate, and whether or not the climate can be controlled for each individual workplace (Baum 1993; Bottom et al. 1998). The latter was not studied here; this study considered only the level of facilities. The variables studied were daylight admittance, the availability of external sun shades and to which extent the windows were operable. In an early stage of the study, also the type of ventilation and air-conditioning was studied. However, the air ventilation and conditioning showed a high level of conformity; most office buildings were found to have systems according to the rules of the building decree (VROM 2003), air-conditioned according to a peak-control system. The functioning of such a system is important; however these data were not retrievable.

To which extent the windows are operable and whether or not the building has external sun shades did not correlate to structural vacancy. Of the comfort variables that were tested, daylight admittance was the only variable that correlated with structural vacancy. Buildings with low daylight admittance, measured as a percentage of the buildings facade, were more often vacant at the 30% level than office buildings with more daylight admittance, while buildings with high daylight admittance had significantly less structural vacancy. Buildings with an almost open facade where 70 to 90 percent of the facade was made of glass and admits daylight show a significantly negative correlation to structural vacancy.

7.5.5 Parking

Structural Vacancy at the 30% level x Type of parking			Type of parking				
			missing	built	outdoor	none	total
Structural Vacancy	<30%	Count	4	59	75	20	158
		Adjusted Residual	1.2	.5	-1.5	1.1	
	>=30%	Count	0	19	33	4	56
		Adjusted Residual	-1.2	-.5	1.5	-1.1	
Total		Count	4	78	108	24	214

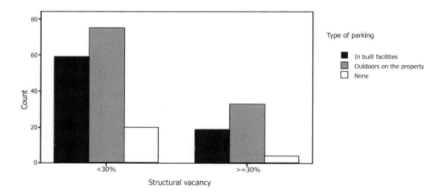

In this study, parking was measured by two variables; square metres lettable floor space assigned to one parking place, and the type of parking facility, i.e. parking in the public domain, on the property though outdoor, or parking in a built facility. The number of parking places available correlated negatively to the level of structural vacancy, something that confirmed the results from former research and from the Delphi survey. The type of parking to a certain extent also correlated to the level of structural vacancy. Few buildings have no parking facilities at all, and most of these buildings are located in the historic city centre. The city centre offers qualities that are not experienced in other locations, and this may be the reason that buildings without any parking facilities actually were not found to have a higher level of structural vacancy than other office buildings; though parking is important, other qualities may compensate this importance. The theory of compensation was described by Baum (1991) and describes that tenants are willing to accept an object that does not have all qualities that were initially required if the value of one of the qualities is high enough to balance the negative qualities. Outdoor parking on the property on the other hand was found to correlate to structural vacancy on the 0.05 level, or as graphically shown in Figure 45. Interestingly, outdoor parking on the property also correlated on the 0.01 level with industrial or distribution locations. These are low density locations with room for parking on the street level and focus on accessibility. These areas have less focus on the quality of the public space. Finally, parking in a built facility showed a slightly negative correlation with structural vacancy, however not on a significant level. What's noteworthy is that built facility parking correlated negatively at the 0.01 level to the square metres lettable floor space assigned to one parking place. It is reasonable to expect that the extra quality of built parking facilities is counterbalanced by the low amount of assigned parking places per square metre.

7.6   Logistic regression model

Finally, the location- and building- variables that were studied were incorporated in the development of the logistic regression models, using < 30% or > 30% structural vacancy as an outcome variable in the first model and structural vacancy in the second model. Developing the models, variables were used that were associated to user preferences according to the Delphi study and that according to the uni-variable analyses had an effect on one of the outcome variable with a significance of $p <= 0.25$. Interaction variables defined by two independent variables were also tested and were added to the model. Examples of such interaction variables were travel time to the highway and the number of office buildings within 500 metres, distance to train stations and the number of office buildings within 500 metres, year of construction and facade quality, and year of construction and type of facade material. Several other combinations were applied to test whether variables that were not found to be significant would become significant if combined with other variables, or if already significant variables would be significantly influenced by other variables. Combined variables with a significant effect on the model were incorporated. Henceforth, the model was developed with the aim of defining a model that explained structural vacancy using as few variables as possible. During this process, variables were discarded that had a negative or no effect on the fit of the total model (Hosmer and Lemeshow 2000).

The models were developed using a forward stepwise method and adding the variables by blocks. First, the building variables were added, in the second block the location variables were added, and in a third block, interaction variables were added. The fit of the models was tested by using a backward stepwise method, and also by adding the location variables in the first block and the building variables in the second block. The resulting models did not differ significantly.

To a great extent the models confirmed the outcome of our Delphi survey, showing the importance of status, parking, flexible lay-out and appearance of the building. The facade material is an important part of both models, in combination with the year of construction. The most important location characteristic from the Delphi survey was accessibility by car. This variable is only part of the first model. The location characteristics that affect the prediction of structural vacancy at the 30% level are variables that describe the status of the location: public space, graffiti and the presence of industry or distribution. In both models, the location variables show the importance of a mixed-use area, as the odds ratio for structural vacancy will increase with the number of office buildings within 500 metres, and decrease with the number of shops for daily necessities within 50 metres. The facade material is an important variable to describe the exterior appearance of a building. This variable is incorporated in the model in combination with the buildings construction year. The models show the association between facade materials and structural vacancy, dependant on the buildings year of construction.

Table 14 Logistic *regression* *model using >=* *30% structural* *vacancy as* *outcome* *variable*	Variables in the equation			Odds ratio (exp b)	95.0% C.I.	
		B	S.E. (B)		Lower	Upper
	Year of construction (categories)					
	1950-64	-18.97	15589.53	.00	.00	.
	1965-79	-.72	1.34	.49	.04	6.67
	1980-94	.52	.78	1.68	.36	7.78
	Parking	-.02	.41	.98	.44	2.19
	Entrance spatiality (categories)					
	Narrow (<8)	.68	.70	1.97	.50	7.74
	Standard (8-15)	-1.19**	.60	.30	.09	.99
	Structural grid (categories)					
	>8 metres	-.50	1.02	.61	.08	4.45
	>5.4 metres <= 8 metres	.85	.75	2.34	.54	10.26
	Graffiti (categories)					
	none	-2.81*	1.71	.06	.01	1.72
	some	-1.78	1.78	.17	.01	5.54
	Travel distance to highway					
	<1 minute	.62	1.22	1.85	.17	20.14
	>= 1 minute, < 2 minutes	1.10	1.16	3.01	.31	28.90
	>= 2 minutes, < 3 minutes	-.31	1.19	.78	.07	7.53
	Distance to metro	.00	.01	1.00	1.00	1.00
	Shops within 50 metres	-2.59	2.29	.08	.01	6.71
	Shops within 500 metres	-.08**	.03	.92	.86	.98
	M2 offices within 500 metres	.00	.00	1.00	1.00	1.00
	Housing within 500 metres	.00	.00	1.00	1.00	1.00
	Public space within 50 metres	-.22	.17	.80	.57	1.13
	Trees within 500 metres	-.01*	.01	1.00	.99	1.00
	Distribution/industrial location	1.21*	.69	3.34	.87	12.87
	Year of construction x facade type					
	1950-64 x natural stone	19.53	15589.53	.	.00	.
	1950-64 x metal, tiles	-.68	21025.52	.51	.00	.
	1950-64 x bricks	-1.69	20459.48	.19	.00	.
	1965-79 x natural stone	-17.73	22904.02	.00	.00	
	1965-79 x glass	2.27	2.15	9.64	.14	648.14
	1965-79 x metal, tiles	2.36	2.09	10.56	.18	629.02
	1965-79 x bricks	5.05**	2.25	155.81	1.90	12773.82
	1980-94 x natural stone	-.50	.98	.61	.09	4.18
	1980-94 x glass	.69	.94	1.99	.31	12.64
	1980-94 x metal, tiles	1.69*	.98	5.40	.80	36.61
	1980-94 x bricks	.73	.98	2.07	.30	14.07
	Constant	.46	1.92	1.59		

* p=<.1, ** p=<.05, *** p=<.01

The models include the explanatory variables that influence the odds of structural vacancy. The odds of structural vacancy (yes/no, <30%/>=30%) are described by the odds ratio (exp b). If exp b for a variable is larger than 1, then this variable increases the odds of structural vacancy. If the exp b of a variable is smaller than 1, then this variable decreases the odds of structural vacancy.

A positive regression coefficient (B) means that the explanatory variable increases the probability of the outcome, while a negative regression coefficient means that the variable decreases the probability of that outcome; a large regression coefficient means that the risk factor strongly influences the probability of that outcome; while a near-zero regression coefficient means that the risk factor has little influence on the probability of that outcome (Hosmer and Lemeshow 2000).

Variables in the equation	B	S.E.(B)	Odds ratio (exp b)	95.0% C.I. Lower	95.0% C.I. Upper
Building size (categories)					
<2500m2	-4.53***	.96	.01	.01	.07
2501-5000 m2	-2.43***	.66	.089	.02	.34
5001-10000 m2	-2.50***	.72	.08	.02	.34
Parking	.96**	.39	2.61	1.21	5.64
Litter (categories)					
None	-2.69**	1.17	.069	.01	.67
Some	-2.09**	.85	.12	.02	.65
Visibility entrance (categories)					
Main road	.53	.81	1.67	.35	8.32
Secondary road	2.30***	.84	9.92	1.90	51.80
Enhanced quality of street furniture	-.94	.62	.39	.12	1.32
Landmark	-2.35*	1.30	1.00	.01	1.22
Entrance spatiality (categories)					
Narrow (<8)	.56	.69	1.75	.46	6.73
Standard (8-15)	-.87	.54	.42	.15	1.20
Facade grid (categories)					
<1.2 metres	-2.13*	1.29	.12	.01	1.49
1.2 - 3.6 metres	-.70	.48	.50	.19	1.28
Daylight admittance as % of facade					
>70%	.55	1.43	1.73	.10	28.74
50-70%	-.96	.61	.39	.12	1.27
Distance to metro	-.01***	.01	1.00	1.00	1.00
Daily supplies within 50 metres	-4.26*	2.24	.01	.00	1.15
Housing within 500 metres	.01***	.00	1.01	1.00	1.00
Offices within 500 metres	.01	.01	1.01	.98	1.04
Water within 50 metres	-.18**	.07	.84	.72	.96
Office location	.50	.34	1.64	.85	3.16
Distribution/industrial location	2.00***	.76	7.38	1.68	32.55
Year of construction * facade material					
1950-64 by natural stone	25.08	14511.70	.	.00	.
1950-64 by metal, tiles	-1.73	1.67	.178	.01	4.65
1950-64 by bricks	.62	1.38	1.86	.12	28.01
1965-79 by natural stone	-1.69	1.74	.185	.01	5.60
1965-79 by glass	20.00	28094.15	.	.00	.
1965-79 by metal, tiles	1.25	1.30	3.50	.27	45.05
1965-79 by bricks	4.06**	1.89	57.84	1.44	2327.75
1980-94 by natural stone	.98	.95	2.65	.42	16.90
1980-94 by glass	.73	.96	2.07	.31	13.62
1980-94 by metal, tiles	1.33	.84	3.79	.73	19.62
1980-94 by bricks	1.16	.87	3.18	.58	17.40
Constant	.30	1.60	1.35		

Table 15 Logistic regression model using structural vacancy (> 0) as outcome variable

* p=<.1, ** p=<.05, *** p=<.01

Table 16 The prediction correctness of the model using >= 30% structural vacancy as outcome variable

Classification Table				
		Predicted		
Observed		Structural Vacancy 30		
		<30%	>=30%	Percentage Correct
Structural Vacancy	<30%	132	13	91.0
	>=30%	19	36	65.5
	Overall Percentage			84.0
a. The cut value is .500				

Table 17 The prediction correctness of the model using >0 structural vacancy as outcome variable

Classification Tablea				
		Predicted		
Observed		Structural Vacancy		
		no	yes	Percentage Correct
Structural Vacancy	no	80	17	82.5
	yes	15	88	85.4
	Overall Percentage			84.0
a. the cut value is .500				

Following the results of the Delphi analysis, a higher contribution to the model by the location characteristics was expected. However, when relocating organisations make decisions in a hierarchical order, starting with location (Koppels et al. 2009) and then choosing a building based on physical building characteristics. Hence, the importance of the building characteristics is explained; within a predefined location an office building is selected, and within this setting, variables describing the exterior appearance of the office building seem to be the most important criteria.

7.7 The physical characteristics of structurally vacant office buildings

Based on the building characteristics found to increase the odds of structurally vacant office buildings, a typology of structural vacancy can be defined. Typologies and type are much discussed in architecture. About the relationship between type and form, Aldo Rossi says: The concept of type is permanent and complex, a logical principal that is prior to form and that constitutes it (Rossi and Eisenman 1985). Eugene Kohn relates office building types to the forces of finance, plan, program and design (Kohn and Katz 2002), while Gunst and De Jong focus on the emergence of the office building as a type (Gunst and Jong 1989). Interestingly, in his more or less standard work on building types, Pevsner (1976) does not recognise the office building as a type, but speaks of it as a subtype to other types, such as government buildings, banks and warehouses.

Office building vacancy is found to prevail in some office buildings more than others. As revealed in the regression analyses, buildings from 1980 to 1995 have the main share in the structural vacancy; while office buildings from after

1995 are more popular. These findings differ from the findings in earlier studies, that found structural vacancy and obsolescence to be a problem mainly in the stock constructed between 1965 and 1980 (Remøy 2007).

The standard office building from the eighties and nineties has a simple shape. Two types are the most dominant (Kamerling et al. 1997; Reuser et al. 2005). First, the tall buildings constructed as floors and columns and stabilised by means of a central core of stairs and elevators shafts, in the older cases with extra stabilisation elements in the facade. The second archetype is the low-rise, rectangular building, also built up of floors with columns and stabilising walls in one or two directions, depending on the floor type. However, by the end of the eighties load bearing facades were used more frequently in the "standard" office building, as office development focused on initial building costs, which are lower for this construction type. A core enclosing the stairways and the elevator shaft is normally located in the centre of the building, while the escape routes are normally found at the buildings ends.

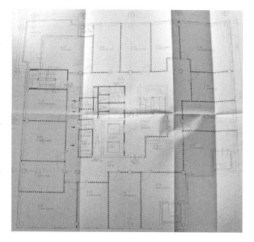

7.7.1 Structure and floors

In the eighties two types of structures and floors were popular: A flat-slab floor on beams along the facade and in the centre of the building, supported by columns and a hollow core prefab floor on facade columns or portals, or supported by the load bearing

Figure 46
Typical office
building with
central core,
constructed in
1990
(OGA)

facade. Both structures are typically linear (Spierings et al. 2004). The flat slab floor is monolithic and consists of two layers, one layer being prefabricated and installed as shuttering for and connected to the second layer that is reinforced in-situ concrete. This floor type spans up to 10 metres and was mainly used in central core tall buildings. The hollow core prefab floor spans up to 15 metres and became popular because of the possibility to span from facade to facade, granting flexibility in the lay out of floors. For the two structure and floor types, standardisation was pursued. The structural grid was more and more a manifold of 1.8 metres, like 5.4 or 7.2 metres.

7.7.2 Floor lay-out, building length and depth

Until the mid-sixties offices in the Netherlands were built for the owner-users who commissioned the design of their office buildings. This tradition also affected the design of rental offices. The Dutch employee is assertive. Company profiles are democratic and not hierarchic. In combination with the Dutch building decree on daylight access, these factors determine the depth of office buildings. Dutch and other Northern European office buildings are narrow compared to buildings in other countries (Van Meel 2000). The required daylight access is expressed in the building decree as the equivalent daylight surface: square metres of daylight that enters through windows or other glass building-parts. The required daylight access in office buildings equals a vertical glass surface of minimum 5% of the square metres usable floor space. For housing, daylight access equalling 10% of the usable floor space is required.

Following the standardisation pursuit in the nineteen eighties, the depth of office buildings was standardised as well, and most low-rise office buildings constructed in this period have a depth of 14.4 metres, possible to span with the hollow core floor. Developed for a lay-out of offices flanking a central corridor, the stairs and elevators were situated on one side of the corridor as well, somewhere central in the building or on one end, with additional emergency exits on the ends of the building.

7.7.3   Facade

The energy crisis in 1973 left its mark on architecture. Insulation of the facade was until then not normal, but in the seventies it became a standard part of the facade. Next to completely glazed curtain walls or strip-window facades, load bearing facades and floor - to - floor prefab elements were used. Insulating and sun-reflecting glazing was developed and the climate-facade and the climate-window were introduced. Window frames and curtain walls were mostly manufactured from aluminium. The completely glazed curtain wall was clearly expressing the curtain wall principle (Kamerling et al. 1997). Often, the windows in buildings developed in the end of the nineteen seventies and beginning of the 'eighties cannot be opened. During the eighties though, thought was given to the well-being of office employees, as attention was drawn to the 'Sick Building Syndrome'. This term points to the fact that office employees became sick from their work surroundings. Some of the problems were caused by facades without operable windows, and the operable windows were re-introduced to the office building, together with individually adjustable heating, ventilation and sunscreens. By standardising the facade measurements, the exterior form of office buildings became more similar.

7.7.4   Stairs and elevators

The location of stairways in office buildings varies. Since the seventies the central stability core with an elevator and possibly staircases and facilities has become standard in high-rise and centrally oriented buildings. Depending on the structure the core is stabilising in one or two directions. Low-rise office buildings have, depending on their length, one or more entrances and elevator-cores and escape routes on the end of the buildings.

7.7.5   Location characteristics

Frequently, office buildings from the 1980s were built on monofunctional office locations outside the city centre. Locations in the city centres were scarce, the plots that were available for office development were small and development in these areas was rather expensive, compared to the larger locations on the city's fringes (Kohnstamm and Regterschot 1994). Additionally, there was a focus on accessibility by car and the locations near ring roads and highway exits were far better accessible than the congested city centres (Louw 1996; Jolles et al. 2003). As the locations were built for cars, there was no need for facilities for employees, the locations were not meant to accommodate other activities than office work. Albeit the locations were well accessible for cars, the parking facilities were not in all cases developed accordingly. In some of the locations a parking ratio of 1 parking place per 100 m2 office space was used, a ratio that would work if the location was well accessible by car and public transport. Moreover, the locations were developed focusing on large back-offices and headquarters of larger corporations, companies that occupy large buildings and have their own facilities like restaurants for the employees. Still, smaller office buildings were also developed in monofunctional locations, creating a need for facilities that was not responded to.

7.8   Predictions of 30% vacancy

The following paragraph presents office buildings with 30% or more structural vacancy well predicted as such, office buildings with 30% vacancy but not predicted as such, and finally office buildings that were wrongfully predicted to have 30% structural vacancy. The buildings are shortly described by characteristics that were revealed to increase the odds of structural vacancy at the 30% level. For presentation, a random selection was made of the buildings belonging to each of the three categories, the fourth and largest category, buildings correctly predicted not vacant at the 30% level, are not presented here.

Location: Slotervaart
Year of construction: 1989
Size: 7550m²
Offices within 500 metres: 10
Facilities: yes
Status: low
Parking: 1/100m²
Facade type: metal
Entrance spatiality: low ceiling
Flexibility: medium

Location: Zuideramstel
Year of construction: 1973
Size: 4700m²
Offices within 500 metres: 18
Facilities: yes
Status: low
Parking: 1/80m²
Facade type: comosite
Entrance spatiality: narrow
Flexibility: low

Location: Westpoort
Year of construction: 1990
Size: 13400m²
Offices within 500 metres: 27
Facilities: yes
Status: high
Parking: 1/70m²
Facade type: glass
Entrance spatiality: lgood
Flexibility: medium

Location: South East
Year of construction: 2002
Size: 13300m²
Offices within 500 metres: 53
Facilities: yes
Status: medium
Parking: 1/100m²
Facade type: glass
Entrance spatiality: low ceiling
Flexibility: low

Location: South East
Year of construction: 1991
Size: 3800m²
Offices within 500 metres: 64
Facilities: no
Status: low
Parking: 1/60m²
Facade type: glass
Entrance spatiality: low ceiling
Flexibility: low

Location: South East
Year of construction: 1988
Size: 3500m²
Offices within 500 metres: 67
Facilities: no
Status: low
Parking: 1/40m²
Facade type: metal/glass
Entrance spatiality: low ceiling
Flexibility: high

Location: South East
Year of construction: 1990
Size: 3400m²
Offices within 500 metres: 65
Facilities: no
Status: low
Parking: 1/40m²
Facade type: natural stone
Entrance spatiality: low ceiling
Flexibility: medium

Location: South East
Year of construction: 1988
Size: 2650m²
Offices within 500 metres: 40
Facilities: no
Status: low
Parking: 1/50m²
Facade type:composite
Entrance spatiality: low ceiling
Flexibility: low

Location: Slotervaart
Year of construction: 1965
Size: 20800m²
Offices within 500 metres: 22
Facilities: yes
Status: medium
Parking: none
Facade type: concrete
Entrance spatiality: good
Flexibility: medium

Location: Oud Zuid
Year of construction: 1989
Size: 7100m²
Offices within 500 metres: 31
Facilities: yes
Status: low
Parking: 1/100m²
Facade type: glass
Entrance spatiality: narrow
Flexibility: low

all air-photos retrieved from Google Maps

7.8.2 5 Buildings wrongfully predicted < 30% structurally vacant

Location: Westpoort
Year of construction: 2000
Size: 2550m²
Offices within 500 metres: 26
Facilities: no
Status: low
Parking: 1/90m²
Facade type: bricks
Entrance spatiality: good
Flexibility: medium

Location: South East
Year of construction: 1997
Size: 22350m²
Offices within 500 metres: 29
Facilities: yes
Status: high
Parking: 1/100m²
Facade type: natural stone
Entrance spatiality: good
Flexibility: medium

Location: Bos en Lommer
Year of construction: 1981
Size: 6550m²
Offices within 500 metres: 4
Facilities: yes
Status: low
Parking: 1/100m²
Facade type: composite
Entrance spatiality: good
Flexibility: medium

Location: Zuideramstel
Year of construction: 1973
Size: 1950m²
Offices within 500 metres: 11
Facilities: yes
Status: medium
Parking: 1/150m²
Facade type: bricks
Entrance spatiality: good
Flexibility: low

Location: Westpoort
Year of construction: 1991
Size: 4400m²
Offices within 500 metres: 25
Facilities: yes
Status: low
Parking: 1/80m²
Facade type: composite
Entrance spatiality: narrow
Flexibility: medium

7.8.3   5 Buildings wrongfully predicted > 30% structurally vacant

Location: South East
Year of construction: 1985
Size: 2500m²
Offices within 500 metres: 57
Facilities: no
Status: low
Parking: 1/50m²
Facade type: glass
Entrance spatiality: narrow
Flexibility: low

Location: South East
Year of construction: 1987
Size: 2850m²
Offices within 500 metres: 64
Facilities: no
Status: low
Parking: 1/40m²
Facade type: metal
Entrance spatiality: low ceiling
Flexibility: low

Location: South East
Year of construction: 1988
Size: 3500m²
Offices within 500 metres: 67
Facilities: no
Status: low
Parking: 1/40m²
Facade type: metal/glass
Entrance spatiality: good
Flexibility: medium

Location: South East
Year of construction: 1988
Size: 2500m²
Offices within 500 metres: 66
Facilities: no
Status: low
Parking: 1/100m²
Facade type: composite
Entrance spatiality: low ceiling
Flexibility: low

Location: Westpoort
Year of construction: 1990
Size: 5500m²
Offices within 500 metres: 28
Facilities: no
Status: low
Parking: 1/50m²
Facade type: bricks
Entrance spatiality: low ceiling
Flexibility: medium

all air-photos retrieved from Google Maps

7.8.4　Fit of the 30% structural vacancy predictions

In total, 168 (84%) of the buildings were correctly predicted. 36 buildings were correctly predicted to be structurally vacant at the 30% level, 19 buildings were wrongfully predicted not structurally vacant at the 30% level, 13 buildings were wrongfully predicted structurally vacant at the 30% level, and 132 buildings were correctly predicted not structurally vacant at the 30% level.

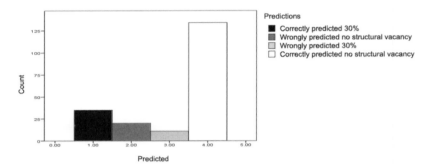

Figure 47 prediction of structural vacancy at the 30% level

The logistic regression model was able to predict 84% of the cases correctly. Following, the buildings that were correctly predicted to be structurally vacant at a level of 30% or higher were studied more closely to reveal to which extent the buildings are described by the main vacancy predictors, which are the location and building characteristics that influence the odds of structural vacancy at the 30% level. A large amount of these buildings
•   were constructed between 1980 and 1995
•   are situated in monofunctional office locations
•   have a glass facade
•   have entrances with poor spatiality
•   have low flexibility

Although 'year of construction' was a strong variable in predicting the structural vacancy of office buildings, 2 office buildings constructed in 2002 were also correctly predicted to be structurally vacant at the 30% level. Both buildings are located in Amsterdam South East, a monofunctional office location. The buildings are both located in a part of Amsterdam South East that accommodates facilities. However, both buildings have poor parking facilities compared to surrounding properties, the buildings are both larger than 10 000 m2, and both have glass facades. Both buildings have entrances with poor spatiality, meaning a relatively low ceiling height compared to the size of the floor space. Finally, the flexibility of both buildings is low. Built for landscape offices, the facade provides only few points for the fitting of interior walls.

Nineteen buildings were wrongfully predicted not structurally vacant at the 30% level. The category shows a large mix of building types. Among these are some typical office buildings from the 'seventies and 'eighties with structural vacancy level higher than 50%. The reason the buildings were wrongfully predicted is described by some important characteristics: the buildings are located in mix-use or central areas with a high level of facilities. Though these buildings typically have a low flexibility due to the small measurements of the main structure, the spatiality of the entrances is good and the facades are well maintained, albeit being technically and visually outdated. The other buildings in this category are buildings constructed after 1995, located in mixed-use locations, with high quality facades of natural stone. From this category, the importance of monofunctionality and lack of facilities as predictors for structural vacancy become visible.

Thirteen buildings were wrongfully predicted structurally vacant at the 30% level. 8 of these buildings are structurally vacant at a lower level though. These buildings share important characteristics with the buildings that were correctly predicted, something that explains why these buildings were predicted structurally vacant. The buildings were all constructed between 1980 and 1995 and are all located in monofunctional office locations without facilities like shops or cafés within 500 metres from the building. Amusingly, the third building shown in this category (7.8.3) is similar to the sixth building in the category of correctly predicted buildings (7.8.1). Building 4 from the category (7.8.3) had a high level of vacancy at the time of assessment, but the vacancy was not structural. These buildings belong to a category that has high odds for structural vacancy.

7.9   Summary and conclusions

The office scan has proved some of the ideas about structurally vacant office buildings to be true and yet others to be false... the chapter was initiated by the hypothesis that was kept from the Delphi study, considering the physical characteristics of office buildings and locations. In the office scan, the hypothesis was tested. Though the location characteristics describing monofunctionality of the location (tested by the functional mix and availability of facilities) were found to be highly influential, building characteristics were found to be the most important predictors for structural vacancy. Office buildings with low flexibility (described by the size of standard floors, measurements of the main structure and the facade grid) were found to have higher odds of structural vacancy, together with buildings with a glass facade. Also, the spatiality of the entrance as a measure for the interior appearance of the building was found to have high impact on the odds of structural vacancy. Measured as the free height of the entrance in relationship to its floor space, the variable describes the spatial proportions of the entrance. Entrances with relatively low ceilings and large surfaces are experienced as low and unpleasant, whereas entrances with relatively high ceilings and small surfaces are experienced as narrow and unfriendly.

This study was conducted parallel to a counterpart study on physical building and location characteristics as determinants for the office rent (Koppels, forthcoming 2010). Interestingly, the results from this study reveal location characteristics as the most important predictors. The explanation for these differences is evident; office users choose office accommodation using a hierarchical decision structure. First, the geographical market characteristics are determined. Secondly, a location is selected, and this location described by its characteristics determines the rent level. Finally, a building is selected, based on building characteristics. Office buildings that have a lower facade quality than surrounding buildings, less parking, lower interior appearance quality and with a less flexible lay-out, have more structural vacancy than other office buildings. Therefore, structurally vacant office buildings are found in all locations.

Location characteristics were also found to affect the odds of structural vacancy in office buildings. As seen in the analyses, a high number of office buildings and employment in the manufacturing or distribution sector, together with a lack of facilities are location characteristics that give increased odds of structural vacancy, enhanced by low quality of land use for public space. These are characteristics that quite well describe the monofunctional locations on the fringes of Amsterdam. Finally, the hypothesis that was defined in the first chapters of this section has been tested and can now be concluded:

Structurally vacant office buildings
- were constructed between 1980 and 1995
- are located in locations with insufficient facilities
- are located in low-status locations
- are located in monofunctional office locations
- have less parking places than other office buildings
- are functionally obsolete (inefficient and inflexible)
- have glass facades
- have a low quality interior appearance
- are in technical decay
- are not described by lack of climatic and workplace comfort
- are not described by accessibility by car and public transport

8   Conclusions Cause

Office buildings and their locations have developed significantly since the construction of the first modern office buildings around 1900. From generic buildings for administration in the city centres, built for specific organisations and therefore with a specific identity, office buildings have developed into specific buildings gor generic organisations, located in locations developed for the sole function of office buildings. With the increase in the business services economy and its need for flexibility to accommodate changing numbers of employees, the office rental market has developed.

Urban development and changes in the built environment are changes of typically static objects and their scenery; it takes several years from the development of new ideas in architecture and urban design until these new ideas become visible as new buildings and urban fabric. The ideas of the modern movement, though developed in the nineteen twenties and thirties, were not developed until after the Second World War, in the nineteen fifties. Similarly, cities and buildings are still developed according to the ideas of the functionalism while actually; there are plenty of signals that this built environment does not suffice. As a result of the changing qualitative demand for office space, new offices are developed though there is no significant quantitative demand for extra office space. A replacement market has developed wherein new buildings drive out bad buildings. In this replacement market office organisations locate to offices with specific characteristics that suit their organisation and other office buildings are left vacant. Because these office buildings do not qualitatively suffice to the demands of the office organisations, they become structurally vacant. Based on literature, hypotheses considering the relationship between specific location and building characteristics and structural vacancy were formulated.

The Delphi survey showed that although the building and location characteristics which are important for office tenants' selection of (re)location are not changing very much, some new trends can be found. The location characteristics accessibility and status of the location and the building characteristics car parking and exterior appearance were found to be the most important characteristics for office organisations. However, the facility level of the location was mentioned as a characteristic that is becoming increasingly important.

The Office Scan was conducted to triangulate and test the results of the Delphi survey. A sample of 200 office buildings in Amsterdam was studied to retrieve variables that describe the location and building characteristics defined from literature and tested in the Delphi survey. The results of the Office Scan show strong associations between some characteristics and structural vacancy, both on building and location level, and by employing regression analyses, location and building characteristics were revealed that increase the odds of a building being structurally vacant.

- The location characteristics that most increase the odds of structural vacancy are: monofunctionality, lack of status, lack of facilities
- The building characteristics that are most closely associated with structural vacancy are: bad external appearance, bad internal appearance, low layout flexibility

Cope

Transformation is a way of coping with structural vacancy of office buildings. Building transformation is a well known phenomenon; inner city buildings loose their function and adapt to new use. In the Netherlands though, the scale on which since 2001 office buildings have lost their function is so far unprecedented; at the end of 2006 about 6 million square metres, equalling 14% percent of the office space in the Netherlands, was vacant. Because of the large surplus of office buildings in the office market maintenance and renovation of the building for the existing use or conversion into a similar use is not interesting. Transformation describes a far-reaching conversion of the building's physical characteristics, and applies to the measurements that need to be taken to make a redundant office building fit for new use. Coping with structurally vacant office buildings by transformation into housing is the main issue of this chapter. There are several reasons for focusing on this specific functional transformation; first, the typology of office buildings matches the typology of housing; second, the location requirements for both functions match, and third, the transformation of structurally vacant offices may offer an outcome to the tight Dutch housing market.

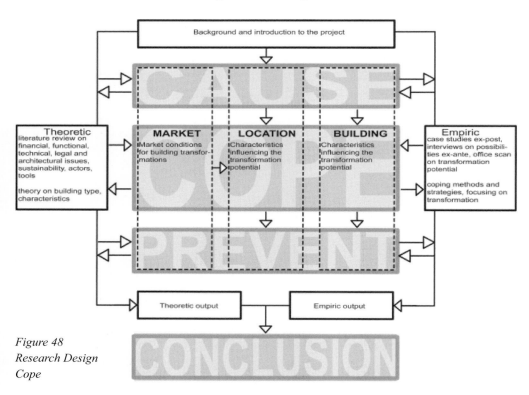

Figure 48
Research Design
Cope

9   Research Design Cope

In this research, transformation as a means of coping with structural vacancy is described by the three aspects market, location and building. This part of the research considers how market conditions and location and building -characteristics influence the potential for transformation of office buildings into housing, the feasibility of the transformation schemes, and the risks and opportunities within each specific project.

Cope introduces new research but also builds forth on the research and results from Cause. The physical characteristics of 200 office buildings in Amsterdam were studied and correlated to structural vacancy. The sample of 200 office buildings contained 106 office buildings with structural vacancy. The transformation potential of office buildings is studied ex-ante by using this sample of 106 buildings with structural vacancy. On a building-location level, the study is quantitative and performed as a cross-case analysis over the sample, though on location-market level the study has more the nature of a single case-study, concerning the transformation potential of the office stock in Amsterdam as a case (Yin 1989; Groat and Wang 2002; Patton 2002). The market conditions and location- and building- characteristics are evaluated, and the financial feasibility of transformation is compared to that of consolidation, redevelopment and adaptation (Muller et al. 2009). The location- and building- characteristics that decide transformation potential and are used in this part of the study are defined in former research (Geraedts and Van der Voordt 2003; Douglas 2006; 2007) that also developed tools for deciding the transformation potential of office buildings into housing.

14 case studies were performed ex-post and were qualitatively compared in a cross-case analysis, validating former research and revealing risks and opportunities that are often not evident in an early phase of the project. The risks and opportunities of the buildings and their locations were related to their physical characteristics through a cross-case analysis.

Finally, a stated preferences study was performed to find out under which market-conditions transformation is interesting to the property developer, and to which extent the physical characteristics of the location and the building influence their choice of which buildings to transform (paragraph 13.4).

9.1   Literature review

The market aspect of Cope considers the market conditions for transformation, and is primarily studied by literature reviews. To study this aspect, literature review was applied to broaden and connect existing knowledge about the topic that was available from different disciplines and different sources (Groat and Wang 2002). The market conditions for transformations comprise office market and housing market issues, such as demand and supply and property values in both markets. Together, these two markets combine as the transformation market (Remøy 2007). This research focuses on the transformation potential of Dutch office buildings as such; hence studied literature concerning specific market conditions is mostly Dutch. However, transformation of offices or other utility buildings into housing is not a Dutch phenomenon and international literature was consulted for the development of a theoretical framework.

Former research (Geraedts and Van der Voordt 2003, 2007; Hek et al. 2004; Zijlstra 2006; Hofmans et al. 2007) produced several instruments to decide the transformation potential and feasibility of existing buildings, considering location, financial, functional, legal, social, cultural, architectural and historic aspects. These studies and instruments were also studied by literature reviews and were thereafter actively used in the empirical ex-ante and ex-post studies comprised in this research.

Literature review was also used as part of the studies of the building and location aspects of transformation, though the role of the literature review was different in these studies. Here, literature reviews were used to focus the research and define the gaps in existing research and literature. As building transformations have already been studied by different disciplines with several points of reference, the literature studies were used to define a theoretic framework and to focus the direction of the study. The literature review was conducted simultaneously with fieldwork, making it possible to inform the field studies, but also letting the field studies influence the choice of literature to be comprised in the studies (Patton 2002), working with the different research methods in an iterative process to develop new theory and to enhance the existing body of knowledge.

9.2 Ex-post study on 14 office buildings transformed into housing

The empirical studies conducted in this part of the research mainly concentrate on the location and building aspects of transformation and consider the location- and building- characteristics of structurally vacant offices and what effect these characteristics have on the transformation potential of the office buildings. Case studies are well suited for this kind of studies, as the following definition is given by Yin (1989) and amended by Groat (Groat and Wang 2002): "A case study is an empirical inquiry that investigates a phenomenon or setting", and Yin adds: "…especially when the boundaries between phenomenon and context are not clearly evident." Case studies can focus on either single or multiple cases, have the capacity to explain causal links, depend on theory development in the research design phase, rely on multiple sources of evidence (as a form of triangulation) and finally, case studies can be used to generalise empirical findings to theory (Groat and Wang 2002). Flyvbjerg (2006) further points out the importance of case studies in the development of knowledge in research fields that are context dependent, as in research on architecture and the built environment. In the discourse on case study research, the selection criteria of the cases and the number of cases that needs to be studied in order to develop generic theory remain unresolved. Patton (2002) refers to Stake (Stake 1995) when he states that "case study is the study of the particularity and complexity of a single case, coming to understand its activity within important circumstances". However, single case studies – like Jacobs (1961) study of New York – often tend to comprise several smaller cases. The context dependency of case-studies makes the multiple case study interesting for many of its applications, which is also the reason why this approach was chosen in this research, and it is also why it is referred to as a multiple case study on the transformation of 14 office buildings, though Patton (2002) would argue that the cases together could be read as a single case on transformation. Eventually, the case should be the main unit of interest and should be described individually while possible cross-case analyses should be of secondary interest.

Having selected a multiple sampling, the type of sampling or the choice of cases to include in the study should be defined. The cases studied in this research were selected for the project analyses (Oudijk et al. 2007) in the book "Transformation of office buildings" (Van der Voordt et al. 2007). The cases were chosen by criterion sampling (Miles and Huberman 1994; Patton 2002) to make it possible to generalise the findings within a specific group of transformation projects (Flyvbjerg 2006). They are all examples of transformation from offices into housing, they are of significant size (the smallest counted 18 apartments) and the transformations studied were carried out during the last ten years, since the quality of the information is better in recent cases and also considering a specific topic of the cases; the legal framework for transformations and adaptations stayed more or less the same during this period. The number of cases to be studied was defined more or less deliberately; the study should present a variety of transformations regarding geographic location, building type and type of new users, though it should also focus on the issue of redundant office buildings. According to Miles and Huberman (1994), after choosing a sampling frame, a number of cases should be chosen that gives confidence in analytic generalisations and that fits with the level of richness and complexity within each case. However, Miles warns that the use of more than 15 cases can make the study unwieldy, containing too many data to study and present visually and too much variation to account for.

The ex-post case studies of the 14 transformations were performed by studying different sources of evidence; studying drawings and documents of the 14 projects, visiting the transformed buildings, and by interviewing the architect and/or the developer of the project. By combining the information from the different media, the location- and building- characteristics that have an effect on the residential transformation potential of offices were revealed and were used to validate or reject characteristics that were defined as important in former research (Barlow and Gann 1993; Douglas 2006; Geraedts and Van der Voordt 2007; Mackay et al. 2009).

After completing the case studies, a cross-case analysis was conducted. In this analysis different aspects of the transformations were compared across the cases. Though the value of generalising based on qualitative research is discussed, it is argued that generalising based on the cross-case analysis of adequately selected cases will enhance the generalisability. Still, to deepen understanding and explanation is seen as a more important reason for cross case analyses (Miles and Huberman 1994). In the cross-case analysis the different cases were compared using a matrix that makes it possible to compare variables from different cases with each other without losing the focus on the case as a whole. As a result of the cross-case analysis, it occurred that the cases that were studied could be classified into groups by their typological characteristics, as such a step towards generalising the knowledge from the case studies.

9.3 Ex ante study on transformation potential

The sample of 200 office buildings that was used for the Office Scan contained 106 office buildings with some level of structural vacancy, and 56 buildings with more than 30% structural vacancy. The buildings that were studied were selected from the supply database of DTZ Zadelhoff, and the relationship between physical characteristics of the buildings and their location and the office user preferences were studied (chapter 7). Henceforward, the characteristics of the buildings and locations in the sample were checked against the characteristics that were defined as increasing the opportunities and enhancing their transformation potential (Barlow and Gann 1993; Benraad and Stuurgroep Experimenten Volkshuisvesting 1994; Heath 2001; Douglas 2006; Geraedts and Van der Voordt 2007). The sample was applied to the 4 investment scenarios consolidation, adaptation (including renovation), transformation and redevelopment, and the financial feasibility of transformations was compared to that of the other 3 alternatives (Muller et al. 2009).

The costs and benefits of transformations are important criteria for classifying the feasibility of transformations, and according to Nutt (Douglas 2006) four key decision criteria should be concerned; the relative costs of options (comparing the adaptation to new-build costs), the relative value of options (by discounted cash-flow analysis), the probable risk of options (business risks and technical risks) and the relative robustness of options (response to rises in interest rates or other changes in market conditions, like demand or rental levels).

Though studying the buildings individually, the focus was on the office building stock, studying the transformation potential of office buildings in general. After completing the studies on transformation potential and feasibility of the sample, the buildings were labelled with a positive or negative transformation advice. In order to generalise the findings, the market, location and building characteristics of the two groups were compared, revealing the characteristics and conditions that generate a positive transformation advice.

As such, the study had the characteristics of a single case study, and generalisation of the findings may be tested on other stocks of structurally vacant office building (Groat and Wang 2002; Flyvbjerg 2006).

9.4 Interviews

Interviews were held with real estate developers and housing associations to study under which market conditions transformation is interesting to the property developer, and to which extent the physical characteristics of the location and the building affect their choice of which buildings to transform. The interviewees came from different types of companies, representing housing associations, independent developers and developers connected to a real estate investor and/or a contractor. At the moment of interviewing (April-August 2008) 50% of the respondents had experience with transformation. The interviews were partly structured and partly open and were analysed both qualitatively and quantitatively. The quantitative analyses were performed by using the software SPSS and the qualitative analyses were analysed using Atlas-ti.

Interviews are much used in qualitative inquiry and were also used for other parts of this research, as part of the Delphi survey and as part of the ex-post case studies. The first parts of this research revealed structural vacancy of office buildings and the possibility for reacting to it by transforming the structurally vacant office buildings into housing. However, few transformations take place and potential actors in a transformation process do not show interest in transformations, hence some bottlenecks or perceived bottlenecks still exist. Interviews allow the perspective of these actors to be presented and discussed, starting with the assumption that their perspective is meaningful and knowable to understand the bottlenecks of transformation (Patton 2002).

10   Theoretical framework: transformation

Transformation means a major change of a building with alterations of both the building itself and the function it accommodates. Transformation is not a new phenomenon, if historical data are consulted, they reveal that transformation has taken place everywhere and at all times, internationally and on different scales contributing to today's beloved historical cities and buildings. Two famous examples are the amphitheatre in Lucca from the 2nd century and the canal-houses in Amsterdam from the 17th century, see Figure 49. The amphitheatre has gone through several transformations and adaptations, and now, 1900 years later, what is left of the original structure is merely its spatial configuration; the theatre scene is now a piazza, and the buildings around the piazza have taken the place of rows of seats. The Amsterdam canal-houses are quite young compared to the theatre in Lucca, and here next to the spatial configuration, also the image of the facades and heights of the buildings are kept, though these were also adapted several times. The functions of the buildings have also changed a number of times together with the interior floors and the rear facade of the buildings.

Figure 49: The amphitheatre in Lucca and the canal-houses in Amsterdam are examples of a durable built environment.

Research on transformation of redundant or obsolete (office) buildings into housing has been conducted both at the TU Delft and at other Academic institutions, in the Netherlands and worldwide. Most research has focussed on the technical and functional aspects that influence the transformation potential and the feasibility of building transformation. SWOT analyses for deciding the transformation possibilities of specific buildings have been developed, and

Table 18 Market, location and building are the 3 topics considered within the 3 themes of this research, Cause, Cope, Prevent. The topics comprise several aspects.

	Cause	Cope	Prevent
Market		Supply and demand, financial, location, building	
Location		Legal, functional, cultural, sustainable	
Building		Legal, financial, functional, technical, cultural, architectural, sustainable	

based on more thorough research tools have been developed for determining the transformation potential of buildings with different original functions and different new functions. In this research however, several other aspects are also considered that are subordinate to and working within a framework of three topics: Market, location and building.

10.1 Transformation, consolidation, redevelopment and adaptation

Property owners have several options for coping with structurally vacant office buildings (Table 19). There are 4 categories of alternatives: consolidation, renovation or upgrading, demolishment and new construction, and transformation. Most owners of vacant office buildings choose a form of consolidation; to do nothing, but to wait for better times. Consolidation includes actions like searching for new tenants and disposal of (or selling) the property. The choice is based on several presuppositions.

The market value of an office building is based on rent value; hence the sale of a vacant building yields less than the sale of an occupied building. The building will not be sold in accordance with its book value, which is often based on a presupposed 100% rent for the entire investment period. Real estate owners and investors in that case regard selling a (partly) vacant building as facial loss for the seller. For housing market investors and real estate developers, high asking prices is a reason for not transforming vacant office buildings into housing. The different real estate markets are separated; office market actors have little knowledge about the housing market, and vice versa, and they tend to have little affinity for each others way of thinking. Among the stakeholders on the real estate market there is a general lack of knowledge about transformation processes. Despite this, several vacant office buildings have been transformed into housing.

Another alternative for coping with structural vacancy is adaptation for other office market segments or renovation of the property. Though smaller renovations are performed every 5 years (Vijverberg 2001; Douglas 2006) at some point the building might be functionally obsolete and a more radical intervention is needed. However, in markets with high levels of vacancy or with location obsolescence, there is a risk that the positive effect of adaptation and renovation will be less than the costs of intervention.

Next to transformation, demolishment and new construction is an intervention that creates possibilities for developing a new building fit to future users' needs, and is especially interesting in a declining office market. However, redevelopment takes time and leads to a delay of income, disrupts both market- and location- development, and if the building is technically in a good state, redevelopment is a waste of resources.

Mothballing a building or temporarily allowing use for anti-squat are not permanent solutions for coping with structural vacancy but may precede adaptation, renovation, redevelopment and transformation, or even be seen as part of consolidating. However, mothballing and anti-squat may both bring about damages to the building and will imply that repair and redecorations are necessary before the building can be rented out again.

Finally, structural vacancy can be coped with by transformation. Transformation may be expensive and disrupt the incomes from and the use of the building. Its future market value accommodating the new function must be higher than for offices. However, if working out successfully, transformation sustains a beneficial and durable use of the location and building, implies less income disruption than redevelopment and has higher social and financial benefits.

	Option	Benefits	Drawbacks
Table 19 Options for property owners to cope with structural vacancy by different types of interventions, derived and refined from Douglas (2006).	Maintain in current state (consolidate)	Preserves the property Sustains existing use Ensures ongoing service and lifespan	Requires maintenance costs though no incomes are generated
	New tenancy – better study of the market	Find a suitable tenant, may ensure ongoing beneficial use of the property	May be time-consuming to find a user for a structurally vacant building, requires maintenance, refurbishment or incentives
	Mothball	Minimizes running costs, such as cleaning, heating and lighting	Costly to keep safe and secure, vulnerable to vandalism and squatting, dust and dirt accumulation, dampness in the building, no rental income
	Anti-squat	Minimizes running costs, secures the building against squatting and vandalism	exposed to wear and tear, inhabitation may influence possible tenancy negatively
	Dispose	Realises asset/site value, reduces management and operating costs	Loss of potentially useful asset, price may not correspond to book-value
	Demolition and new building	New building tailored to meet users preferences	Disruptive and expensive, delay of income, location characteristics cannot be influenced
	Adapt and renovate	Enhances the physical and economic characteristics of the building, delays deterioration and obsolescence, reduces the likelihood of redundancy, sustains the buildings long term beneficial use	Disruptive and expensive, extended lifespan is unlikely to be as great as a new building, upgraded performance cannot wholly match that of a new building, location characteristics cannot be influenced
	Transform	Enhances and alters the physical and economic characteristics of the building, prevents deterioration and obsolescence, sustains the buildings long term beneficial use, sustains social coherence in the area	Disruptive and expensive, market uncertainty, location characteristics may not suit new function, building costs may be out of control, new rental function may not be the core-business of the owner

10.2 The stakeholders

10.2.1 Commercial Office Investors

Structurally vacant office buildings are usually property of an investor or a private owner. However, real estate markets are segregated and the different types of actors in the different market sectors generally have little affinity with other actors and segments. Investors in the office market reside in the management part of the real estate life cycle and therefore rarely participate as actors in a transformation project (Figure 16). The previous chapter showed the possible actions that can be undertaken by the owners of structurally vacant office buildings. Different forms of consolidation are the normal reaction from owners and especially from larger investors or investors with a certain distance to the market (physically or psychologically). One reason for consolidating is the expectation of future market improvement and new tenants for the buildings. Other reasons are land-speculations; the owner waits for the value of land to increase as a result of new urban plans for the area (such as a change in the zoning plan allowing for more built volume on the location), expectations of economic growth, or changes in neighbouring properties. In the known cases where a transformation was initiated by an investor, the property was sold to a property developer for transformation with an engagement for buying the property or parts of it back after completion of the transformation (Oudijk et al. 2007). Hence, the investor is typically not active in the transformation and the ownership of the property always changes in advance of the transformation. Of course, holding on to a structurally vacant building means that there will be no direct income or revenues from tenancy while the operation costs and possible interests must be paid. However, as long as the indirect revenues of the property are high, the investor is not inclined towards selling the property against a lower market value than it is accounted for.

10.2.2 Housing Investors and Housing Associations

Two of the most active stakeholders in transformation processes are housing investors and housing associations. For instance, the Dutch housing investor Vesteda invests in upmarket rental housing. Focusing their investments in inner-city areas, transformation or redevelopment are the two possibilities for housing development in these areas. The user target group of Vesteda are dinkies (double income no kids), either young people without kids or the so-called "empty-nesters", couples or singles above the age of 55 whose children moved out.

Housing associations have a much larger share of the housing market than the commercial housing investors. Approximately 34% of the Dutch housing stock is owned by the housing associations. Housing associations have different reasons for being interested in transformations. They also focus on developments in inner-city areas since one of their target groups consists of young people with a low income and no children, and prefer living in the city centres. Another reason for housing associations to be interested in transformation is the location of some structurally vacant office buildings: In the 1970s office buildings were built in mono-functional housing locations. Transforming office buildings on these locations is a way of acquiring more control over the quality of an area and is

Figure 50 Two examples of transformations from offices into student housing, the GEB tower and the Bredestraat, both by Stadswonen in Rotterdam

used as a strategy if the housing association owns a critical amount of the properties in an area.

A Dutch housing association with extensive transformation experience is Stadswonen in Rotterdam (Stadswonen 2008).The association so far bought and transformed 18 office buildings into housing, all in the centre of Rotterdam. Their user target groups are students and young starters on the housing market. Stadswonen, like several other housing associations, work closely with a developer (Stadswonen is linked to Kristal) for the housing development.

10.2.3   Real Estate Developers

Knowledge and experience with transformation is in practice foremost available among real estate developers. Redevelopment and transformation of existing buildings and locations are interesting to developers because the locations are often situated in central urban areas where it is otherwise difficult to find land for new developments and where the financial benefits of housing are high, and for an experienced developer the revenues of transformations are therefore interesting. Transformation has become an expertise to some developers; most of these are combined development and construction firms, giving the advantage that the expertises of developers and constructors can be combined at an early stage in the projects. Contract forms such as "design and construct" are more common in these projects than in "conventional" new construction projects.

Developers may work on projects in cooperation with or for investors, as is common for housing associations, or they may develop a project for their own account and sell it when it is completed. If working with an investor market risks are (for the developer) eliminated though development and construction risks will still be accounted for by the developer. The Dutch housing market is stressed, and while the market risk of office developments are seen as high, the risks in the housing market are normally limited. This may be the reason why in general, developers take on transformation projects on their own, or as in large-scale projects cooperate with another developer.

Generally, the first step in a transformation project is to calculate the potential benefits of the project, then estimate the transformation building costs, costs for design and development and other additional costs. Based hereupon a residual value for the existing building and site is calculated. This value is the price that the developer is willing to or able to pay for the building in the existing situation in order to secure revenues from the project. However, the residual value is not connected to the market value of the existing building like it is calculated by the investor or owner of that particular building. This divergence between the point of view of the developer and the perspective of the investor is one of the obstacles for transformation as a way of coping with structural vacancy.

10.2.4 Architects

Architects play an important role in the transformation of office buildings. The assessment of the functional feasibility of transformation from offices into housing is – in most cases – done by architects, and while new construction projects start with a program of requirements from the developer, in transformation projects the program is often developed by the architect and the developer together in the first phase of the project. Architects also typically have specific expertises within their own field and some architects work exclusively with renovations or transformations of existing buildings. Coxe et al. (1987) divides architecture firms into three types: the strong idea-, the strong service- and the strong delivery- office, who all have different views on how to tackle assignments in general. While the strong idea office poses its idea onto the assignment and is unwilling to discuss design with the developer or other implied parties, the strong service office will analyse the existing situation thoroughly and involve other parties. The strong delivery office on the other hand will follow the rules that are put by the commissioner and fulfil the assignment as efficiently as possible. Developers are well aware of how different architecture offices work, and often the strong service- or the strong delivery- offices are chosen. A strong idea office is chosen in cases of transformation of a significant urban location, well-known building or in the case that a lucid idea is needed to add new architectural and commercial value to the development.

Figure 51 example of a transformation design for the former Rotterdam post-office by UN studio (UN Studio)

10.2.5 Municipalities and government

The role of municipalities in transformation projects as well as in other types of projects is that of facilitating legal processes by maintaining zoning plans, the building decree, the monument act and other municipal legislation. However, municipalities see structural vacancy as undesirable and therefore have interest in transformation to increase the image and quality of life of specific areas and to increase the interest for new developments of office space. Also, especially the municipalities with a high structural vacancy have the most stressed housing market and see transformation as a way of adding inner-city housing to the market and to increase the functional mix in some areas (Decisio 2006). The differences are large between the different municipalities. Only a few municipalities have knowledge about the extent of vacancy within their own borders (Harmsen and Waal 2008). The municipality of Amsterdam created a function for an "office pilot" whose task it is to stimulate transformation on the one hand and on the other hand lessening the amount of new office developments.

The core-task of the municipalities is to maintain the zoning plan and the building decree, including the fire-prevention legislation. However, the different municipalities have different policies for how to react on building permit applications for transformations and the laws and rules in this field are considerably flexible, and are also interpreted differently by the municipalities. Since the Dutch

Figure 52
The "Solids"
developed by
the housing
association
Stadgenoot in
Amsterdam can
functionally
hold all "urban
functions". This
development
requires flexible
zoning plans!
(Stadgenoot)

building decree holds different rules for existing buildings than for new buildings, the discussion regarding transformation projects always hinges on this point. Zoning plans are the other legal obstacle for transformation projects and are local plans that are locally maintained by the municipalities. Changes in a zoning plan must always be reported to and approved by the province. However, a zoning plan may be flexible towards which activities may be performed within the area of the plan and may also give a bandwidth of height and density instead of exact numbers. Such plans are applied to most inner-city areas.

Knowingly, transformation projects demand more from municipalities than do new-build projects. The official in charge must be more flexible, spend more time on checking the content of the building decree towards the project in question, and must be able to understand which consequences maintaining one rule may have on maintaining other rules. However, the same municipalities are in short of locations for new construction. Therefore, redevelopment and transformation of areas and buildings should be an important task for municipalities in the upcoming future.

The authorities see transformation as a possibility for sustainable development but so far they did not influence the industry significantly. The parliament from time to time gathers interest for transformation by asking parliament-questions to the sitting minister of Housing, spatial planning and the environment. After questions to the minister in 2005 a study was performed to find out how big a share of the yearly housing production comes from transformation, and a policy was formulated that governmental office buildings that are disposed should not be demolished but renovated or transformed for new use.

10.3 Market

The transformation potential of structurally vacant office buildings into housing is dependent on the supply and demand for housing and offices, and also of the value or the price of structurally vacant office building and of the possible yields of housing on the same location. Structurally vacant office buildings are seen as redundant and therefore continued use as offices is not seen as a possible development for these buildings. From the interviews held with property developers and housing associations, more than 50% mention the price of structurally vacant office buildings as the biggest obstacle for transformation. The reason lies in the differences among the actors in the real estate market. Property developers' appraisal of structurally vacant office buildings is based on their potential for transformation, adaptation or redevelopment, and is contrasting the valuation of the owners of these buildings.

Transformation of offices into housing is a small though welcome part of the housing production, and also the production has increased during the last few years. The share of new housing developments in existing buildings as part of the total housing production has increased from 5% in 2001 to 10% in 2005. There are no specific statistics available about the amount of residential transformations of commercial office buildings, though it is reasonable to aspect that the increase has also partially taken place in this segment. In my letter dated September 30th 2003, regarding actions to be taken to stimulate the housing production (Kamerstukken II 2003/04, 29 200 XI, nr. 3), the following point of reference was used: The amount of dwellings added to the total housing supply as a result of changes in the existing building supply stays the same for the period 2005-2010. In 2003, these additions accounted for roughly 5000 dwellings, compared to a total of approximately 60000 dwellings as a result of new constructions. In my letter this trend is continued for the period until 2010. The transformation of offices is seen as part of the dwellings that are realised in the building supply that did not accommodate housing functions before. This supply comprises public buildings, office- and industrial buildings, but also dwellings that were added by dividing existing dwellings. Statistics on new dwellings as a result of dividing existing dwellings is not separately available. Furthermore, it is not possible to retrieve how many dwellings are realised in buildings that previously had no housing function. (like offices). A careful estimate shows that each year approximately 300 dwellings or housing units are realised in former offices; that is 6% of the additions. Nevertheless, residential transformations have increased substantially since the 'nineties. In 1990 the total transformation accounted for 4% of the housing production (4015 dwellings). Per 2005 this amount has increased to 10% (7354 dwellings) of the total housing production. I aspect this share to increase further during the next years, foremost as a result of the high available supply in the office market (estimated to 5 million square metres) and the disposal of outdated public buildings. Many buildings will not be suitable for housing due to mal-adaptability or unsuited location. However, experience from practice and feasibility studies that were conducted show that 10% of the office buildings are transformable, considering only office buildings of which continued use as offices is not realistic. This means that we should not regard the current oversupply of 5 million square metres as potential transformation projects, only the half of this supply will not be rented out as offices again. Of this supply (2,5 million square metres) 10% has a potential for residential transformation. Hence, the actual potential for transformation applies to approximately 2500 dwellings for the period 2006-2010. If this task is realised, it means doubling the current amount of residential office transformations.

Box 1 extract from Minister Dekker's letter to the Dutch parliament; Approach for transformation of offices into housing. Date June 16th 2006

10.3.1 The financial value of structurally vacant office buildings

The appraised market value of office buildings is normally based on the income approach; described by the rent paid by its tenants, from which also the book value of the property is derived. However, a structurally vacant office building has no tenants and also no perspective of future tenancy and hence also comparisons using transactions in similar properties are pointless. Still, appraisal of structurally vacant office buildings is in most literature (ten Have 1992, 2002; Hendershott 1996; Hordijk and van de Ridder 2005) based on potential tenancy of the property, even in situations of market disequilibrium such as studied by Hendershott, using either the cap rate, depreciated replacement cost methods, or discounted cash flow methods calculating the Net Present Value (NPV).

The depreciated replacement cost method is based on the costs of the value of the land plus the development costs of the building minus technical and economical depreciation, and seems quite interesting at a first glance. However, the investment market, in which the property is traded, is different from the land and construction market, in which the property is produced (Schiltz 2006). Therefore this valuation method is traditionally only used for types of properties for which there is no investment market. Vacancy is not considered a permanent characteristic of a property and does not mean that the property will be permanently illiquid, though it can be argued that structurally vacant office buildings are redundant and thus illiquid. Also, calculating economical depreciation is done by using reference projects, meaning that again we'll compare the vacant property to let properties. Also this method comprises another problem. Theoretically, the only moment at which the replacement costs equals market value of a property is at the moment of completion of a property (DiPasquale 1996). It can be concluded that this method does not work, with the remark that the lowest possible price of any property would be the land value minus the costs of demolition and clearing.

On the other hand, using the discounted cash flow method every future cash flow an asset attains is discounted to today's value by using a discount rate, and so the cash flow and the discount rates must be estimated. The method is convenient for calculating the market value of properties with existing long term tenancies, but cash flows of potential future tenancies are unknown and comprise future market risk. The discount rate on the other hand is obtained from the general type of investment and by the estimated risk of the investment (Rust et al. 1997). This method, like the traditional capitalisation method, sees vacancy as a correction post and simply estimates the duration of the vacancy. Structural vacancy or redundancy of office buildings is not covered by this method. The discounted cash flow method is the most widely used method among real estate investors; however estimating the market value of structurally vacant office buildings using this method is nonsense!

The market value of structurally vacant office buildings is experienced as too high for the developers of transformation projects, who calculate the land and existing building value residual, by subtracting the transformation costs from the total estimated investment. On the other hand, this value is found too low by the owners of structurally vacant office buildings. As long as these two ways of calculating the value of structurally vacant office buildings are not compatible, the price of structurally vacant office buildings will be experienced as too high by property developers.

10.3.2 Housing market: demand and supply

Structurally vacant offices are valuated by their potential future rent incomes, yet the revenues of the property developer are determined by the costs and benefits of the development. The developer typically bases his appraisal of a transformation object on the residual after the building costs have been subtracted from the estimated incomes, so if the estimated income is high, the appraisal of the transformation object will be proportional high. In specific markets such as Manhattan, New York the price per square metre housing is higher than the price per square metre office and the office market also comprises several functionally obsolete office buildings that would need radical adaptation in order to be let out again as offices (Beauregard 2005).

The Dutch housing market is tight. In 2005, the shortage of dwellings was approximately 180.000 dwellings, or 2.5% of the total housing stock. Simultaneously, the number of households is increasing (CBS 2006) and a large part of the housing stock will need to be replaced, leading to an expected shortage of 3% of the total housing stock if the production of housing is not increased. The government aims at reducing the shortage to 1% in 2020, which implies that 1.1 million dwellings should be completed before this year (Otter et al., 2005). Though the demand for housing is partly driven by population growth, it is also caused by a decreasing average household size, with an increasing number of one- and two-persons' households. At the same time, the space use per person is increasing. The production of dwellings should therefore be 85000 to 90000 per year until 2020. According to the CPB, these numbers are not realistic, as the average from 2005 through 2008 was 75000 dwellings per year (CBS 2006).

The Dutch housing market comprises 54% privately owned dwellings and 46% rental dwellings, of which most are owned by housing associations. The associations own 34% of the total Dutch building stock. After the Second World War and until 1990, housing was developed in urban expansion areas typically with 70% for the social housing sector and 30% for the free market. In the 1990s this policy was changed in most Dutch cities, focussing on the development of up-market housing for the free market. The vinex-locations developed in these years are typical examples; here 30% are built as social housing and 70% for the up-market private property. Moreover, the housing production has become more sensitive to conjunctures, leading to a low of the housing production in 2003 with only 60000 dwellings constructed. In such a cramped market, the poorer groups of the population have problems finding a dwelling that fulfils their needs. Especially students and other newcomers on the housing market experience problems finding a suitable dwelling. Senior citizens with a low income also belong to the group that needs special consideration, albeit this group is often prioritised to other groups by housing associations.

A logic solution to these housing market problems seems to be development of housing for starters on the housing market. However this solution might still not be that logical, according to the Dutch Association of Developers, the

NVB (Rietdijk and NVB 2005). To realise inexpensive housing, money is saved by decreasing quality. Building expensive or mid-income housing on the other hand, might be just as effective to avail the housing market. Constructing expensive housing creates a relocation chain of 3-4 mutations; hence more households are accommodated according to their demands. Moreover, expensive housing typically has a high quality and future value.

According to Boelhouwer, professor of social housing at Delft University of Technology, there are many reasons to aim instead at a differentiated housing production. Developing expensive housing costs both more time and money than developing inexpensive housing and the likelihood of failure is high. Also, if the production is decreasing and the demand increases, lower income groups are not served. Third, by the development of large scale locations differentiation is important in order to prevent concentration of low-income groups elsewhere. Finally, when restructuring inner city locations current occupants should not be forgotten. For those who cannot or will not move to more expensive housing, affordable housing should be offered in their own neighbourhood (Boelhouwer, 2005). The future of the housing market is depending on government policies and macro-economic developments. What may happen to interest-levels, subsidies on rents for social housing and the position of housing associations will be of great importance. Because of these uncertainties, investors in real estate are careful to invest in housing, even though investments in housing accounts for more than 50% of the Dutch investments in real estate. Investors do see potential growth in housing for senior citizens for whom quality and comfort is important. Combining housing and care is also seen as an interesting investment market.

10.3.3 Transformation market

Transformation of structurally vacant offices into housing may contribute to extending and broadening the housing supply and at the same time create possibilities for office buildings of which the current office function is no longer interesting. The location of the office buildings is an important factor to consider. Locations in the city centre, in housing areas or on the edges of such areas are possibly suitable for transformation into housing, while transformation of office buildings in office parks will need further consideration, possibly as part of an urban area development. Transformed office buildings in the city centres are a valuable addition to the existing building stock. These buildings normally have a size that implies transformation into apartments. Considering the functionally realisable apartment types as well as the location of office buildings, interesting target groups (buyers or renters) may be found. One of the most important differences between target groups is the difference in income. The price that a target group is willing to pay for an apartment residually decides the sum of the building costs plus the purchasing costs of the existing building.

10.4 Location

Building transformations have taken place at all times and all places. However, office buildings in mono-functional office locations are not regarded fit for transformation into housing while most structurally vacant office buildings are situated in such locations. In these cases, the location itself would need to be transformed, possibly by a redevelopment of the whole area, or by transformation of a substantial part of the buildings on the location. Industrial and harbour areas, the so-called Brown-fields, were once developed on the fringe of the cities but are now pocketed in central urban areas. The same goes for some of the first office parks, planned in the 1930's and developed shortly after the Second World War. The redevelopment of such locations is triggered by the renewed interest for inner-city living by the emerging creative class and is therefore evidently not taking place in all cities with an industrial legacy; it is restricted to cities that experienced a growth in financial and business services and a shift from industrial production to informational and creative production (Hall 1999; Florida 2004; Hamnett and Whitelegg 2007). In larger European and American cities these developments have led to gentrification of inner city areas that used to accommodate harbour and industrial areas with housing for the working

Figure 53 The former AKZO headquarters building was transformed into housing initiating a redevelopment of the whole location, a former office- and industrial-location near the centre of Arnhem. (Klaassen Vastgoed))

class. In Dutch cities this development is seen in the Amsterdam harbour area, where artists and squatters moved in as the harbour activities came to an end, and where the development of high end housing blocks followed (Avidar et al. 2007; Smit 2007).

The first generation office parks together with post-war factory locations were developed on the city fringes according to the ideals of the modern movement and are now located within the urban fabric of the larger cities that experienced strong growth after the Second World War. The characteristics of the locations are similar to those of the housing locations from the same period and are also located in the vicinity of these housing locations (Hoek et al. 2007). Some of the factory locations, like the Akzo location (Figure 53), were already redeveloped; these are well connected to public transport and road networks, and housing locations and facilities such as cafes and restaurants are found in or near the location.

The office locations that were developed from the nineteen seventies onwards are located further away from the city centres. Urban areas were expanded in this period; the locations are typically well accessible by car and public transportation and the locations were developed as monofunctional office locations. Some of these locations are now becoming redundant and obsolete and show a downward spiralling development of financial yields while the public space is neglected and the maintenance of the buildings seems to be minimised. New initiatives are essential to prevent further downgrading of the locations and depreciation of the properties. As the locations are well accessible and the locations do not accommodate hazardous activities, transformation of these locations into housing would be possible (Muller et al. 2009). However, an integral redevelopment of the location would be essential, and the redevelopment should

125

be seen as part of a development towards multi-functional urban areas (Beauregard 2005; Schalekamp et al. 2009).

10.5 Building

Numerous examples of successful building transformations are known. These are often buildings with a cultural-historical value, symbolic value, use value, intrinsic value or value of experience; often traumatic experiences that have led to an ending of the buildings initial function (Benraad and Remøy 2007). These aspects often referred to as cultural or historic aspects may also play a role in the choice of transforming an office building, though their importance is higher if the building has a recognised monumental value, such as the Van Nelle Factory in Rotterdam (Figure 54). Recently, buildings that were built until 1955 were added to the Dutch list of monuments, including a few office buildings. Most office buildings though were constructed later, as the need for office buildings grew with the growth of the service economy from the 1950s onwards.

Figure 54
The Van Nelle
Factory in
Rotterdam,
completed for
refining and
packaging
coffee, tea and
tobacco in 1931,
transformed into
the "design-
factory", a work
environment for
design-related
companies
(NAI Archives)

Financial/economic, functional, technical and legal aspects are considered more important in the transformation of newer office buildings that are not (yet) listed (Barlow and Gann 1995; Douglas 2006; Geraedts and Van der Voordt 2007). The availability of inexpensive (obsolete) office buildings and a tight housing market are found to be the most important triggers for transformation (Heath 2001; Beauregard 2005). Most office buildings with a high level of structural vacancy are built between 1980 and 1995 (chapter 7) and are not renowned for interesting architecture or beauty; rather the quality of their external appearance is assessed as poor. For the current owners of these buildings and for possible buyers, the future yields are more important aspects than cultural aspects. In some cases, the urban sustainability and future value of the location are also important triggers.

Functional and technical aspects of the building are aspects that often translate into financial feasibility, as there are few functional or technical aspects that make transformation impossible. However, the measurements of the buildings structural grid is an aspect that is found to be of critical importance to the feasibility of the transformation (Douglas 2006; Geraedts and Van der Voordt 2007). Other functional and technical aspects are considered seriously before deciding for transformation of an office building, balancing the functional and technical (im) possibilities with the financial consequences. The functional adaptability of modern office buildings is dramatic, compared to that of office buildings from before the real estate boom. Office buildings were designed as "cockpits" to fit closely around the function they were meant to accommodate, and were overfitted; working with the concepts of open offices in the 1960s, energy efficient in the 1970s and smart in the 1980s (Brand 1994). This overfitting threatens the functional feasibility of transformation into housing.

Legal aspects again may reduce the financial feasibility of transformations. As the requirements for residential buildings and other buildings that accommodate overnight-stay are stricter than for other functions, such as offices, in some cases adaptation of the buildings structure, stairways and facade is needed. In these cases, the transformation costs possibly become too high compared to the expected benefits; transformation is not financially feasible (Geraedts and De Vrij 2004).

Some successful Dutch examples of residential transformations of modern office building were presented in the book "Transformatie van Kantoorgebouwen" (Transformation of Office Buildings) (Van der Voordt et al. 2007). Typically, these buildings were purchased for a low price, had a floor plan that facilitated adaptation into apartments, got subsidy from the government or were bought and transformed by housing associations that in general work with long-term investment scenarios and do not require profit-maximisation.

10.6 The Netherlands vs. international examples

Internationally, transformations are studied and described in several publications (Barlow and Gann 1993; Tiesdell et al. 1996; Coupland and Marsh 1998; Heath 2001; Beauregard 2005; Ogawa et al. 2007), describing transformations in London, New York, Toronto and Tokyo. Though extensive search for transformation studies in other countries did not deliver compelling results, more studies on this phenomenon probably exist. The studies all show transformations of redundant office buildings in central urban areas or downtown locations.

The cases of London and Toronto are described by Heath (2001), describing popular office to residential transformations as a very successful means of redeveloping inner cities during the nineteen nineties. Both the City of London and the Toronto city core were areas characterised as office districts with little housing that experienced an exodus to the suburbs at 6.00 PM. As the offices were ageing and becoming obsolete, the opportunities for transformation arose. Office-building booms in the late-1980s and an economic recession in the early 1990s resulted in a large stock of vacant offices and a dramatic reduction in rents, resulting in a replacement market where tenants moved to newer accommodations at comparable rents (Barlow and Gann 1995). The planning authorities in Toronto and London reacted quite differently to the vacancy problem. While in Toronto, the planning system played a key role in bringing forward developments, the London planning system was supportive though not proactive. In Toronto, in the early-1990s 9000 dwellings were added to the downtown area. By 2000, the impetus for transformations had slowed down; the office vacancy had fallen to 9%, the most suitable buildings were already transformed, and since the downtown now had a strong residential market, many obsolete buildings were demolished and new residential accommodation was constructed. While transformations in Toronto were concentrated to the downtown area, in London transformation was taking place more dispersed, in the different boroughs and in the City of London. The driver for transformations in London was the opportunities that occurred as office rental values fell below those of residential accommodation. The triggers and obstacles of transformation in Toronto and London were numerous; the triggers included demographic and household compositions, changing attitudes and housing demand, causing city centre living to become more popular. In addition, there was little or no demand for the vacant office space from existing or alternative uses. However, the most important factor was the rent-gap between the functions offices and housing; as by 1994 in some situations the return on housing was estimated to be 90% higher than that for commercial rented property. In London, the effect was increased by office owners refusing to accept the lower rents, and thereby contributing to an increased obsolescence. The five major triggers and obstacles to the transformation process were found to be physical/design aspects, location, financial/economic aspects, demand and legal aspects.

In the 1960s, the erosion of Lower Manhattan as a business centre signalled the starting point for the government to invest in the quality of the area. A world trade centre, improved public transport, the "Alliance for Downtown" by corporations located there, and the reintroduction of middle-class housing were the four issues that were incorporated in the governments plan. The aim was to improve the Downtown office market. It partly succeeded, though in the late 1980s offices relocated out of Manhattan as a reaction to the economic slump, part of a cyclic development comparable to that of London and Toronto; after an economic boost in the late eighties, the recession in the early nineties left a huge amount of downtown office buildings structurally vacant (Barlow and Gann 1995). Between 1992 and 1995 the office vacancy rates were about 20 per cent. Office tenants who still preferred Manhattan moved to Midtown, as the buildings there were newer, bigger and of a better quality. A large amount of the office buildings Downtown were obsolete. As a reaction, in 1995 the New York City government initiated the Lower Manhattan Revitalisation Plan to enable and subsidise the transformation of obsolete Lower Manhattan office buildings into apartments (Beauregard 2005). Subsidies were given for the transformation of office buildings completed before 1975. The government focused on transformations into studios and small apartments for first-time renters, though the transformed offices were also popular with other groups, as the rents were kept relatively low because of the subsidies. However, the area lacked basic services seen as substantial for families or elderly. The triggers of the successful transformations in Downtown Manhattan were the tight housing market and a high supply of obsolete office buildings. From 1995 to 2005 more than 60 office buildings were transformed, and the number of inhabitants in the area grew. Still, the worker population in Lower Manhattan is 3-4 times larger than the resident population and there are few services and facilities for residents.

In Tokyo, some developments were found that are equal to the New York developments. As the office market was climbing up from the recession in the nineties, new office buildings were added to the market. However, the take-up of offices lagged behind and had not yet recovered as the dot-com crisis hit the market in 2002-2003. Older and smaller office buildings, located in secondary streets were becoming obsolete, and transformation has been taking place, though at a smaller scale (Ogawa et al. 2007). Different from New York, albeit the value of the existing buildings is low, the tenancy perspectives for new and large office buildings are still good. Therefore, demolition with new construction has in general been a more interesting option than transformation, often resulting in an increase in scale of the urban fabric. The local government has had little influence on the urban developments, though recent focus on conservation of the urban fabric and urban sustainability might enhance the opportunities for building adaptation and transformation (Minami 2007).

10.7 Durability and Sustainability

The Brundtland commission defines sustainable development as 'development that meets the needs of the present without compromising the ability of future generations to meet their own needs' (WCED 1987). This definition can be broadened to discuss the expected lifespan of a system or of parts or aspects in the system. From this proposition sustainability goals can be defined and achieved, nowadays resulting in climate emission restrictions and aims for reduction. While during the nineteen nineties sustainable development was mostly understood as development without growth, this thought of train has resigned for the ideas of cradle-to-cradle developments that consider recycling or upcycling of second hand building materials (McDonough and Braungart 2002) and extended lifespan (De Jonge 1990) that reduce waste production and energy use in construction.

In the Netherlands, the building industry is responsible for 25% of the road-traffic, 35% of the waste produced and 40% of the energy consumption and CO_2 emission (Lichtenberg 2005). Several approaches for reductions were proposed. One example is the proposal for Industrial, Flexible and Demountable building systems, abbreviated IFD. IFD buildings are built up of industrial developed modules that can be demounted when the buildings are no longer needed or whenever major adaptations are required. The scope of the IFD system is to develop adaptable, transformable buildings that are better suited to accommodate the functions of a society with user preferences that are rapidly changing (Durmisevic 2006). It is meant to decrease the production of waste from the demolition of buildings and at the same time trigger the reuse of building material and thereby limiting the production of new building materials and the emission of CO_2.

Extended building life span is another proposal to improve both the sustainability of the built environment by increasing the durability of the buildings, considering the buildings technical, functional and economic lifespan (De Jonge 1990). From this perspective, change is seen as a constant, while the implications of the changes are seen as uncertain (Leupen 2006). The building is seen as a frame, or bookshelf, and possible functions or activities are seen as books. A slightly different approach focuses on buildings that are robust and flexible in use but specific in appearance and that can accommodate several programs, like the 'Solids' of housing corporation 'Het Oosten' (Het Oosten 2004). By developing new buildings with a sturdy structure and without a functional program, a proposal is made for buildings that should become dear to its users and that should last for at least 100 years.

According to Zijlstra (2006) durability is a product of continuity and changeability. Changes react to continuity, and although demolishment of a building is also a change and a possible reaction to continuity, the continuity would then be broken and durability would not be the result. Changes add quality to existing buildings and make new programmes possible. The lifespan of buildings may be prolonged as a result of adaptation, whether considering adaptation of a building for the original function, or considering transformation of a building. In housing, if a building is adapted, an expanded lifespan of 30 years following the adaptation is expected (Douglas 2006). Rental offices respond much faster to market and user preferences, and so the extended lifespan expectation of each adaptation will be lower.

In this research, durability is seen as one of the main contributors to sustainable buildings and urban areas. As transformation contributes to a longer lifespan for functionally obsolete buildings, developments by transformation are by definition sustainable.

10.8 Summary and conclusions

Transformation is a way of coping with structurally vacant office buildings. The alternatives are consolidation, renovation or upgrading, or demolition - possibly with new construction on the site. Consolidation is most often chosen as a solution – to do nothing but wait for better times. Structural vacancy is a problem to the owner of a structurally vacant office building as the building does not deliver any direct yield. However, structural vacancy is also a societal problem. Locations with several structurally vacant office buildings develop in a downwards spiralling movement; the buildings deteriorate and are devaluated, causing financial loss to the owner and to the municipality by lower taxes and land lease incomes. Enhancing transformation possibilities by facilitating legal processes and developing policies on transformations is the task of the municipality. Real estate developers, housing associations and housing investors are potentially interested in transformation of structurally vacant office buildings, though the purchasing price of structurally vacant office buildings is found to be too high by these actors.

The valuation of office buildings is based mainly on the direct yield or potentially direct yield by rent income. As there is no potentially direct yield for structurally vacant office buildings, theoretically the value should be zero, or the value of the land minus the costs for demolishing the existing structure. In practice, potential future rent is still used for calculation, using a discount rate to account for vacancy risk. Developers valuate structurally vacant office buildings using a residual cost method. As long as the two ways of calculating the value of structurally vacant buildings do not match, transformations can hardly take place.

The locations of structurally vacant office buildings to a great extent determine the buildings transformation potential. Monofunctional office locations are not found suited for housing, unless the location is transformed as well by adding more housing and facilities to the location. Office buildings with cultural-historical, architectural, symbolic, intrinsic values or values of experience are often successfully transformed. The transformation potential of newer office buildings depend more on financial/economic, functional, technical and legal aspects, influencing the financial feasibility of transformations. As seen in international examples, if the housing market is tight, the housing prices rise and the transformation potential of office buildings increases. The focus on financial feasibility and revenues is easily explained as the actors in transformation processes are commercial parties. However, to become more sustainable, actors in real estate development and investment should consider transformation more often and weigh financial profit against sustainability goals. Increasing buildings lifespan, e.g. by transformation, is a way of achieving a more sustainable built environment.

11 Tools for analysing transformation potential

Based on research results, different tools and instruments have been developed to analyse buildings' transformation potential and the feasibility of transformations (Hek et al. 2004; Zijlstra 2006; Geraedts and Van der Voordt 2007; Hofmans et al. 2007) and may be of use at different stages of the transformation process. Most of the tools were developed as check-lists, and are based on thorough studies of building transformations. At Delft University of Technology, numerous tools, instruments and methods were developed (Van der Voordt et al. 2007), though many of these are comparable to or deduced from the tools described here and will not be used or discussed in this research. Three of the tools that are discussed are developed at Delft University of Technology, one is developed by a construction managing company and one describes the architects approach to transformation projects.

11.1 The transformation meter

In order to be able to judge office buildings on their potential for transformation into housing the "transformation meter" was developed by Geraedts and Van der Voordt (2003; 2007) as a quick-scan. This tool consists of criteria to assess the value of a building and its location for housing, based on the physical aspects of building and location and with some criteria considering organisational aspects and market aspects. While only a few internal building criteria are absolute, more of the location criteria can be the source to a negative transformation advice. Depending on the target group, the transformation of the building can be financially feasible; the location though is not that easily changed. The transformation meter has been developed to assist decision making at the beginning of a possible transformation trajectory.

The vacancy duration is seen as one of the most important criteria before considering transformation as a means of coping with vacancy, and transformation may be advised for buildings with structural vacancy. Also the municipal policy and the zoning plan for the area where the building is situated is taken into consideration. The demand for housing within a specific area is the next issue that is discussed. However, in the Dutch housing market the demand is higher than the supply and specifically in the denser areas where most office buildings are located, and the demand for housing is also rising.

Assessing the transformation potential of a building using the transformation meter happens in five steps; first, the so-called veto-criteria are assessed. These are demand for housing, urban location (considering the two aspects zoning plan and serious public health risk), dimension of the building structure (considering 2.60 metres free height of the floors), and on organisational level there must be an enthusiastic developer, (the building must fit within the developers portfolio and the owner of the building must be willing to sell or to redevelop). One could argue that the organisational veto criteria are actually superfluous since transformation and using the transformation meter will not be considered if there is no one interested in transforming the building.

LOCATION	GRADUAL CRITERION	APPRAISAL
FUNCTIONAL		(yes/no)
Urban location	Remote industrial or office park	
	Building gets little or no sun	
Distance to and quality of facilities	Shops for daily necessities > 1 km	
	Public meeting space (square, park) > 500 m	
	Hotel/restaurant/cafe > 500 m	
	Bank/Post Office > 1 km	
	Education, sports, basic medical facilities > 1 km	
Public transport	Distance to railway station > 1 km	
	Distance to bus/metro/tram > 250 m	
Accessibility by car	Obstacles; traffic congestion	
Parking	Distance to parking place >250m	
	<1 parking place per housing unit	
CULTURAL		
Status of neighbourhood	Situated near city edge (e.g. near motorway)	
	No housing in immediate vicinity	
	Poor green space in neighbourhood	
	Area has poor reputation/image; vandalism	
	Noise or stench (factories, trains, cars)	
LEGAL		
Urban location	Noise load on facade >50 dB (limit for offices 60dB)	
Ownership of land	Lease	
BUILDING		
FUNCTIONAL		
Year of construction	Office building built or modified <3 years ago	
Vacancy	Building vacant <3 years or partly vacant	
Features of new housing	<20 units of minimal 50 m2 can be realised	
	Unsuitable layout for selected target group	
Extendibility	Not horizontally or vertically extendable	
TECHNICAL		
Maintenance	Poorly maintained	
Structure dimension	Building depth < 10m	
	Structural grid <3.6m	
	Distance between floors >3.6m <5.5m	
Support structure	In poor condition, not sufficient for housing	
Facade	Not adaptable, impossible to attach interior walls	
	Windows cannot be reused	
Installations	Impossible to fit vertical ventilation shafts	
CULTURAL		
character	Lack of identity	
Access entrance	Unsafe entrance	
LEGAL		
Environment	Acoustic insulation of floors	
	Poor thermal insulation	
	Too little daylight; less than 10% of equivalent floor area	
	No elevators in buildings higher than 4 floors	
	No emergency stairs or not sufficient stairways	

Table 20: feasibility scan using gradual criteria: adapted from Transformation Meter by Geraedts and Van der Voordt (2007), the total number of criteria met is a measure of unsuitability for transformation.

Step two and three using the Transformation meter is a scan of the transformation potential of the building and its location based on gradual criteria, (Table 20). In this step, the characteristics of the building and the location are weighted; the location criteria are multiplied by 5, being more important than the building criteria which are multiplied by 3. 23 location criteria are used and 28 building criteria. However, once the veto criteria were assessed positively, when applying the Transformation meter to a sample of office buildings no negative assessments were attained by the gradual criteria. The valuation of the criteria may therefore be argued upon!

Step 4 in the Transformation meter is a financial feasibility scan. This scan uses cost outlines from reference projects from student housing. This part of the scan is actually not so much a tool, but may be used to raise awareness about the effect of the level of intervention on the transformation building costs, and is based on a cross-case analysis of 11 transformed buildings (Geraedts and De Vrij 2004). The study revealed that changes in the structure, facade, installations, inner walls, ceilings and fixed interior increase the building costs the most, together with the total contractor costs and the purchasing costs. However, interior walls, ceilings, electrical installations and fixed interior costs were considered costs that are always made, whereas changes in the structure, facade and mechanical installations depend on the state of the original building. Geraedts and De Vrij described these differences as having a low or high influence on the variation in building costs, see Table 21.

Finally, the Transformation meter is concluded by step five, assessing possible risks of the development and construction phase, followed by opportunities for eliminating the risks. If using the transformation meter for assessing the transformation potential of a building, most of the issues in the risk list are already known. In 4.5, a cross case study of 14 transformations from offices into housing, this risk list is evaluated and adapted.

Table 21: The influence level of transformation costs

High costs, high variability	High costs, low variability
Structure	Inner walls
Facade	Ceilings
Mechanical installations	Electro-technical installations
Total contractor costs	Fixed interior
Acquiring costs	
Low costs, high variability	Low costs, low variability
Roof	Foundation
Floors	Elevators
Stairs, ramps, railings	Domain

11.2 Programmatic quick scan

Hek developed an instrument consisting of 4 phases (Hek et al. 2004). The first phase considers defining possible functions based on the location characteristics, financial, societal, technical and procedural aspects. The study is hierarchical, starting with the location characteristics, and then tuning to arrive at a definition

134

of possible functions. In the second phase, combination possibilities of different functions should be studied; starting with possible interaction and synergy effects between the different functions, and then developing a concept for fitting the functions in the building before positioning the different functions in the building. In phase 3 the program is fitted to the building using sketches, and in phase 4 the financial feasibility of the plan is assessed based on the preliminary sketch plan. The instrument refers to the transformation meter in its use of check-lists. In every phase, a check list should be filled in, assigning scores to decide the feasibility of transformation of the building and the potential for reusing the building for a specific function. Following, the scores are weighted and the feasibility of transforming the building into the chosen function(s) is assessed.

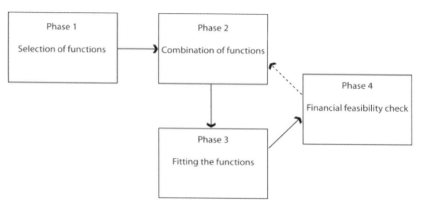

Figure 55 The phases of the programmatic quick scan (Hek et al. 2004)

11.3 Architectural value

According to Zijlstra (2006) buildings are about the past, the present and the future. Interventions in a building should therefore be preceded by a study of the buildings contextual aspects (i.e. original commission, location and architect), next to a study of the buildings architecture, in order to decide the potential changeability of the building. More of a method than a tool, this method assumes three levels of time; commencing, ageing and continuing. Within these layers of time the building elements space, structure, substance and services are studied. The technical lifespan and the technical state of the building are important, as technical decay is often seen as the most important aspect of the ageing of the building, and since it is also important for continuing the building.

Analysing buildings with these aspects in mind, new possibilities are created, offering possibilities for a different way of living, working and recreating. By studying the possibilities before starting the design process, buildings can be kept for continuation instead of being lost to decay. The extra layer of time that existing buildings offer generates urban continuity and additional quality to the functions accommodated in the building (Zijlstra 2007).

11.4 The architects' method

The architects approach to redesign and redevelopment of a building is not so much a tool or instrument developed for anyone to use, but rather the methodical way of studying and analyzing a specific building, a case, in order to conclude the study by making a design for transformation. An understanding of the values (architectural value, value in use, historic and cultural value) of the existing building and an interpretation of these values that makes the building fit for new use is the contribution of the architect to transformation (Coenen 2007). The architects study in this case needs support by a financial feasibility study and, if applicable, a historic study. The architect's assessment of the buildings transformation potential is a kind of backwardly reasoning based on possibilities, departing from ideas of possible future functions and designs for the building, using intrinsic knowledge of typology, construction, space-use and dimensions of both the existing building and the possible new functions in order to find a programme that suits the building and enhances the buildings architectural quality (Oudijk et al. 2007). The architect's method is, together with a thorough study of financial feasibility a method often used for assessing the transformation potential of office buildings.

11.5 The ABT method – an instrument developed in practice

ABT is a Dutch multi-disciplinary consultancy firm in structural engineering. The firm has contributed to several transformation processes and has developed a quick-scan for assessing the transformation capacity of existing buildings, seeing two issues as the most important to assess, i.e. possible new functions in the building and the costs of transformation. The ABT quick-scan consists of three steps, inspecting the building, controlling (legislation) and valuing (meaning evaluating the technical state, functionality, flexibility, architectonic, historic and "visual and emotional" quality, assessing five aspects of the building – structure, facade, entrances, fixed interior and installations – on condition, legislation and

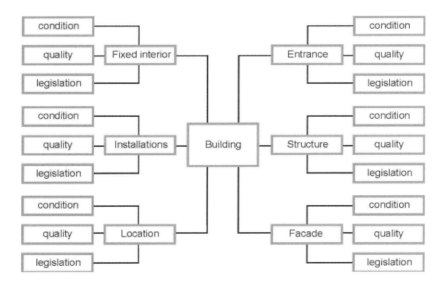

Figure 56: tree diagram ABT method

quality), and also assessing the condition, legislation and quality of the location (Hofmans et al. 2007). The method is structured as a tree diagram, see Figure 56, where the building is central and where the location is seen as a sixth aspect of the buildings attributes.

11.6 Summary and conclusions

The several instruments that are presented here may one by one be of use for studying the transformation potential of buildings and locations. The Transformation Meter is an instrument that is easy to use for a first quick-scan for residential transformation. The Programmatic Quick Scan adds an analysis for defining a new function for the redundant building. The study of architectural value is an interesting instrument to use parallel to a transformation feasibility analysis, while the architects' method is not as such an instrument but rather the methodical way in which architects approach a study of transformation possibilities. Finally, ABT developed an instrument for studying transformation potential that has parallels to the Transformation Meter. In this research, the definitions and characteristics described in the Transformation Meter have been used, as the characteristics defined here use the same terminology and are comparable also to the characteristics defined in Cause (chapter 6), based on REN (Stichting REN 1992) and studies of (office) user preferences (Baum 1991; Louw 1996; De Jong 1997; Korteweg 2002; Venema and Twijnstra Gudde 2004; NVB 2006). Based on the next chapter "Fourteen transformations analysed ex-post" the Transformation Meter checklists for assessing the location and building will be adapted (chapter 12).

12 Fourteen transformations analysed ex-post

This study is based upon a cross-case analysis of 14 cases (Oudijk et al. 2007; Remøy and Van der Voordt 2007) with the purpose of identifying risks and opportunities for transformation. The cases were selected for the book "Transformation of Office Buildings" that was published in January 2007 (Van der Voordt et al. 2007). The cases to be studied were chosen by random purposeful sampling (Miles and Huberman 1994; Patton 2002) to make it possible to generalise the findings within a specific group of transformation projects (Flyvbjerg 2006): They are all examples of transformation from offices into housing., They are of significant size (the smallest counted 18 apartments). The cases chosen were carried out during the last ten years, since the legal framework stayed more or less the same during this period. Table 22 gives an overview of the 14 cases that were studied. The studies were performed after the transformation.

The original buildings represent three different construction-periods: buildings constructed before 1950, between 1950 and 1965, and buildings developed between 1970 and 1990. The typological characteristics of office buildings changed over time. Buildings from 1950 to 1990 have the main share in the structural vacancy; while office buildings built after 1990 are more popular. These findings correspond with the obsolescence of the supply from this period (Remøy 2007). The vacancy concentrates in the buildings from 1970 to 1990; while in buildings from 1950 to 1970 it is less significant. An analysis is performed concentrating on the office buildings developed between 1970 and 1990, revealing their typological characteristics.

The 14 cases that were studied are presented in key figures on the pages 152-165, including a short description of the most important opportunities and obstacles of the transformation process.

Table 22: 14 transformation cases

		Delivery	Trans-formed	Units	Type of dwelling	Inter-views
1	De Stadhouder	1974	2005	70	Starters buy	1
2	Lodewijk Estate	1954	1999	24	Seniors, buy, rent	1
3	De Enk	1956	2006	69	Starters, buy	2
4	Schuttersveld	1915-1923	2003	104	Luxury, buy	2
5	Westplantsoen	1970-1980	1999	45	Students, rent	1
6	Billiton	1938	2004	28	Luxury, buy	2
7	Hof ter Hage	1935-1967	1998	*97	Mixed, buy	2
8	Wilhelmina Estate	1969	2007	*43	Mixed, buy	2
9	Granida	1958	2005	*30	Luxury, rent	3
10	Residence De Deel	1959	1999	18	Seniors, buy	1
11	Twentec Building	1960-1965	2002	*87	Luxury, rent	2
12	Eendrachtkade	1980	2004	83	Students, rent	1
13	Churchill towers	1970	1999	120	Mixed, rent	2
14	Puntegale	1940-1946	1999	*210	Starters, rent	2

*Other functional programs were added, such as shops, health care and commercial space.

12.1 Method

The case study evidence includes material from several sources; the situation before transformation was studied through documents; text, photos and drawings, and the situation after transformation was studied through documents and visits to the building. Interviews with stakeholders were held to gain insight in the process and to retrieve additional information about the situation before transformation. In any building project, several actors are involved; the client, the developer, the architect, the structural engineer, the installation engineer and finally the contractor. Ideally, two interviews were performed per project, one with the architect and one with the developer. In some cases though, there was no architect involved, while in two cases the client was also interviewed. The interviews were semi-structured, based on an interview protocol (Yin 1989; Mason 1996), evolving during the six months period in which they were held.

12.1.1 Interviews

In the interviews, project specificities were discussed. The first issue was the project initiative. Typically, the project was initiated by the developer, but sometimes by the local municipality or the owner of the vacant building. Following, questions were asked about the spatial program, the appointed user and feasibility. Also, the relationship with the local municipality and the municipality's role in the project was questioned. Next, questions were asked about the design phase. Usually, information about this part of the project was retrieved from the architect, but due to the project character, other stakeholders played more important roles than they would have done in a typical new construction project. The executive project leader was sometimes the architect, sometimes the developer. Questions were then asked about the construction phase, a stage in which technical obstacles typically surfaced. Finally, questions were raised about delivery, use and building management; process evaluation, financial feasibility and user satisfaction.

12.1.2 Additional data, the project documents

The buildings were visited and the new situation was photographed. In some cases, the inhabitants were informally interviewed. Photos of the existing situation and the architectural drawings of the building before and after transformation were used. In many cases, these drawings gave a good overview of the existing structure, stairways, elevators and exterior and structural walls, while the interior walls had often been changed. The interiors of office buildings are often adapted without updating or making new drawings. The written documents consisted of magazine- and newspaper- articles. These were especially useful in the study of buildings that were transformed several years ago and where the interviewees had forgotten important details.

12.1.3 Data analysis cross case

24 interviews were held about 14 projects. For each project, project and process descriptions were written; distilled from the interviews and the written documents. The drawings and photos were used to explain the situation. The stories were written based on the interviews and sent to the interviewees for feedback and

accordance. When the interviewees did not agree on the story a second round of feedback was held. The stories written up from only one interview were validated by another stakeholder in the same project. A cross case analysis by manual comparison was the last step of the analyses. The data were arranged in a matrix and analysed for patterns (Yin 1989). As a result, the projects could be divided in three categories; buildings from before 1950 (or designed before 1950), buildings from 1950 to 1965 and buildings from 1965 to 1980.

The 5 buildings constructed before 1950 share several characteristics; they are monumental in their appearance, and 3 are listed monuments. The buildings have structural, solid outer walls and considerable size. Four were built

Figure 57: Twentec building, the facade was completely stripped and renewed. (Vesteda)

to accommodate specific governmental services. 4 buildings were built between 1950 and 1965. During the fifties, new construction methods entered the market. The buildings of the Akzo headquarters, De Enk, in Arnhem and the GGD Building, Granida, in Eindhoven have structural columns in the facade with additional columns in the centre of the building, while the Estate De Deel and the Twentec Building are early examples of structures with columns and open floor plates. Of the 5 buildings newer than 1965, one of them has a structural facade in the form of facade columns, four have a construction of columns and open floor plates. Of these four, in two of them the columns are placed directly behind the facade, while in the other two the facade is kept completely free from the construction.

12.2 Transformation risks

Former studies (Geraedts and De Vrij 2004; Geraedts and Van der Voordt 2007) developed checklists to determine development risks (Table 23) and finally instruments to decide office buildings potential for transformation. The cross-case analysis of the 14 cases was performed focusing on the risks and unforeseen problems that surfaced during the building phase of the project. The four risk-categories (legal, financial, technical, and functional/architectonic) of these studies were used.

The projects were all completed, which implies that the requirements made in the zoning law and in the building law were met satisfactorily. Asbestos was found in seven of the fourteen projects. The removal of asbestos follows strict rules and therefore incurs high expenses. In all the projects though, eventual removal of asbestos would be paid by the seller of the building. What was stated as a risk in previous research is taken into account by developers of transformation projects, and has gone from being a risk to being a cost that can be calculated.

Apartments in the projects studied were let or sold without problems, except in a few cases; in one case luxury apartments without a private outdoor space and with incidentally low ceilings (not according to the building rules) were sold only after lowering the price. In another case, some apartments with daylight

Location and Market	Aspect
1. Legal	Zoning law Land ownership Soil pollution
2. Financial	Purchasing costs of vacant office buildings Housing market and revenues of the new function
3. Technical	Stench pollution Noise pollution
4. Functional / Architectonic	Bad reputation, unsafe area Amount of parking places Amount of facilities in the area Accessibility by public transport Routing of the area

Building	Aspect
1. Legal	Presence of asbestos Monumental status Dutch building decree, including fire regulation Municipal building act
2. Financial	Acquirement / purchasing costs Initial phase investments Financial feasibility
3. Technical	Incorrect technical assessment Inadequate pipes, ducts, electricity system and water supply Inadequate acoustic insulation of the floors Inadequate thermal insulation of facade, openings and roof Damp / condensation in structure Joints of brick walls in poor condition Daylight < 10% of the appointed living-space Sunlight; building is poorly situated Inadequate / poor state of main structure or foundation
4. Functional / Architectonic	Incorrect assessment of functional possibilities Low recognisability of the building and its entrance Building too slender or too deep Too loose fit, too high floors No basement Windows not operable Few or poor quality of interior walls, few points for attaching interior walls to the facade No balconies or roof terraces Not enough elevators and staircases

Table 23: Checklist of potential risks, adapted from Geraedts and Van der Voordt (2007)

from the north only, were not sold for the initial asking price. In all cases, the difficulty of selling the apartments in transformation projects did not exceed that in other projects. In some cases, model apartments were furnished to boost the sale, occasionally even before initiating the transformation. Any developer, assisted by an architect, needs to be aware of the users' wishes. Even in a tight housing market, quality and willingness to pay correspond, especially in the upper part of the housing market.

3 out of 5 buildings from before 1950 were not built according to the construction drawings, or the construction differed and had different measurement from floor to floor. In one of the five projects, the differences were anticipated from the start, the floors were radically different. In the first years after the Second World War housing was prioritised over commercial in the Netherlands. It was difficult to get building materials, and in many cases contractors used the materials they could find without changing the drawings. Two of the four buildings from 1950 to 1965 were not built according to drawings and the construction materials and measurements were different per floor. The buildings constructed after 1965 showed no such differences. The risk of inconclusive drawings and differing construction is strong in buildings dating from before 1965. Building methods and measuring methods were not as precise.

The main structure was found to be in an unsatisfactorily state only in one of the 14 projects, Granida. The concrete of the external columns was rotting and was renovated and reinforced. The repair itself added extra costs to the project, but additionally, as a result of the repairs the columns became wider, and the design needed to be modified. In another project Billiton, concrete rot was found in part of the facade but required only a minor investment to repair. Rotting wood or concrete, or oxidising steel can raise the price of a transformation, but in most cases, these problems can be seen in the preliminary phase and will not be a risk. Adding weight to the structure was problematic in only one case. Office buildings are constructed to carry more weight than housing, hence in most cases, an additional floor can be carried by the existing structure.

Apartments are normally smaller than office units and more shafts are needed for electricity, water and plumbing. In the buildings from before 1965, floors were penetrated and shafts were placed without problems. After 1965, reinforced concrete was commonly used, making larger span without columns possible. The problem of reinforced concrete though, is that it loses strength when the reinforcing steel cables are cut. In three of the five buildings built after 1965, reinforced concrete was used. Nowadays, reinforced concrete is the most common material to use in buildings. When renovating or transforming a building newer than 1965, the construction method should be taken into account. Designing apartments with a minimum of shafts is a challenge for the architect. The problem can be solved; the accurate place of the steel trusses can be located with metal detectors.

Reinforced concrete was not used in building constructions before 1965. The measurements of the structural grid were smaller. The small spans came with thin, light floors. These floors are strong; they are constructed to allow for the weight of office equipment, which before 1965 was heavier than it is now. The problem of transforming these structures into housing is the acoustic insulation of the floors. It is reasonable to say, that floors from before 1965 will need to be acoustically improved to meet the requirements of modern building standards. This can be done, as seen in the cases, by adding a floating floor and a suspended ceiling.

The Dutch building code requires a higher level of thermal and acoustic insulation of the facade for housing than for offices. The facades in 6 of the buildings were removed and new facades were added. In 7 projects, the thermal and acoustic insulation of the facades was improved, for 5 of the projects there was no other possibility because these were monumental. The facade of only one project was not altered.

In the initial phase of a transformation project, before deciding to buy the property, the developer, alone or with the architect and other experts, made quick scans of the possibilities for transformation. Sketches were made, when possible based on the original drawings, to make an estimation of the possibilities to fill in apartments or other functions.

In addition to the risks already identified, some new risks appeared in this study. The municipality not allowing exceptions from the zoning plan is a risk. But based on these cases, the risk was recognised of the municipality slowing the process where a change or an exception of the zoning plan was needed. One of the chances of transformation projects is the short time span from first sketch till delivering the apartments. Long lasting procedures may slow the process and delay income, spoiling the financial feasibility of the project.

When a first scan is made of the building to transform, the height of the floors needs attention. In most cases, office buildings have higher floors than requested for apartments, but when both a floating floor and a suspended ceiling are needed, excess height is required. To be sure to obtain a free height of 2.60 meters inside the apartments, the height from floor to floor should be 3 meters, allowing for mechanical ventilation above the suspended ceiling and a minimum height of 10 centimetres for the floating floor.

Not really an additional risk, but a result of other risks is the financial feasibility. A lowered ceiling and floating floor can be placed; constructions can be repaired and reinforced, shafts can be made through reinforced concrete floors and municipalities will allow changes or exceptions to the zoning plan. But the transformation costs will rise as a result. Several of the risks recognised by Geraedts and De Vrij could easily be assessed in the initial phase of the transformation and are not seen as risks. After analysing the 14 cases, the risk-list could be shortened.

12.3 Transformation opportunities

The short development time-span from the first sketch till delivery of the apartments is an advantage for transformation projects. The project Stadhouder was developed in only two years from the first sketch till delivery. While still working on the design, the facade was removed and the building stripped down to structure, stairs and elevator. Not only was time saved because the main structure was already there, but also because of this, there were fewer unworkable days because of bad weather.

The "WYSIWYG-factor" is another advantage for transformation projects: What You See Is What You Get. Model apartments can be furnished

Aspect	
1. Legal	Zoning law: Impossible to meet requirements (function, form, size)
	Dutch building decree: Impossible to meet requirements from the (VROM, 2003), including noise-level prescriptions and fire-precautions
	Municipal building act: The municipality is unwilling to cooperate
2. Financial	Development costs: Slow handling of procedures (loss of income)
	Vacancy: Failing incomes from exploitation or sale of the property
3. Technical	Incorrect or incomplete building structure assessment
	Inadequate / poor state of the main structure or foundation (rotten concrete or wood, corroded steel)
	Insufficient shafts available; Construction allows no extra penetrations or shafts being made
	Inadequate acoustic insulation of the floors / Thin floors
	Insufficient thermal and acoustic insulation in the facades
	Insufficient daylight for housing
4. Functional / Architectonic	Incorrect assessment of functional possibilities: Preliminary sketches prove worthless; "unusable" space

already before demolition starts. Most people cannot interpret architectural drawings, while this communication form may better inform potential buyers and boost the apartment sales. The project De Stadhouder demonstrates that the financial feasibility of transformation projects can be improved by taking advantage of the existing fiscal rules: Increasing the financial feasibility of transformation projects is reduced of conveyance duty on the land and existing building (6% instead of 19%). If the apartments are sold within six months, the conveyance duty only has to be paid for the second sale and is then paid by the buyers. The full VAT (19%) is then only paid over the building activities.

Transformation of vacant offices is an opportunity for development in an already organised context, in central urban areas. The transformation of an already existing building normally attracts fewer objections from neighbours or neighbouring users than the demolition of an existing building and new construction. Finally, the redevelopment of a building in an area of high vacancy, obsolescence and dilapidation can give a boost to the area and increase the value of the land within reasonable investment time-perspectives. This gives developers and investors a chance to increase the financial feasibility of a project, for both social housing corporations and corporations active in the unregulated housing market.

Finally, transformation of vacant offices is a sustainable alternative to demolition and new build. Transforming vacant office buildings into housing saves building materials and building materials transportation, and produces less waste than demolition and new construction. A frequently heard argument for demolition is that the thermal insulation in older buildings is not adequate. Demolition is in this case used as a sustainability argument. However, the case studies show that the performance of existing office buildings can be adapted to the level of the Dutch building legislation law as well as to the level of comfort expected by the relevant user group.

Most of the risks that were recognised in the cross-case analysis were found in the technical category. The risks within this category turned out to depend on the date of construction of the existing building. Fewer technical risks were experienced in the transformation of the 5 buildings that were originally built between 1965 and 1980. The construction drawings of these buildings were correct and the state of the construction was good. The floors in the buildings from the later part of this period, De Stadhouder, Westplantsoen and Eendrachtskade, had sufficient acoustic insulation for housing. The Eendrachtskade had double glazing. The thermal insulation of the facade was sufficient for housing; but the acoustic insulation was not. In this case, the municipality made an exception from the building code since students (the expected occupants of the transformed building) are considered to tolerate noise well. If the relevant user groups had been seniors, the acoustic insulation of the facade would probably have had to be improved. In the financial category few risks were recognised. However, all technical, legal and functional risks reduce the financial feasibility of the project. Hence, it may be concluded that most risks are also financial risks.

Figure 58: Granida. To the left the entrance galleries, right interior of a top floor apartment

The projects included in this study are completed transformation projects. One of the legal risks was the municipalities' cooperation on zoning plan changes and building code exemptions. However, the parties involved in all 14 transformations were satisfied with the municipalities' cooperation. One of the questions remaining unanswered is whether the projects would have failed without municipal cooperation.

In the analyses of the 14 cases, the aim was to reveal the factors that influence the projects financial feasibility. The developers who were interviewed stated that the earnings on transformation projects are too low compared to new construction. Also, other actors in the transformation processes complained about overrun budgets and too many hours spent to develop specific solutions to problems that occurred during the building-process. Of the 14 cases, only one developer was willing to share financial information regarding the project. In one case, the developer informed us that the financial goal was not achieved, because of failing occupation. In the other 13 cases, the developers claimed that there were no financial losses, despite the fact that the budgets were overrun.

12.4 Typology

The lessons learnt from the ex-post cross case analysis shows how opportunities and obstacles of transformation are closely related to the architectural characteristics of the existing buildings. To be able to use the information from the ex-post cases to study other buildings ex-ante, the transformation potential

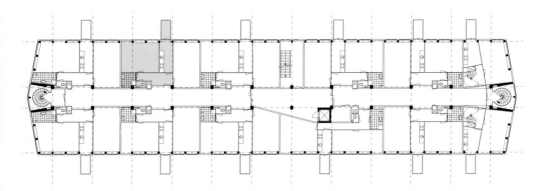

Figure 59: The 5,4m structural grid of the "Westplantsoen" was beneficial for transformation into student housing. The existing facade was upgraded. An additional floor was added on top of the building.

of the common office types as described by the office scan (7.7) was studied theoretically. This study concerned finding the characteristics that describe a building type and that also influence its transformation potential, e.g. structure and floor span, facade characteristics, floor lay-out and the length and depth of the building, and the number and situation of stairs and elevators. These characteristics were identified through case-studies (Remøy and Van der Voordt 2007).

12.4.1   Structure and floors

The main load bearing structure in standard office buildings most commonly has a span or bay width of 7.2 metres, though a structural grid of 5.4 metres is sometimes used and in some cases a larger grid of 8.1 metres. In Dutch housing 5.4 metres has long been a standard measurement for the width of single family housing and apartments, while in some newer apartments a structural grid of 7.2 metres or even 8.1 metres is used. In transformations of older office buildings with flat-slab beamless floors, the large number of columns may cause a partition problem. The linear structures from the 1980s have larger spans perpendicular to the long walls and are more easily adapted to new use. Beams under the floors may cause problems, because the free height of the floors is incidentally lowered, and when adapting new installations these need to be fitted in under the beams. The floors in office buildings are normally constructed to carry more weight than in housing (In offices, 300kg/m2 is required, in housing, that is 175kg/m2), a positive characteristic for transformation of these buildings. However, office buildings are normally constructed using precast concrete floors. The limited possibility of penetrating these floors makes it difficult to add vertical shafts. The steel cables in the floors may be located, but are not always located on the same place in all floors. Floors of this kind may be of hindrance for transformation, but do not make it impossible. Solutions could be found by smart reuse of the central existing shafts.

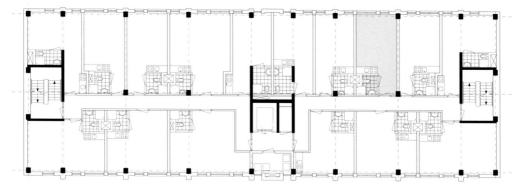

The floor height of office buildings is normally sufficient for conversion to housing; the Dutch building decree requires 2.6 metres free floor height in housing. The acoustic insulation of typical office building floors is not sufficient for housing. In most transformations adherence to the building code requires the addition of acoustic insulation following the box-in-box principle, with a suspended ceiling and a floating floor. When lowering the floor height locally because of existing beams, exceptions from the requirements to the free floor height may be given.

Figure 60: The "Eendracht-kade" was transformed from office building to student housing without altering the facade. The floor lay-out with a central elevator caused an awkward routing.

12.4.2 Floor lay-out, building length and depth

An efficient lay-out of housing on an office floor may be thwarted by the office floor plan. The location of the central elevator and staircases may be inconvenient for housing. Moving the elevator core and staircase is usually not possible, because the core also contributes to the stability of the structure. Placing a new elevator in many cases would only be possible outside the existing building, so that no extra shafts have to be made in the existing floor. However, applying radical changes to the buildings staircases or elevator cores critically increases the building costs of transformation. The depth of office buildings is mentioned as an obstacle for residential transformation, but if the normal depths of Dutch office buildings built in the 1980s are actually similar to the normal depths of Dutch apartments. In many cases, the depth of office buildings is even a positive aspect when considering transformation. The building depth may be an obstacle for the transformation of older office buildings; buildings from the 1960s were generally deeper and with less day-light access.

12.4.3 Facade

Interventions in the facade represent the most substantial costs and represent a critical factor for the financial feasibility of transformation projects. Completely replacing the existing facade of an office building implies a high transformation building cost, though it was found necessary in 7 of the 14 cases that were studied. In examples of transformation of office buildings into student housing the financial targets were met because the facade could be retained. When office buildings are transformed into more expensive housing more serious changes can be encountered.

147

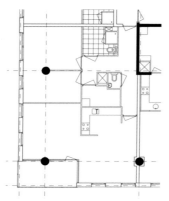

*Figure 61:
Private outdoor
space inside the
facade envelope;
a winter garden.*

The Dutch building code was recently altered. Until 2003, a balcony or other private outdoor space was mandatory. Though for a few years the new building decree did not prescribe a private outdoor space, most people demand or desire dwellings to have a balcony or a terrace, especially in more expensive high-end apartments, and so the decree was changed back in 2008. Until the seventies, modernism had a great effect on the design of floor plans. The Domino-principle by Le Corbusier was incorporated in its pure form with columns and floors, with cantilevering floors and a curtain wall facade. Such a structure though makes the addition of balconies difficult. Adding a loggia is an alternative; the floors need to be wrapped in insulation and an undesired height difference between inside and outside would be the result. French balconies or winter gardens are possible solutions.

12.4.4   Stairs and elevators

Office buildings are designed for more people per square metre and more traffic than apartment buildings. Therefore, the number of elevators available for the new function is a positive aspect for transformation. Elevator shafts that are not needed after the transformation into housing may be reused as shafts for ventilation, electricity, water supplies and sewer. Since the shafts are often used to provide for the stability of the structure, the possibility for alterations or making holes in the shaft walls may be restricted. The requirements for escape routes however, are stricter for housing than for offices. Adding extra stairs may be necessary, though most new office buildings have sufficient escape routes.

	Positive	Negative	
Structure and floors	Structural grid 5.4metres or 7.2 metres: common in housing Columns; free plans Constructed for heavy carriage; 300kg/ m2 required, 175kg/ m2 required for housing	Dense grids Low ceilings under existing beams Reinforced concrete: complicates floor penetration Thin floors: acoustic insulation insufficient	*Table 25: The typological characteristics that influence the buildings transformation potential*
Facade	Facade grid 1,8m and load bearing walls: possible to attach interior walls to facade	Curtain walls:, inadequate technical state, no attachment-points for interior walls Cantilevering floors: complicates adding balconies Remove and rebuild facades	
Floor lay-out, length and depth	Depth of standard office buildings enhances the transformation potential	Centrally placed elevators and staircases	
Stairs and elevators	Excess number of elevators	Insufficient number of escape routes Space occupied by stairs and elevators: Excessive	

12.5 Summary and conclusions

Location

The only location characteristics that could be said to be a veto-criterion for residential transformation are:

* noise level at the facade
* level of stench and fine dust in the air

If the requirements for low noise level and clean air are not met, then residential transformation is not feasible. Other location characteristics are less critical, depending on the target group and the combination of characteristics. However, other housing projects nearby is a "soft factor" that influences the transformation potential. 13 of the 14 transformation projects that were studied are located in established housing locations or mixed-use locations. Only the transformation project "Churchill Towers" has different type of location; on the edge of an industrial/logistics area, near a housing area. Transformations of buildings in industrial areas were not considered attractive by the housing associations or developers, who are the primary actors initiating most transformations. Still, residential transformations for specific target groups are possible in monofunctional office locations, i.e. if the location is situated near the central business district and near areas with social and commercial facilities.

Figure 62: Characteristic pieces of art integrated in the building "Enka" were kept.

Building

Summarising the characteristics that have an effect on a building's transformation potential, there are few building characteristics that make transformation into housing impossible. A building is more easily manipulated than its location. The characteristics of the structure and the floors are the most crucial for the transformation potential. The scale of the structure must allow separation into usable spaces. While older office buildings were not built according to standard measurements, office buildings from the 1980s onwards often have a structure that is a multiple of 1.8 metres, such as 7.2 metres, and is well suited for accommodating housing. A specific risk with older office buildings is that measurements and materials used do not always correspond to the construction drawings, and the plan sometimes differs between floors. Another potential risk with older buildings is poor maintenance and deterioration of the structure, e.g. concrete rot.

The floors of office buildings normally provide enough strength for residential transformation. Problems may occur though when manipulating the floors. A typical floor in an office building is made of pre-stressed hollow core slabs. If the steel in the floors is cut, the floors loose strength. Apartment buildings require a higher density of vertical shafts than office buildings. Penetrating the floors to create shafts for water, electricity and sewer is one of the problems of transforming offices into housing. Though several building characteristics represent potential risks for the legal, functional, technical and cultural feasibility and thus also for the financial feasibility of transformation projects, only one characteristic represents a veto criterion: The floor to ceiling height must equal or exceed 2.6 metres.

The characteristics of the facade influence the transformation potential of office buildings significantly. Though the facade is often adaptable, all adaptations imply extra building costs, and hence reduce the financial feasibility of a transformation. As the requirements for thermal and acoustic insulation are higher for housing than for offices, adaptations of the facade are needed in most transformation projects.

Finally, the image of outdated office buildings does not always trigger positive reactions from potential residents. Though some office buildings are listed monuments or renowned buildings that have a specific image or are even able to provide a specific identity to a whole neighbourhood, most office buildings are very ordinary and have an image too strongly related to office work. In these cases, the facade is often replaced, even if it is technically well maintained and meets the requirements for housing. The location and building characteristics that influence the residential transformation potential of office buildings are summarised and presented as a checklist (Table 26).

LOCATION	CRITERION
FUNCTIONAL	
Urban location	Monofunctional industrial or office park
Distance and quality of facilities	Shops for daily necessities > 500 m
	Public meeting space (square, park) > 500 m
	Restaurant/cafe > 500 m
	Bank/Post Office > 1 km
	Education, sports, basic medical facilities > 1 km
Public transport	Distance to railway station > 1 km
	Distance to bus/metro/tram > 250 m
Accessibility by car and parking	Distance to parking place >100m
	<1 parking place per housing unit
CULTURAL	
Status of neighbourhood	Situated near city edge (e.g. near motorway)
	No housing in immediate vicinity
	Poor or no public space in neighbourhood
	Area has poor reputation/image; vandalism
	Noise or stench (factories, trains, cars)
LEGAL	
Environment	Noise load on facade > 50 dB (limit for offices 60dB)
	Level of fine dust above norm
BUILDING	
FUNCTIONAL	
Features of new housing	<20 units of minimal 100 m2 can be realised
	Unsuitable layout for selected target group
Extendibility	Not horizontally or vertically extendable
TECHNICAL	
Maintenance	Poorly maintained, deteriorating structure
Structure dimension	Building depth < 10m
	Structural grid <3.6m
	Distance between floors <2.6m or >3.6m <5.5m
Support structure	In poor condition, not sufficient for housing
Facade	Mal-adaptive, impossible to attach interior walls
Installations	Impossible to fit vertical ventilation shafts
CULTURAL	
character	Lack of identity or negative image
	Image not adaptable
LEGAL	
Environment	Poor Acoustic insulation exterior and interior
	Poor thermal insulation
	Too little daylight; less than 10% of equivalent floor area
	No elevators in buildings higher than 4 floors
	No emergency stairways or not sufficient stairways

Table 26 Checklist for location and building characteristics that influence the residential transformation potential of office buildings negatively

1. "Stadhouder" in Alphen aan den Rijn

Completion office building: 1974
Completion transformation: 2005
Commissioner: Giesbers Maasdijken Ontwikkeling
Architectural design transformation: Herms van den Berg
General Contractor: Giesbers Maasdijken Bouw
Area: 5500m2
Area after transformation: 7500m2
Purchase costs: 4.5 million euro (2005)
Construction costs: 5 million euro (2005)

In 2002, the owner of the office building foresaw vacancy and contacted the property developer to make a plan for transformation of the building or the site. Within the zoning plan the site was designated for housing. The potential profit was calculated for both transformation and demolition and construction of a new housing development. The revenues for transformation were the highest. The target group for the new development were starters in the housing market. Commercial developments of the ground level were considered, however a market analysis was not positive, and so the base was designated for entrances and storage space for the housing. The structure of the building turned was robust and two extra floors could be added on top of the building. By adding maisonettes to this part of the building, the existing staircases and elevators could be reused. The facade was technically outdated and was stripped. The floors were made of pre-stressed concrete slabs that did not allow for holes for large vertical shafts. The service shafts were therefore placed on the outside of the buildings facade. The contractor, a subdivision of the developer, was involved in the project from the beginning, together with the architect. This, and strict adherence to the zoning plan enabled a short development- and construction- period: From the first sketch it took 2 years to complete the transformation.

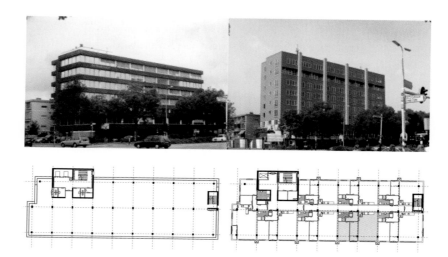

2. "Lodewijk Staete" in Appingedam

Completion office building: 1954
Completion transformation: 2002
Commissioner: Woongroep Marenland (housing association)
Architectural design transformation: Martini Architecten
General Contractor: Bouwbedrijf Kooi
Area: 4400m2
Purchase costs: 1.1 million euro (1999)
Construction costs: 2.2 million euro (1999)

The 'Willem Lodewijk van Nassau Kazerne' was built in 1954 as quarters for the air-force, after which it was used as governmental offices until 1999. Even before the government moved out, a transformation feasibility study was performed by the owner, the Dutch government (RVOB). The housing association Marenland bought the building to transform it into apartments for elderly people. 24 apartments, partly privately owned, partly for rent, were developed. Designing for the elderly implied spacious apartments that could accommodate a wheelchair. The architect calculated the construction costs, by comparing the project to earlier transformations. The large entrance on the ground floor was reused and connected to a new atrium at the back of the building with entrance-galleries, an elevator and staircases making the 2nd and 3rd floor accessible for wheelchairs. In the facade balconies and sun-porches were added, on the 3rd floor these were cut out of the roof. The main structure of the 3rd floor diverged from the 1st and 2nd floor and also the floors were thin, so no extra weight could be added to the 3rd floor. For the same reason the acoustic insulation was insufficient and floating floors and suspended ceilings were added. The large entrance hall is appreciated by the residents, a quality quite specific to transformed buildings. The building is also widely appreciated for its historical meaning and value.

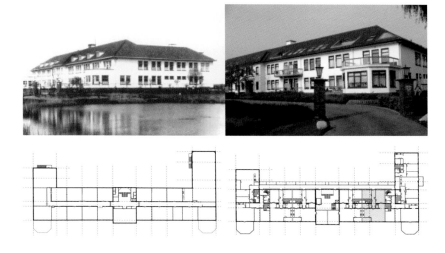

3. "Enka" in Arnhem

Completion office building: 1956
Completion transformation: 2006
Commissioner: BAM, Klaassen
Architectural design transformation: Bureau voor Harmonische Architectuur
General Contractor: BAM and Klaassen
Area: 6600m2
Purchase costs: -
Construction costs: 7.3 million euro (2005)

The building was developed as the head quarters of Akzo Nobel. By the end of the nineties it lost its function, and was sold. The building is a listed monument and may not be demolished. Given the advantageous housing market, the owners chose to transform the building into housing for starters. The market pressure in this category was high, and the building was suitable for this purpose: the entrance to the apartments is via a gallery, and since the building is a monument, no balconies could be added. Both characteristics are not favoured by higher income target groups, while for starters they are not a problem. The existing staircases and elevators were reused, keeping the character of the building and also adding to the financial feasibility of the project. The building's specific monumental characteristics determined the division of the building into apartments, entrances and public space. Open spaces were kept where artwork had been incorporated. The load bearing structure turned out to differ between the floors; hence new inner walls had to be lightweight. Some parts of the ceiling were too low according to the Dutch housing standards, but exemptions from the decree were obtained. The transformation of this monument implied that compromises had to be made regarding both the quality of the apartments, and monument and building regulations. The building is well known in Arnhem as the head office of a firm where many people worked. The building still has this identity and imposes it to its surrounding; the whole area is now being redeveloped as the Akzo Housing Estate.

4. "Schuttersveld" in Delft

Completion office building: 1923
Completion transformation: 2003
Commissioner: ABB
Architectural design transformation: Feekes & Colijn
General Contractor: ABB Construction
Area: 16100m2
Area after transformation: 26150m2
Purchase costs: 4.1 million euro (2000)
Construction costs: 17.9 million euro (2000)

The building was owned by the TU Delft and accommodated offices and the university's library. As a new library was built on the university campus, the building became redundant and was sold, however claiming that it would be reused since parts of it was listed. ABB bought the building for transformation into housing, reusing as much of it as possible. Only a small part which was of poor technical quality was demolished. Though 10.000 extra m2 were realised the weight had to be kept low for the existing fundaments to suffice. During the design phase, the building was mothballed. Since it was not heated, damage was done to the characteristic interior of the stairwells and entrance space. The storeys were partly too low according to the building decree, and exemptions were made. However, potential buyers dropped out for this reason. The apartments on the ground floor have gardens, the apartments on the top floor share a terrace on the roof of the new part of the building. The apartments in the new part all have balconies. Balconies for the roof apartments were cut out of the roof. New windows resembling the originals were placed in the original openings. Windows with original glass paintings were kept and insulated by a second glass layer on the inside. After transformation, the whole building except for the new built part was listed.

5. "Westplantsoen" in Delft

Completion office building: 1970'es
Completion transformation: 1999
Commissioner: Housing association DUWO
Architectural design transformation: Karina Benraad Architecture office
General Contractor: ERA
Area: 5400m2
Area after transformation: 6000m2
Purchase costs: 1.3 million euro
Construction costs: 3.0 million euro

The former tax-office had been vacant for 5 years when the housing association DUWO bought it for transformation into student housing. Demolition and new construction was considered but was regarded to give lower revenues. Based on market studies, DUWO decided to develop 2 room apartments, since these could also be let to other target groups. Financial feasibility studies were negative, hence subsidies were granted by the TU Delft and the municipality. The structure of the building was adaptable with columns and a facade grid of 1.8 metres. The facade was technically outdated and looked sulky. Therefore, it was insulated and a new outer layer was added. The fire-escapes were reused, but the main staircase was relocated from the centre to the perimeter of the central axis where a corridor now facilitates the apartment's entrances. The original entrance was situated above street level and could only be reached by outdoor stairs. To allow for wheelchair access it was moved to the basement. As private outdoor spaces were required by the building decree balconies were added, providing the building with a completely new appearance. The simple shape of the building contributed to an efficient transformation-design. The adaptability of the structure was one of the critical success factors of this transformation, together with the system of floors: These could easily be removed and service shafts could be added.

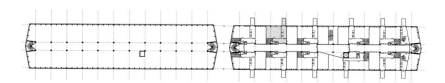

6. "Wilhelminastaete" in Diemen

Completion office building: 1969
Completion transformation: 2007
Commissioner: Rabo
Architectural design transformation: Rappange & Partners
General Contractor: Heddes constructors
Area: 6700m2
Area after transformation: 8500m2
Purchase costs: 3.2 million euro
Construction costs: 6.3 million euro

The former Rabo bank office was technically and functionally outdated and finally redundant. The location was no longer considered suitable for offices, and due to the technical state of the building a retrofit would imply a thorough renovation. Rabo development took initiative for transformation. Studying the feasibility of transformation they saw housing for the elderly as an opportunity because of high local demand for housing within this target group. The municipality was supporting the transformation plans. Together with the architect, a functional programme was developed that would fit the building and the intended target group. The building was equipped with spacious entrances to fit wheelchairs and strollers. On the ground floor, a small bank and a library were realised, together with some parking. Due to the technical state of the facade (the sheet stone facade was literally falling off) it was stripped, and a new facade was added. The new facade was designed as a typical housing facade, vertically laid out instead of horizontal, like the old facade. Transformation of the building into housing was feasible because of an adaptive structure of columns with suitable dimensions. The existing elevators could be reused. The existing stairways were reused as escape-routes, and no additional staircases were needed.

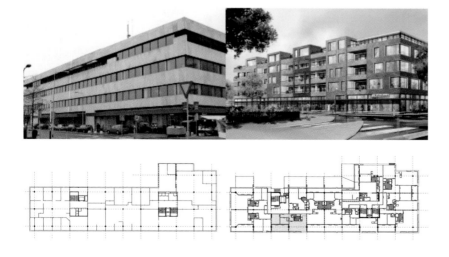

7. "Granida" in Eindhoven

Completion office building: 1958
Completion transformation: 2005
Commissioner: Van Straten, Woonveste
Architectural design transformation: Architecture Office Ton Kandelaars
General Contractor: Van Straten
Area: 7800m2
Purchase costs: 2 million euro
Construction costs: 8.4 million euro

This office building was built for the municipal health service (GGD) who moved out in 1995 after which the building served as temporary offices for the municipality. The building was owned by the municipality who decided that the building should not be demolished, but would be sold to the developer with the best transformation plan. The winning development scheme considered transformation into apartments. The size of the apartments was dictated by the buildings structure, and large luxury apartments were developed which were later bought by the investor Vesteda. The existing staircases, elevators and entrances were reused, resulting in much larger common space than in new apartment buildings. To eliminate the effect of thermal bridges in the structure the apartments were designed like boxes that fit into the existing structure. The demands of the building decree for new housing were followed, though the elevator-doors were too low, the steps of the stairs were too high, in some apartment the floor-height is in some places too low. Exemptions were made for these issues. During the construction the measurements and materials of the structure turned out to differ from floor to floor, concrete rot was discovered and parts of the structure was too weak, according to the fire-safety legislation. As a result, the "apartment-boxes" that were prefabricated did not fit and had to be refitted, accumulating extra costs. Though the original building was not listed, the municipality of Eindhoven found this building significant for a historical period of architecture related to one of the most important periods of growth that Eindhoven experienced, and therefore decided to preserve the building.

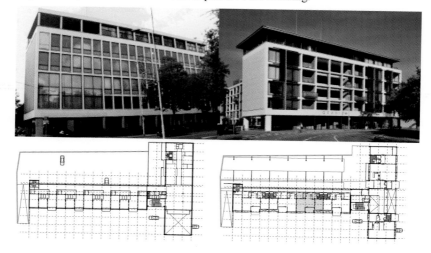

8. "Residentie de Deel" in Emmeloord

Completion office building: 1959
Completion transformation: 1999
Commissioner: WEN
Architectural design transformation: G. Stuwe and C.P. van den Bliek
General Contractor: Haase
Surface: 1980m2
Purchasing costs: 0.4 million euro (1999)
Building costs: 1 million euro (1999)

The office building was owned by the Dutch government and accommodated offices for the water-management bureau. Its typology with small spaces around a large typing-hall made it functionally obsolescent for modern offices. The facade was technically and thermally outdated. WEN saw possibilities for residential transformation and bought it. The typology and structure was seen as suitable for senior citizen housing; the typing hall was transformed into an entrance-atrium. Though the dimensions of the structure were unsuited, parking could be realised in the basement. The floors were an early example of precast concrete floors; thin and without sufficient acoustic insulation to fit housing standards. Weight was added, and also a suspended ceiling. Because of the renewed heavy floors, the walls had to be light and were built from steel frames and gypsum boards. Originally, the building had a curtain wall facade, a light facade hanging on the outside of the construction. To spare weight in the new design, lightweight concrete was applied. Balconies were designed as loggias. All parts of the building turned out to be in a poorer state than estimated, accumulating extra building costs.

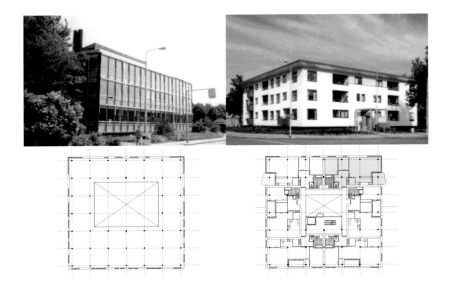

9. "Twentec" in Enschede

Completion office building: 1960-1965
Completion transformation: 2002
Commissioner: Dura TePas
Architectural design transformation: A12 architects
General Contractor: Dura TePas
Area: 11940m2
Purchase costs: 2.8 million euro (1999)
Construction costs: 8.3 million euro (1999)

Originally, the two towers on a joint base were developed as offices for the textile industry. From 1977 onwards the buildings were used as offices until becoming redundant in 1995. The municipality was planning redevelopment of the area, including a large parking garage partly under one of the towers. To boost new developments, Vesteda, the owner of the towers, decided to reuse one tower while demolishing the other. Because of estimated low building costs and short development time transformation was favoured over demolition and reconstruction. Luxury apartments for senior citizens were developed. The existing facade was technically and visually outdated and was stripped of, and a new facade was added. The dimensions of the existing structure were appropriate for transformation into apartments. Since the floors were cantilevered, balconies could not be added to the facade. However, private outdoor space was required, so enclosed loggias were placed. Enclosed loggias implied a fire-safety problem, imposing the use of highly fire-preventing materials, raising the building costs. The estimated short development period was one of the motives for transformation, but eventually the transformation took longer than planned, causing rent loss and higher costs. However, the actors involved in the process considered the project highly successful.

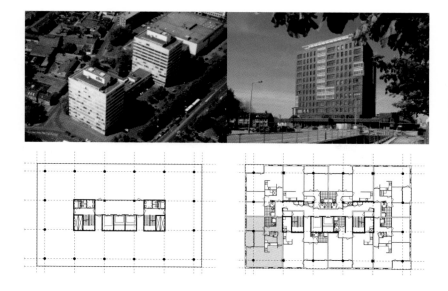

10. "Eendrachtskade" in Groningen

Completion office building: 1980
Completion transformation: 2004
Commissioner: Housing Association Stichting In
Architectural design transformation: Scheffer van der Wal /Stichting In
General Contractor: Ballast Nedam
Area: 3800m2
Purchase costs: 2.5 million euro (2004)
Construction costs: 1.8 million euro (2004)

This office building was property of the ING and was vacant from 2002. The housing Association In found the building interesting for transformation into student housing. The purchasing price was first too high, but as the general contractor agreed to be part of the development team, the building was bought. The housing association owned more student housing units in the area, and found the property interesting for enhancing the housing function of the area. To keep the building costs low, the housing association sought to reuse as much as possible of the building. The building "was not a beauty" but quite new, with a technically well-functioning facade. Each bay of the structure provided at least one window that could be opened, so the facade was kept unchanged. The ground floor and the entrance were slightly changed to give space for post-boxes and door bells for the 84 individual studios. The stairways and the elevator were reused. The studios could be fit efficiently into the existing structure. Placing vertical shafts for services in the pre-stressed concrete floor was problematic; the reinforcement bars had to be located using a detector. The time span from purchase to delivery of the studios was one year and according to planning. Since the building was relatively new, there were no unpleasant surprises during the construction period and the building costs were roughly like calculated.

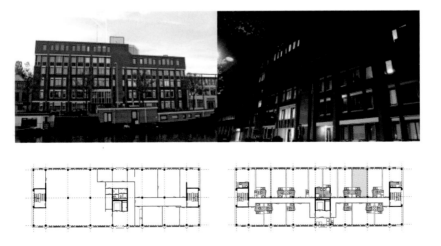

11. "Billiton" in Den Haag

Completion office building: 1938
Completion transformation: 2004
Commissioner: Van Hoogevest
Architectural design transformation: Van Ede Architecten
General Contractor: Van Hoogevest
Area: 25000m2
Purchase costs: 6.2 million euro (2004)
Construction costs: 5.3 million euro (2004)

The office building was built for Billiton in 1938. Billiton became part of Shell and the building was left and sold to an investor in 1988. However, the building was functionally outdated and partly vacant, partly rented out to a school for low rents. Van Hoogevest saw transformation potential in this building and contacted the architect who made a functional feasibility study of the possibilities of housing, with a positive result. The building was technically in good state, despite of some concrete rot. Demolition was no option since the building was a listed monument. The zoning plan allowed for housing and other reasons for transformation into housing were the image of the building, the measurements and adaptability of the structure and good parking possibilities in the basement. An approximate program of requirements was made by van Hoogevest, though the building was the decisive factor. As the building was a listed monument the front facade could not be altered. On the back though, the windows were enlarged and balconies were added. Two extra stairways with elevators were added. High groundwater level had to be taken care of to make the basement suited for parking. By using the "box in box" principle the acoustic insulation between the floors was improved by adding floating floors and suspended ceilings and the insulation of the facade was improved by adding insulation on the inside. The monument-act decided the level of intervention in the building. However, the fire-safety regulations had to be met and also the level of comfort described in the building decree were met.

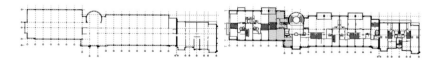

12. "Hof ter Hage" in Den Haag

Completion office building: 1935/1967
Completion transformation: 1998
Commissioner: BAM
Architectural design transformation: ONB, Witt & Jongen
General Contractor: BAM
Area: 22000m2
Area after transformation: 25000m2
Purchase costs: 3.2 million euro (1998)
Construction costs: 10 million euro (1998)

This city block of offices was built over 30 years for the National Mail and Telecom Company. As the telephone was digitalised, the building lost its function and was sold to BAM, who saw the building as a prestigious housing project on a prime location in Den Haag. Financial and functional feasibility studies were conducted, concluding to transform parts of the block and settle for demolition and new construction for less adaptable parts. A short program of requirements was set up, locating shops on street-level while the upper floors would be transformed into housing. The basement was assigned for parking. A design and build contract was applied, involving all parties in an early stage of the project. The existing building was dimensioned for heavy floor-loads and was easily adapted. Balconies were located on the courtyard side since the streets are quite noisy and to maintain the buildings appearance. Though the building was not a monument, it was characteristic and renowned. A variety of apartments were developed, depending of the structure and street-facade of that part of the building. Large apartments accessible by a stairway and elevator per two apartments were located on the widest streets. The transformation process was complicated because of the location in the city-centre: there was no construction site! Also, the building was also very robust, a negative aspect for the partial demolition, and a reason that the building-costs were finally higher than calculated.

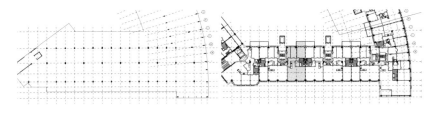

13. "Churchill Towers" in Rijswijk

Completion office building: 1970
Completion transformation: 1999
Commissioner: Geerlings Vastgoed
Architectural design transformation: Oving Architecten
General Contractor: Gebroeders Verschoor
Area: 20700m2
Area after transformation: 24000m2
Purchase costs: 6. 7 million euro (1999)
Construction costs: 8.2 million euro (1999)

The two towers were built in 1970 on a common base accommodating parking. In the beginning of the 1990s the building became redundant. It was seen as functionally outdated with deep floors intended for open office landscapes. The building was in technically good state, though the facade was outdated. A design and build contract was used for the transformation. The architect and the developer together studied the functional and financial feasibility for transformation into housing, and decided to let the buyers decide the size of their apartments. A model apartment was built to give potential buyers an idea of the possibilities. The thermal insulation of the facade was insufficient for housing. The original glass facade was kept, and a second facade was placed on the inside. In-between these layers, private outdoor spaces were realised. The original concrete corners, constructed to enhance building stability turned out to be superfluous and were removed, opening up the facade. The existing stairways and 2 elevators were reused. 2 elevators were removed and the shafts were reused as service ducts.

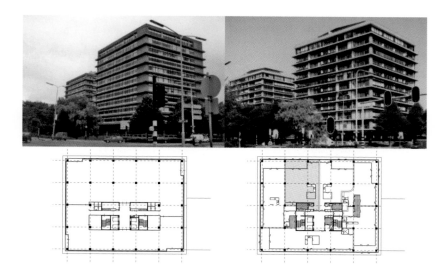

14. "Puntegale" in Rotterdam

Completion office building: 1940-1948
Completion transformation: 1999
Commissioner: Housing Association Stadswonen
Architectural design transformation: De Jong Bokstijn Atchitecten
General Contractor: Moeskops bouwbedrijf
Area: 25700m2
Purchase costs: 3.4 million euro (1996)
Construction costs: 12.1 million euro (1996)

Built as offices for the tax and customs administration, the building became redundant when this service moved to a new building in the beginning of the 1990s. The building was nominated for listing, and could not be demolished, but was functionally obsolete. The sturdy structure, large dimensions and characteristic facade made it interesting for housing. Stadswonen had experience with transformation and found this building interesting for transformation into housing for students and starters in the housing market, the so-called young potentials. Though thermal and acoustic insulation was applied on the inside of the facade, the building is situated on a heavy trafficked road and acoustically some parts of the building were not suited for housing. These zones, along with the ground-floor, were assigned for small offices. The building had high floors, and the 3 lower floors were so high that maisonettes could be realised. The original entrance and stairways were reused. New elevators and fire-escapes were added. The original Pater-Noster elevator was kept though not for daily use. The apartments were made accessible by corridors. The back of the building had galleries that were reused for private outdoor spaces for the apartments on this side of the building. Since the building is a monument, balconies could not be added, and the apartments on the front-side have no outdoor space. Instead, a common roof terrace is realised. Stadswonen sees the building as a trigger for new development in this area. The transformation is financially interesting in the long run, since the value of the building and the location are expected to increase.

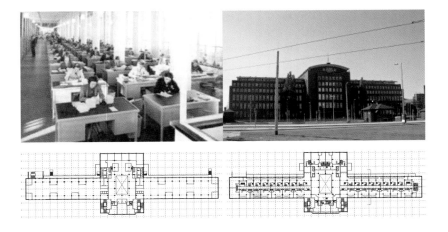

13 Transformation potential and feasibility of the Amsterdam case

In the Office Scan the physical characteristics of office buildings were assessed, and a relationship was sought between office user preferences and the characteristics of structurally vacant office buildings. In the sample of 200 office buildings, 106 buildings have some level of structural vacancy and 56 buildings have more than 30% structural vacancy. Transformation is a way of coping with structural vacancy. In this chapter, transformation potential and feasibility in the Amsterdam office market are studied based on the sample of 106 office buildings with structural vacancy, and will be referred to as the Office Scan Ex-ante. The findings from this study are generalised to predict the transformation potential of office buildings in general, based on a study of market, location and building aspects.

The transformation potential was studied at the building stock level, considering the market conditions that are characterised by a surplus of offices and a shortage of housing. Following, the transformation veto criteria of air quality and noise level of the location together with requirements of the minimum measurements of the buildings were applied to rule out buildings that are not suited for residential transformation. These veto criteria were revealed in the ex-post transformation studies (paragraph 12.5). Subsequently, a comparison was made of four different options for coping with structurally vacant office buildings (consolidate, renovate, transform, demolish and rebuild) revealing which option is the financially most interesting. Finally, interviews were held with housing associations and commercial developers to study under which conditions transformation is perceived as feasible.

13.1 Market aspects

The Amsterdam office market is characterised by a high level of vacancy, the average for Amsterdam is 16% (BHH 2008). The level of structural vacancy varies between the different locations, and in some locations the level is even higher; in specific locations in South-East more than 40% of the office buildings are vacant. The housing market on the other hand, is one of the tightest in the Netherlands, and also has the highest prices. According to research (Heath 2001; Beauregard 2005), these are two of the most important market conditions for residential transformation of office buildings. However, the housing prices also vary between the different locations, and are the highest in the city centre, while the areas Teleport and South-East have the lowest prices. Teleport has very little housing; the larger part of the area accommodates harbour activities while the location nearest the city centre is a monofunctional office location (Figure 63).

13.1.1 Government policy and incentives

The municipality of Amsterdam is well aware of their structural vacancy problem. From October 2006 an "office pilot" was appointed, an official from the municipality who got the task of initiating measures to decrease the structural vacancy by encouraging transformation of redundant and obsolete office buildings. Also, studies were made on the planned new office building stock and by discussions with investors and real estate developers the municipality sought to decrease the level of speculative office developments. The most apparent effect has been that several parties and actors have acknowledged the problem of structural vacancy, and so several investors and housing associations are playing a more active role in the initiation of transformation processes.

13.1.2 Land ownership

The system of land lease was introduced in Amsterdam in the 15th century, though the current system has been in use since 1896. Two third of the land within the borders of Amsterdam is owned by the municipality (OGA 2006), and the municipality's policy is to buy all available land supply within its borders. The land is rented out to users of a plot by means of a land lease system, where the leasing

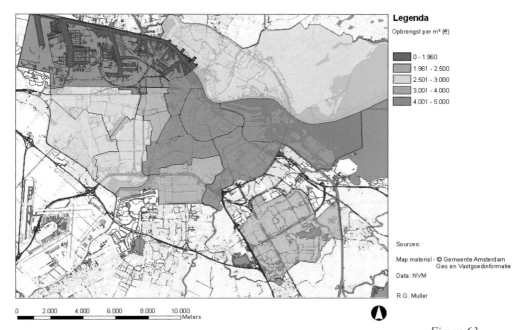

Figure 63
Purchasing price
of apartments
in Amsterdam,
price in euro per
square metre

party rents the land for 50 or 75 years, and the lease price per year is a percentage of the land value. The lease level depends on the function that is accommodated on the plot and the number of floors and amount of square metres that are realised. The land value is assessed at the beginning of each lease period, and the lease price may be multiplied several times. The land lease system is a considerable source of income for the municipality with a result of 60 million euro in 2006. Also the land lease gives the municipality the possibility to reclaim land for new developments from current users, though in practise, this intervention is hardly used.

As such, the land policy is found to reduce the transformation potential of office buildings. When large changes are made in the use of a plot or if the building on a plot is sold, the value of the plot will be assessed and the municipality may raise the rent price if the land value has increased and if the new use of the plot is likely to yield more than the old use. Likewise, if the assessed value of a building is becoming lower, the municipality may be forced to lower the value of the plot and thus lower the rent price. However, the land lease system may also be used by the municipality as an instrument to encourage transformation by lowering the lease level for transformed buildings, by lowering the land value of redevelopments, or by raising the land value for new developments in natural areas or green cultural landscapes.

13.2 Location aspects

For transformation to be a feasible way of coping with structural vacancy the following location veto criteria should be met (see paragraph 12.5). These consider noise from airplanes, railroads and highways, and air-quality, specifically focusing on fine dust. Other location criteria that affect the potential for and feasibility of transformations are less critical, though if none of these criteria are responded to, the transformation potential is low or the transformation will not be feasible. The location characteristics of the sample with structural vacancy were studied and their influence on the transformation potential was tested.

13.2.1 Urban development

Transformation of office buildings in central urban areas happen and can take place on the scale of a building. Several examples in Amsterdam are known, many of them just outside the canal district. This area was mainly developed between 1920 and 1940, though in the 1960s a large part of the plots were redeveloped. The scale of these buildings was larger than the early 20th century developments (Figure 64) and was a result of the Reconstruction Plans from 1953 (Jolles et al. 2003). These transformations were feasible also because of their location; the buildings are easily accessible by car and public transport, they are located near the city centre, the location has a high level of services, facilities and retail. Within the canal district, the municipality was very restrictive on permitting transformation of residential office transformation, since it was worried that employment would disappear from the city centre and leave the canal district a housing area and tourist attraction (Heim et al. 2006).

13.2.2 Functional

The functional use of office locations is described by its characteristics as defined in the Delphi Survey. Travel time to the highway and parking possibilities, distance to the railway station, the level of facilities and services in or near the location, and the mix with the functions housing and offices and facilities are the most important characteristics. Except for the city centre, most locations are well accessible by car. The locations South-East and Westpoort/Teleport are also located within short distance from intercity stations. A high amount of office space is located in these locations, while on the other hand neither facilities nor housing are found here. The other locations have more facilities or housing, or a combination of both, and also accommodate less office space. While South-East and Teleport score high on accessibility, the other locations score high on facilities and the mix with housing. The lack of facilities and housing in the locations Teleport and South-East is problematic for the transformation potential of the locations. As also recognised by Beauregard (2005) a certain level of facilities are needed for successful residential transformation of offices, even in a tight housing market. Transformations in these locations are not per se impossible, though the possibilities of adapting the locations by adding housing and facilities on the scale of the location need consideration. A successful transformation will eventually depend on the quality of the built environment, a mix of functions with housing and offices and facilities on the scale of the neighbourhood.

13.2.3 Legal and policy aspects

In the Netherlands, The Spatial Planning Act is the main legal document that influences the transformation potential of office buildings on a location level. The Spatial Planning Act describes the design and use of zoning plans and is used for communication between central and local governments. Building locations, nature and cultural landscapes are described and also possible developments of these. An important aspect in the Spatial Planning Act is environmental legislation, considering not only conservation and cultivation of nature, fauna and flora, but also health issues related to the built environment. One specific issue that reduces the transformation potential of office buildings is the legislation on noise levels and air quality, as the law is stricter for housing than for offices on these issues.

   When new developments are initiated, local governments are obliged to develop zoning plans fitting within the legal frames of the Spatial Planning Act. A zoning plan may apply to a part of the city, a location or a small part of a location. Within the physical borders of the zoning plan public space, building envelopes, parking rules and functions are described. The municipality decides the level of detail of a zoning plan, varying from a precise description of building height, building materials and function to less specific plans describing envelopes and functions within certain margins. The transformation potential of office buildings is closely related to the zoning plan. If offices is the only programme described for a specific location, site or building, the zoning plan must be adapted before a building can be transformed into housing. Likewise, if a zoning plan describes a building envelope of – let's say – 10mx10mx10m, the zoning plan must be adapted before the building can be enlarged. From January 2010, the Spatial Planning Act is less strict, though it will still need to be adapted to allow transformation. The procedure of adapting zoning plans requires time. The municipality needs to elaborate a new zoning plan or revise the existing and the plan must be submitted for public inspection before

Figure 64 Three transformed office buildings in Amsterdam Sloterkade (Kother Salman, Vandenhoeven, Kentie & Partners)

it may be approved. As such, the procedure of zoning plan adaptation requires at least half a year if no objections are lodged. The time consuming process of adapting the zoning plan is experienced as a problem by real estate developers. As municipalities need to adapt the plan for each building that is changed, the process of zoning plan adaptations may take longer than half a year, depending on the capacity of the municipality's planning department.

A first step in testing the transformation potential of the Amsterdam office market was conducted by applying the noise contours of the airport, highways, railway and industry onto the map of office buildings with structural vacancy (Muller et al. 2009). As shown in Figure 65, a great part of the office buildings located in Teleport is not suitable for transformation following the noise contours of the harbour area in Amsterdam West. Except for a few buildings near the highway and airport and some buildings in other harbour areas, the transformation potential of the other buildings from the Office Scan is not influenced by the noise contours. Fine dust is another critical issue that influences the transformation potential of office locations. The areas with raised levels of fine dust appeared to overlap with the noise contours, and as such have no influence on the transformation potential of the sampled office buildings. Of the sample with 106 office buildings with structural vacancy, 21 buildings were located within the noise contours and are not suited for transformation. Within the contours, another way of coping with structural vacancy is needed. The possibilities are demolition, renovation or keeping a status quo, hoping for new tenants to be interested in this office space.

13.2.4 Financial

Office rents are determined primarily by their location. Assuming that the right location increases the organisations profitability, the willingness to pay for locations with preferred characteristics is increased and is expressed in rent levels and asset prices (Koppels et al. 2009). However, the influence of location characteristics on structural vacancy is less strong, structurally vacant office buildings are found throughout Amsterdam, also in the office locations with high rents.

Housing prices also vary per location (Figure 63 Purchasing price of apartments in Amsterdam, price in euro per square metre) as some housing locations are also more popular than others. The interesting possibilities for transformation emerge in locations where the housing prices are high and the structural vacancy of office buildings as well. In locations with expensive office space however, the asked price for structurally vacant office buildings is likely to be high, since the financial devaluation of office buildings is lagging behind on the structural vacancy. In all locations with housing prices at the same level or higher than the price for office space, transformation is interesting. Especially in the old centre of Amsterdam, housing yields more per square metre than offices. Also, some locations, like the Teleport location, are monofunctional office locations without an existing available housing supply and no examples for comparison. Housing prices in these locations are likely to be comparable to prices in neighbouring locations.

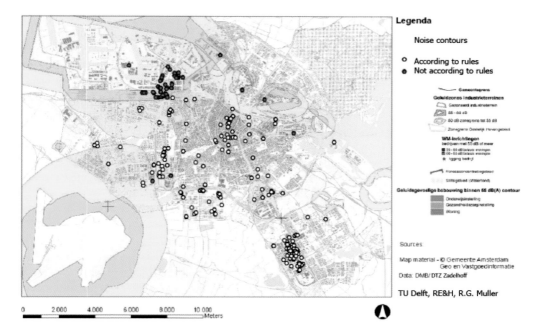

Legenda

Noise contours

○ According to rules
● Not according to rules

~~~ Gemeentegrens
Geluidzones industrieterreinen
◯ Gezoneerd industrieterrein
◎ 55 - 60 dB
◎ 60 dB zonegrens tot 55 dB
Zonegrens Oostelijk Havengebied
WM-inrichtingen
bedrijven met 55 dB of meer
■ 51 - 60 dB brivis woningen
■ 60 - 65 dB brivis woningen
★ ligging bedrijf

Hoofdassenhoofdwegennet
Stiltegebied (Waterland)

Geluidgevoelige bebouwing binnen 55 dB(A) contour
■ Onderwijsinstelling
■ Gezondheidszorginstelling
■ Woning

Sources:

Map material - © Gemeente Amsterdam
Geo en Vastgoedinformatie
Data: DMB/DTZ Zadelhoff

TU Delft, RE&H, R.G. Muller

0   2.000   4.000   6.000   8.000   10.000
▬▬▬▬▬▬▬▬▬▬▬▬▬▬▬▬ Meters

13.2.5 Location transformation

50% of the 106 structurally vacant office buildings that were studied are located on monofunctional office locations, whereas these locations are not found suitable for housing because of their intrinsic monofunctionality, (often) isolated location and low quality of the public space. The structural vacancy as well as the ownership is dispersed; in Amsterdam South East investors typically own one or two buildings and though numerous buildings have some level of structural vacancy, few of these are 100% structurally vacant. Transformation of office buildings in Amsterdam South East will not take place on building scale. Structural vacancy pushes the location in a downwards spiralling development. The municipality experiences this development as a problem, since this image of the location hinders new take-up of office space, the location starts dilapidating, the value of properties depreciate, and so also the municipality's income from land lease will at some point be lowered.

A large scale intervention is required, adding a number of housing units that will generate this demand (Schalekamp et al. 2009). A functional transformation of one building will not be successful, as it will not generate enough demand for facilities and services that are needed in or near a housing location. As a consequence, the transformed office building will not be a successful housing project, and will not trigger new transformations as expected by Post (2007). The effect of one transformation is not significant and the timeframe from the first transformation until the emergence of a mix use location will be too long to attract real estate investors. Geraedts and Van Der Voordt (2007) brought up the idea of starting a transformation of the location from its edges; if the monofunctional location is located near a mix-use or housing location with the facilities and services needed for housing, transformation may take place next to these locations.

Figure 65 The noise contours of the airport and industry are shown in the map. Within the orange contour, housing is prohibited, within the yellow contours; housing is possible if measures are taken for improved acoustic insulation.

Anyhow, the two latter strategies are inherent to consider a longer development time-span than an integral approach. A negative effect of the two step-wise approaches is the possible increase of purchasing prices of structurally vacant office buildings as an effect of speculation. If the first transformations would be successful, the purchasing prices for office buildings would rise, if transformation would not be successful, new transformations would certainly not take place, and the obsolescence, deterioration and further downgrading of the location would be continued (Schalekamp et al. 2009).

An integral approach to transformation of monofunctional office locations has its flaws. As the property in the locations is in most cases dispersed, counting just as many or even more owners than buildings, starting up an integral urban development is complicated; a director would be needed, being an investor sensing the urgency of redevelopment, aiming at transforming his property, being the municipality making an effort to improve the office market or the viability of office locations within its boundaries, or being a developer seeing possible revenues from a location transformation. Depending on the size and built volume of the location, a considerable part of the owners should contribute to redevelopment of the location, together forming a coalition. The size of the coalition or the number of office buildings to be transformed cannot as such be determined, however the amount of 'free-riders', owners who don't contribute to the redevelopment albeit profiting from it, should be minimized as they discourage other owners contribution.

Still, one more option for initiating a location transformation is thinkable. In former redevelopments of brownfields, artists and other 'urban pioneers' played an important role using the redundant buildings and locations for working and dwelling (Avidar et al. 2007; Hamnett and Whitelegg 2007; Smit 2007). This group find it less problematic to live in locations without the typical facilities that are normally found in housing locations. However, the group is normally not eager to pay high rents for living or working space, hence the owners of the properties need to see the sense of this kind of 'incentives'. Again, the possibility for this development is threatened by the dispersed properties, the owner's attitude and a prisoner's dilemma; as other parties will profit from one owner's investment, the owners will await the initiative from other owners. One example of a successful redevelopment where the transition from redundancy to liveable location was enhanced by pioneers is "Strijp S", a central though isolated location in Eindhoven, and former property of Philips. The location had a mix of offices and larger light-industrial buildings. The housing association Trudo bought the location and let pioneers inhabit it, knowing that the sheer size of the location would set the time frame of the redevelopment to several years (interview with Thom Aussems, July 23rd, 2008).

Though the process of transforming office buildings in monofunctional office locations is more complex than transforming solitary office buildings in central urban areas, it is not impossible. However, the complexity of a location transformation requires time, effort, finance and collaboration, and the sense of urgency for such transformations have so far not been constituted in Amsterdam.

13.3 Building aspects

For transformation to be feasible, one criterion is employed as a veto criterion by the Transformation Meter (Geraedts and Van der Voordt 2007); the possibility for realising a free floor height of at least 2.6 metres, as required by the Building Decree. Other building characteristics are one by one influential, though the characteristics that describe the buildings structure, facade and installations together influence the buildings transformation potential. After studying the location characteristics of the sample with structural vacancy, buildings were filtered out that have no transformation potential. The transformation potential of the remaining buildings was again studied by discussing the building characteristics' influence on the transformation feasibility.

13.3.1 Legal and policy

The main legal issues that impinge on the residential transformation of office buildings are in the Netherlands described by the Dutch Building Decree. The building decree considers issues relating to the safety, usability, health, energy use and environmental impact of the buildings for a specific use, with different requirements for housing than for offices. Office buildings can be transformed to apply to the most requirements for housing, and some requirements are equal for the two functions. However, measurements of the base-building are hard to change, and one of the requirements for housing is a free floor height in living areas of 2.6 metres. As the requirements for office buildings are also 2.6 metres and as office buildings normally have a free floor height of more than 2.6 metres, the issue does not seem very intriguing. Nevertheless, as residential transformations of office buildings often require the addition of a floating floor and a lowered ceiling to cope with the acoustic insulation requirements for housing, the 2.6 metres free floor height can sometimes be hard to realise, especially in redundant offices from the 1970s and 1980s that were built according to a "narrowest fit" concept.

The requirement is much debated; until 2005 the Building Decree required a free floor height of 2.4 metres, making more offices suited for transformation. Since most existing housing in the Netherlands have a floor height of 2.4 metres, it may also seem strange to require higher ceilings in transformed existing office buildings. However, the 2.6 metres free floor height is experienced as an extra quality and as new housing is developed with this height, residential transformations with a lower ceiling height may be experienced as having a lower quality – of course again depending on the potential inhabitants of the transformed office buildings. The floor height of the sample was tested. All buildings could possibly be transformed with a free floor height of 2.6 metres after transformation.

Also important are the regulations on safety issues. In the case of fire, the main structure of offices is required to hold for more than 90 minutes if the building is taller than 5 metres. The same goes for housing taller than 7 metres and lower than 13 metres, while housing taller than 13 metres is required to hold for more than 120 minutes. Moreover, laying out apartments in existing office buildings complying with the requirements of fire-escapes in housing is seen as a challenge. At least two exits are required from the front-door of an apartment, a measure that might imply that additional stairs must be added. These requirements may be responded to by a smart design solution and do not directly threaten the transformation potential of the sample. However, meeting the requirements increase the transformation building costs.

13.3.2 Financial

Considering the feasibility of residential transformations of office buildings, the financial feasibility is the most important to actors like investors and real estate developers. Housing associations strive to meet with other aims and targets; their investment perspective is normally set for 30 years and not for 10 or 15 years which is common for investors, and unlike the financial goals of real estate developers who normally develop housing projects and directly sell the units. Normally housing associations also require a lower return on investments. In some cases, as in transformations of monuments, other aspects might be more important than the financial feasibility, and sometimes projects are also taken on for experience or exposure within new markets in order to acquire new projects.

Financial feasibility is defined by the building costs and profits and the required return on investments. A financially feasible project meets the required return on investment that was defined beforehand by the developer, investor or housing association. Depending on the different financial requirements and spreadsheet techniques, large differences occur in the calculations. A project that is financially feasible for a large housing association may not be financially feasible for a small developer.

13.3.3 Architectural, functional and technical

Most structurally vacant office buildings come with 13 in a dozen, with moot architectural qualities. These buildings are not kept for their architectural or emotional value, and also not for their historic or cultural value, rather the value of these buildings is their intrinsic value and the loss of value by demolition.

Buildings that are considered for transformation because of their architectural value are few. The building that was owned and occupied by the ABN-AMRO bank in the centre of Amsterdam (Figure 67) is a curious example. It was built in the 1960s and designed by Duintjer, and though it was not a listed building, when the bank decided to move and sell the building, the municipal heritage committee started a procedure to get the building listed, as it is seen as an important example of modernistic architecture. Additionally, the building represents a paradigmatic change in urban planning and thinking. Its construction in the 1960s led to loud protests; hence the consideration of listing the building again shows interesting developments in architectural conservation and urban planning (Schoonenberg 2006). The direct incentive to the procedure was a redevelopment plan by the new owners who reconsidered their development partly because of these procedures. A residential transformation scheme for the building is being developed in 2009, with possible construction in 2010.

An intended future example is the Zuidas. Effort is taken to develop the location under the supervision of a master-architect, employing famous architects in order to achieve a high architectural value of the buildings and thereby contributing to the status of the location. However, it is difficult to predict which, if any of the buildings, will be appreciated for their architectural value in the future.

13.3.4 Strategies for coping with structural vacancy

Transformation can be compared to other strategies for coping with structurally vacant office buildings, like consolidation, renovation and demolishment with new construction (Vijverberg 1995; Douglas 2006). Monumental, architecturally interesting buildings and buildings with specific visual qualities may be transformed despite being maladaptive and despite high transformation costs, either because they are listed monuments, found important by interest groups, seen as interesting acquisition projects by developers or seen as image lenders for a larger development. However, most office buildings with high structural vacancy are typical office buildings. Though transformation is a sustainable way of coping with structural vacancy, the financial feasibility, or rather, the financial revenues of transformation as opposed to other possible strategies decide the transformation potential of these office buildings. The financially most interesting strategy can be found by calculating the NPV (Net Present Value) for different possible strategies. Using market conform calculation methods, the NPV was calculated for the sample of structurally vacant office buildings in Amsterdam (Muller et al. 2009). As many of the actors in the market are still sceptical towards transformation, a worst case scenario was calculated for the transformation building costs, and a best case scenario (from the investors' perspective) was used for calculating the value of the structurally vacant office buildings.

*Figure 66
the Mahler 4
development in
Zuidas
(www.flickr.com)*

The study used an IRR (Internal Rate of Return) of 7% for the different strategies, making a comparison of the strategies possible. The buildings value was determined using the cap-rate method; calculated as the product of the estimated first year rental income divided by the Gross Initial Yield (GIY). The estimated risk and future value thereafter decide the choice for a strategy. The NPV for consolidation was calculated using a 10-year operation period of the existing building, anticipating that 50% of the building will be let during the whole period. The NPV calculation for renovation was conducted assuming that a newly renovated building is more attractive to office users. Therefore, the NPV was calculated anticipating that 75% of the office building would be let during the whole 10-year period. In the case of transformation, a worst case scenario was assumed, using 1450 euro/m2 as input variable for the building costs. The alternative was calculated assuming purchase of the land and the existing building and selling the whole development after 2-3 years. The last alternative considered demolishment and construction of new housing on the same plot.

In 40% of the cases studied, the NPV calculations revealed transformation to be financially interesting. As the purchasing price per building was not known but estimated, a positive NPV would give an idea of the space for negotiation with the current owner of the building. The financial feasibility of transformation could be additionally enhanced by extending the building horizontally or vertically or by adding a commercial program like retail or leisure functions to the ground floor of the building. The possibilities depend on the location and the building. Not all locations are suitable for retail or leisure functions, although most office buildings are already located in locations where the ground floor has a public character. A vertical extension could be possible for a large amount of the existing office buildings as these were sturdier constructed than the standard apartment buildings, and so most office buildings could be extended vertically by 1-2 floors. Horizontal extensions could also be interesting, depending on the size of the building plot. While in the city centre of Amsterdam most office buildings are built on small plots or even adjoining other buildings, office buildings on the city edges and in office locations are built on larger plots providing enough space for extensions. On the other hand, parking possibilities and other functional studies were not part of this study and should be considered in subsequent assessments.

Evaluation of the strategies

Calculating the value of a structurally vacant office building means that future rent is not expected, and its value would be zero – except for the value of the remaining land lease minus the costs for clearing the site. Keeping this in mind, the value of structurally vacant office buildings should be lower than calculated in this study. For example, if the building is let for 50% and the remaining 50% is structurally vacant, calculating the buildings market value by the cap rate method using a GIY of 7% is rather opportunistic, as the GIY is based on a completely rented out building. A much higher GIY would be more realistic, and in that case the coping strategies transformation and demolishment and new construction would become more interesting.

The calculations considering building costs, new rents or sale are calculated on a highly abstracted level. The building costs for office renovation are retrieved from numbers on standard office developments; the building costs used for the transformation strategy are based on the highest building costs observed in the 14 ex-post cases (12). Though the building costs in the ex-post studies varied between 500 euro/m2 and 1500 euro/m2, estimating the building costs for a transformation projects implies a more thorough study of the specific building, and so the costs calculated here were kept high to stick to a worst case scenario. Calculating a best case scenario would conclude transformation to be the best coping strategy for an even higher percentage of the structurally vacant office buildings.

The purchasing price of apartments differs in different locations (Figure 63) as does the rental price for offices. Following, the transformation potential in some locations were much higher than in other locations. The city centre scored well on transformation potential (76% of the structurally vacant office buildings), together with the location Baarsjes (95%!) but also small, old office locations, enclosed within popular housing areas, such as Westerpark, Oud-West, Geuzenveld/Slotermeer and Oud-zuid show a transformation potential above 70%. On the other hand, some locations with high structural vacancy like Zuidoost, Oost/Watergraafsmeer and Zuideramstel, all have a transformation potential lower than 40%. The reason is that all the office buildings in these locations are relatively new, and also the structural vacancy of most of these buildings is only partial, and so the value of the office buildings is relatively high. As the structural vacancy of these buildings would endure or increase, the buildings value would decrease and such depreciation would cause transformation to become the best coping strategy for an even higher percentage of the structurally vacant office buildings. This study shows the differences between the various coping strategies and most importantly, the importance of the different variables in a development scheme. The following paragraph will show how developers and housing associations think about transformations.

13.4 Interviews on conditions and characteristics

As introduced in paragraph 9.4, 21 Real estate developers and 10 housing associations were interviewed, discussing under which market conditions transformation would be interesting and whether specific location and building characteristics influence the transformation potential and feasibility. 10 of the 21 developers had no experience with transformations. Two of the housing associations were at the moment of the interviews working on transformation projects, though they did not previously complete transformation projects. The mayor opportunities for transformation were described by the characteristics of the location and secondly by the intrinsic characteristics of the building. The purchasing price was found to be the most important obstacle for transformations. The interviewees were allowed to give multiple arguments.

Though the most argued opportunity, the location, was seen as important by all the interviewees, housing associations seem to find the location more important than developers. Additionally housing associations find the strategic possession of land an important opportunity, albeit this is hardly mentioned by developers. Also, the possibility for developing housing for specific target groups was mentioned by the housing associations, while this was not at all an issue for the developers. On the other hand, the buildings image and its intrinsic characteristics were found important by the developers though not by the housing associations. The main differences between firms with and without experience is their view on the building and the location: though both groups find the location the most important, groups without experience find the building more than twice as important as firms with experience.

The most important argued obstacles for transformations were purchasing price, building and location characteristics. While developers found the building to be the largest obstacle, housing associations thought the location and the purchasing price to be most problematic. While firms with experience considered the purchasing price the largest obstacle, firms without experience considered the intrinsic building characteristics the most important obstacle. In the interviews, the interviewees were confronted with specific statements based on assumptions from the ex-post case studies, and were asked whether or not they could agree to the statements. The reactions to some of the statements were expected, though others were not and are therefore quite interesting.

- Half of the respondents agreed that the development risks of transformations are higher than for new constructions
- 77% agreed that the risks during the construction phase of transformations are higher than for new constructions
- Hidden flaws are a big risk
- There's no agreement that the building costs or benefits are significantly different from new constructions
- 40% of the respondents thought that "13 in a dozen buildings" could better be demolished
- 60% agreed that a new facade is needed because of its technical performance, but most of all because of the bad image of existing office facades - although there's a strong agreement that people don't mind living in transformed offices
- There's agreement that the zoning plan, building decree and public policies hinder transformation
- Changing the installations is not a hindrance
- 84% think that developers have an obligation to act sustainably
- While 77% thinks this can be achieved by keeping the existing buildings

The location was found to be the most important success factor for transformation, and housing associations pointed out the importance of the right location for specific target groups. As housing associations develop and manage their buildings, often with long investment perspectives, this is an important difference with developers, who mostly develop and sell the properties, or in some cases are involved during the first few years after completion of a project. Knowing this, the housing associations interest in strategic land possession can be explained, as the quality of a location can be enhanced by large scale ownership and developments. One of the housing associations expressed it like this: "we try to build up land possession in certain areas of the city. In that way, we can upgrade the quality of a larger area and in the course of time the value of our properties will increase. This way, what seems as a financially not feasible plan to others, is a good investment for us."

This statement shows the importance of using the right variables (also) when calculating the feasibility of transformations. The time factor is important and to housing associations who are involved in student housing or housing for first-time renters, vicinity to the city centre and universities are important reasons for getting involved in transformations; these locations are normally already developed and transformation is in many cases found to give higher revenues than redevelopment. Housing associations developing for students are more likely to find existing office buildings fit for transformation. Developing small housing units, typically for one or two students, the new lay-out in the existing base building is changeable. Also, a low status appearance of interior and exterior is less important for this target group, and less money is therefore invested in upgrading the appearance of the building and in finishes, though the required technical quality of the facade is met and the transformed buildings are in compliance to the building decree.

	Market conditions						Building and location characteristics		
	Revenue	Obsolescence	Strategic possession	Sustainability	Company profile	Target group	Image	Building	Location
Total	19	23	19	13	13	16	23	26	61
Developer	29	29	10	5	14	0	29	38	52
Housing association	0	10	40	30	10	50	10	0	80
Experience	11	22	17	11	17	-	22	17	67
No experience	19	23	23	15	8	-	23	39	54

Table 27 Opportunities for transformation – conditions and characteristics found important by the interviewees, expressed as percentage of the interviewees in the category.

	Market conditions		Building and location characteristics			
	Purchasing price	Legislation	Building costs	Hidden flaws*	Building	Location
Total	52	19	16	3	45	42
Developer	43	19	19	5	52	33
Housing association	70	20	10	0	30	60
Experience	61	17	17	6	33	39
No experience	39	23	15	0	62	46

mentioned by only one developer with experience.

Table 28 Obstacles for transformation - conditions and characteristics found important by the interviewees, as percentage of the 31 interviewees who found it important

To developers the building is far more important, and interestingly it is just as often found an opportunity as an obstacle. As typical apartments vary in size between 80 and 120 square metres, and sometimes bigger, the lay-out of the existing building is important. Developers also state the importance of adaptable design, where the existing building is guiding. However, fitting larger apartments into existing buildings leaves a bigger part of the building unsuited for use, though this extra space may also be experienced as a quality. As one developer expressed this dilemma; each building keeps a "gift" for the one who's able to find it. Another developer argued that the emotional and historic values of existing buildings are reasons to be interested in transformations, and if the revenues of transformation are lower than for new developments, that would be less important – though the development should be financially feasible when selling the apartments as the development is completed. Furthermore, one interviewee stated that transformations are only financially feasible if the new use – housing – is adapted to the building, and not if the building is adapted to housing…looking at is that way, even the most silly office building may be interesting.

Figure 67 The two buildings and locations that were discussed in the interviews. To the left, a building and its site in the centre of Amsterdam, to the right a building and its site in Amsterdam South East

The location is also important to developers, and many examples are known of office buildings in central urban locations that are transformed into high-end apartments or housing for first time buyers. For the location to be suitable for housing, vicinity of other apartment buildings and daily facilities are found important. Possibly, one characteristic building may be used to pull a larger development. In that case, the situation of the location in the city is the most important and the existing building should have the quality to provide identity to the whole location. In that case, the usability of the existing building is less important, if its historic or emotional values are sufficient.

Assessing the transformation potential of two buildings and locations

The Amsterdam case study (The office scan) shows the transformation potential of the Amsterdam office building supply. The two locations with the most structural vacancy were the City Centre and Amsterdam South-East, a monofunctional office location developed in the 1980s. Roughly described by their location characteristics, the largest difference between the locations is the presence of other functions and facilities in the area, and the status of the locations. The city centre has developed through hundreds of years and is a mix of all possible functions in co-existence with each other. On the contrary, Amsterdam South East was planned as part of one of the city extensions described in the General Extension Plan from 1935, including housing, offices, and distribution and logistics, again separated by railway and ring roads. The building in the centre is approximately 30000 square metres and quite large compared to the buildings in Amsterdam South East that is 2600 square metres.

As part of the interviews, the respondents were asked to assess the transformation potential of two different buildings on two different locations, one in the city centre and one in Amsterdam South east (Figure 67). They were asked if they as developers would be interested in taking on and transforming one or both buildings. Of the 30 respondents, 5 thought the location in Amsterdam South-east to be interesting, though 2 of the 5 thought that functions like a long-stay hotel or a health-clinic would be a more interesting function than housing. All interviewees thought the location and building in the centre of Amsterdam to be interesting except of two, these two took into concern that the purchasing price of the building would probably be high and form an obstacle to the financial feasibility of the transformation. The respondents first reaction was not to be interested in transformation of the building that is located in a monofunctional office area, the building in Amsterdam South-east. Since their first reaction was based on both the building and the location, they were asked to first argue their view on the building, then on the location.

The reactions towards the buildings were mixed, and could partly be explained because of the background of the interviewees. To small-scale developers the building in South-east was interesting because of its scale, while the sheer size of the building in the centre of Amsterdam was seen as an obstacle. Also half of the housing associations reacted positively on the building in South-east, seeing a potential for transformation into student-housing. For the same reason, the larger developers considered the building in the centre more interesting. While all respondents had the idea that transformation of the building in the centre will be functionally, technically and financially feasible, given that the purchasing price would be "reasonable", some respondents questioned the feasibility and sustainability of investing in the transformation of the relatively small scale building in South-east. As it would need a new facade in order to be suited for housing and as problems were foreseen for adapting the installations to a housing scheme, the transformation building costs would probably be high. Some suggested rather investing in a new building with high initial quality and a less strict functional scheme.

The location in the centre did not trigger much discussion. All interviewees would consider the location a scoop, though some again opted that the owner of the location – given any knowledge of the real estate market – would ask a high purchasing price. The location in Amsterdam South-east generated more discussion. Few of the interviewees were initially interested, but discussing the possibilities for transformation, three approaches were opted for, all three starting with the outlook that the whole area will need to be transformed. One development option mentioned was a stepwise redevelopment, to first transform some buildings into shops, gyms, restaurants and other services, then in a second phase adding housing to the program, partly by transformation and partly by demolition and new construction.

A second option mentioned was to start transformation of buildings adjacent to existing housing, facilities or public transport, applying the so-called "ink-stain method" to slowly improve the quality of the area. The ink-stain method departs from the idea that transformation of one office building into housing may inspire other actors to transform or redevelop buildings in the vicinity, and so a whole area can be transformed with small means. However, the risk is high that the redevelopment takes a long time and investors drop off along the way. The third and most preferred option would imply an urban area development, considering the whole area as one development. Regardless of the preferred solution, transformation of one building in this area is not seen as feasible. The area lacks facilities, public transport and is not regarded socially safe. One interviewee made a point, representing the meaning of most other respondents as well: "look at it this way; organisations don't want to locate their offices here. Why would anyone want to live here?"

13.5 Summary and conclusions

The transformation potential of the sample of 106 office buildings in Amsterdam with some level of structural vacancy (8%-100%) was studied. Transformation was found to be the best coping strategy for 40% of the buildings. The potential was defined through a stepwise hierarchical study of the market, location and building characteristics considering:

- The purchasing price of apartments and office rental prices in different locations
- The location characteristics, focusing on functional, legal and policy issues, specifically considering monofunctionality
- Legal issues like air quality and noise
- The building characteristics, focusing on legal, policy and financial issues
- Financial feasibility, as the studied sample consists mainly of standard office buildings without a recognised monumental or architectural value

In this study, the financial feasibility of residential transformations was decided based on general building characteristics, only the free floor height was considered a veto, giving the buildings a negative transformation advice. In a more detailed study, the influence of technical and functional issues on the transformation potential could be assessed. In this study, a worst case scenario of the building costs was anticipated, based on the highest level that was found in the ex-post case studies in chapter 12.

Within the given limitations, transformation is the best strategy for coping with structural vacancy in 40% of the cases. However, monofunctional office locations will need extra attention as the transformation potential of buildings in these locations will also depend on the willingness of actors in transformation processes to invest in these locations. Moreover, investors and owners of office buildings still need to be convinced of the opportunities of transformation or sale anticipating transformation. Interviewing commercial developers and housing associations, discussing under which market conditions transformation would be interesting to them and whether building and location characteristics influence the transformation potential and feasibility, the location characteristics were found to have the most influence on the transformation opportunities. The purchasing price was found to be the most important transformation obstacle. Transformation of office buildings in monofunctional locations was only regarded possible if the location as a whole would be transformed.

14 Conclusions Cope

Transformation is a way of coping with structural vacancy and takes place especially in city centres or in central housing areas. The most important aspects that influence the residential transformation potential of office buildings are

- the demand for housing
- the segregation of real estate markets; actors roles
- the purchasing price of office buildings for transformation
- the buildings' location characteristics
- the building characteristics
- the transformation building costs

In the Netherlands, the housing demand is high, and in some locations the housing prices are higher than the office rent. In these locations, like in the centre of Amsterdam, residential transformation is especially interesting. The real estate market is segregated and office investors are not keen on investing in the housing market. Investors who are interested in transformation have the choice of transforming for sale or appointing the narrow private rental market. Housing associations on the other hand have no interests in the office market, but see residential transformation of office buildings as an interesting way of acquiring central urban locations. The same goes for housing developers for whom the most important transformation triggers are revenues and acquisition possibilities. Investors may choose to sell obsolete office space to housing associations or real estate developers. This way, they can reinvest their profit in new office buildings. Governmental subsidies are not a transformation trigger for any of the parties; rather municipal cooperation on policies and legislation is found to be important. The price for obsolete office buildings is often too high for transformation to be feasible, while owners are not eager to sell buildings with financial loss. However, as the market value of an office building is related to its potential yield, investors need to consider realistic and convincing future yields to calculate a credible market value for their structurally vacant properties. When refusing to devaluate their properties, they seem to have forgotten a basic principle from general economic theory: never consider the investments made; only the possible future yields.

70% of the office buildings in the Netherlands are located in monofunctional office locations. Studying Amsterdam, many of the buildings are located in locations with no adjacent housing locations and no facilities. In general, the accessibility of the locations is good, both by car and by public transport. Possible scenarios for residential transformations in these areas are developments starting at the edges of the locations, developments in phases starting with the addition of facilities, the "ink stain" development method, or integral urban developments. While the last option seems to be the most successful, it is also the most complicated. However, as complete office locations are deteriorating, such approaches will be interesting.

The intrinsic characteristics of office buildings that decide whether or not a building is acquired for transformation are the measurements and technical state of the buildings structure. Subsequently, building characteristics are considered that have a more direct effect on the transformation building costs; these are characteristics of the facade and installations and costs related to the level of finishes of the new housing program. As the building costs add up to 50% of the total investment costs, a good estimate of the building costs is important. Though in 40% of the cases studied transformation was found to be the best strategy for coping with structurally vacant office buildings, the various obstacles mentioned in the interviews reduce the residential transformation potential of the office building stock. If nothing happens, transformation will continue to be a marginal possibility for coping with structural vacancy.

PREVENT

Prevent

Prevent considers possibilities to limit structural vacancy on market, location and building level ex-ante and builds forth on the two preceding parts – Cause and Cope. Unlike the two foregoing parts this part will not present new empiric studies, but uses the empiric material and results of the foregoing analyses, introduced by a literature review. The foregoing analyses have revealed market conditions, location and building characteristics that cause structural vacancy. Henceforward, market conditions, location and building characteristics that enhance the transformation potential of structurally vacant office buildings were discovered. Based hereupon, the following section will discuss the possibilities for influencing the office market by governmental interference. Building and location characteristics that reduce the risk of structural vacancy and that enhance the transformation potential of office buildings are defined. Finally, these sets of characteristics are used to define a framework for office buildings with low risk of structural vacancy and therefore a longer functional lifespan, or for buildings with high transformation potential and multiple lifespans.

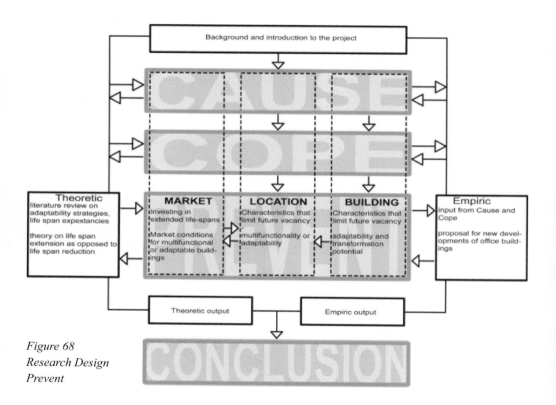

Figure 68
Research Design
Prevent

15 Research Design Prevent

Market mechanisms cause a mismatch in the demand and supply of office space and are as such the cause of structural vacancy. Hence, interventions in the market or the market conditions may seem like the most logical way of preventing structural vacancy. However, departing from the fact that structurally vacant office buildings are functionally outdated, increasing the functional lifespan of buildings or making several subsequent uses possible is a way of preventing structural vacancy. Quantitative and qualitative mismatches in the supply and demand in the office market are seen as structural vacancy in specific locations and buildings and vice-versa; user preference for specific locations and buildings are revealed in the market as highly performing office buildings or locations.

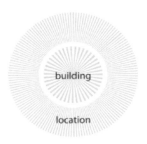

Though the cause of structural vacancy is analysed in the first section, the problem analysis is not per definition a problem solution. The results from the analysis form input for the design of a product, theory or model that aims at solving the original problem (Simon 1996; Groat and Wang 2002). In part 2, Cope, transformation as a solution to the problem of structural vacancy was suggested and evaluated based on ex-post and ex-ante studies. The results of these evaluations are again used as input for this study. The cyclic and iterative character of research recognises the different phases of inquiry, data-collection, analysis, and theory development. In architectural and engineering research this cycle looks slightly different, as there is often a normative goal of improvement of a situation, or of the development of a product, design or model (Simon 1996; Baarda and Goede 2001; Groat and Wang 2002). This research type resembles design studies with a research cycle consisting of evaluation of the existing situation, modelling, programming and optimisation. Eventually, both fields aim at detecting elements of the general pattern that our society embodies, and both fields are drawing nearer to each other (Giedion 1967). Imposed onto this research, the foregoing two parts (Cause and Cope) comprise ex-ante and ex-post evaluations and modelling, while this part considers programming and optimisation (Van der Voordt et al. 2005). In the two preceding parts, the relation between market, location and building were sketched; the market regarded as context for the location and the building, or as a hierarchical system from market to location to building (Figure 69). Both models express the importance of the market for the cause of structural vacancy and the influence of the building as subordinate to the location.

Figures 69 the office market seen as context for location and building, or market, location and building seen as a hierarchical system.

However, as commercial developers and investors develop or invest in office buildings from a portfolio point of view, the building is the starting point. The location becomes a characteristic of the building and the market conditions are considered in order to calculate future costs and benefits of the development. All is taking place within a social and economic defined framework. This shift from market to building is immanent to the shift from study to design, as the office building is the object of study while the market conditions are the forces that determine the functioning of the object.

15.1 Literature review

As from the 1930s onwards buildings were designed to fit only one specific function, research has been conducted on how to design flexible, adaptable and polyvalent buildings (Habraken 1972; Frampton 1992; Van der Werf 1993; Brand 1994; Duffy 1998; Kendall 1999; Leupen 2006). Though not all studies had the same point of departure, all had the aim of developing buildings suited for multiple uses. The literature review was therefore applied to broaden and connect existing knowledge about a topic that was available from different sources and published over a longer time span (Groat and Wang 2002). This research focuses on adaptability as a means of increasing the potential for residential transformation of office buildings, aiming at preventing structural vacancy of office buildings in the design and development of new properties. As such, structural vacancy is experienced as a threat towards the sustainability of the built environment, which is enhanced by durable buildings. This idea of sustainable urban environments is represented by several architects, planners and academics (Lynch 1960; Norberg-Schulz 1980; Rossi and Eisenman 1985; Pallasmaa et al. 1994) and relates to the broad view on sustainability, defined by Elkington as the "triple bottom line": People, Planet, Profit (1994).

15.2 Evidence from Cause and Cope

This section uses the data collected in the two preceding sections; new empiric material is not collected. By induction, the evidence from Cause is treated reversely, as this section describes how to avoid the conditions and characteristics that correspond with structural vacancy (Groat and Wang 2002). Likewise, results from the analyses in Cope are used to describe conditions and characteristics that enhance the transformation potential of office buildings, using the same logic of induction: Implement into a design the characteristics that enhance a buildings transformation potential, and the building is more likely to be transformed – if necessary.

Market

Though the preceding explains the focus on the office building in this part of the research, the office market stays the context and market conditions remain the main cause of structural vacancy. The office market comprises a stock of office buildings of a certain quantity and with specific qualities that can be described by the characteristics of the office buildings and their locations. In part 1, Cause, the market conditions that cause structural vacancy through an oversupply of office space were described. Furthermore, the Delphi Survey and the Office Scan revealed the relationship between the user preferences for certain physical office location and building characteristics. These two phenomena together explain the cause of structural vacancy and in which office locations and buildings structural vacancy concentrates.

Interventions in the market may prevent structural vacancy. The government may intervene by influencing the supply, by bringing market parties together, by adapting policies and legislation or by stimulating adaptation and transformation financially (Decisio 2006). The market may also be influenced by private actors; investors, owner-users or developers. Real estate investors may contribute to lower structural vacancy by devaluating structurally vacant office buildings and sustain transformation and by investing more money in fewer, more sustainable and durable office buildings.

In the current situation the demand for office space is not growing. Office buildings are developed for replacement of existing office buildings, though the technical lifespan of the replaced buildings is not ended and structural vacancy and obsolescence occur. Investing in adaptable office buildings that can accommodate different office concepts or different functions, or that can more easily be transformed into different functions can be a way of preventing structural vacancy and simultaneously increasing the sustainability of the office stock. Henceforth, the possibilities for influencing the market causes of structural vacancy can be discussed based on literature reviews on the functioning of the office market.

Location

The location of new and existing office buildings or the characteristics of these locations may be altered to reduce structural vacancy and this way contribute to the development of sustainable urban areas. Currently, neighbouring municipalities compete to attract new office organisations and do so by issuing new land for office developments near to ring roads and on the city fringes. The Office Scan revealed that the location characteristics of most structurally vacant office buildings describe monofunctionality. Moreover, the Cope analyses render the difficulties of residential transformation of office buildings on monofunctional office locations.

Other location characteristics, like accessibility by car or public transport, the availability of other services and facilities, and the status and image of the location influence office users' preferences. In the following, based on the findings from part 1 and 2, location characteristics that are related to structural vacancy or that reduce the transformation potential of office buildings will be described and recommendations will be made for how to avoid these characteristics in future developments. Conversely, location characteristics that are preferred by office users or that enhance the transformation potential of office buildings will be described and recommendations will be made for how to incorporate these characteristics in future developments of office locations.

Building

The Delphi survey and the Office Scan revealed several characteristics of the building that correlate to structural vacancy. One characteristic is the year of construction of the office building. The correlation between the ageing of office buildings and structural vacancy sustains the idea of a replacement market; the functional lifespan of office buildings is getting shorter because new office buildings are available. Though the existing buildings are functioning, the new buildings are more attractive. This is described by characteristics of the aesthetic, maintenance and image of the building. A small part of the structurally vacant office building stock is characterised by more severe shortcomings. These are typically related to flexibility characteristics or to comfort characteristics. However, the market value of obsolete office buildings is not related to its depreciation, and the purchasing price of these buildings is too high for a feasible transformation scheme.

Other office building characteristics have an effect on the transformation potential; of which typological characteristics are specifically influential to the financial feasibility of the transformation scheme. These are characteristics such as the technical quality and construction of the facade, size of the structural grid, the floor height and the availability and quality of stairs and elevators. These characteristics are again related to the construction year of the buildings. In the following, based on the findings from part 1 and 2, building characteristics that are related to structural vacancy or that reduce the transformation potential of office buildings will be described and recommendations will be made on how to avoid these characteristics in future developments. Conversely, building characteristics that are preferred by office users or that enhance the transformation potential of office buildings will be described and recommendations will be made for how to incorporate these characteristics in future office building developments.

16 Theoretical framework: adaptability, lifespan and sustainability

The lifespan of office buildings is determined by financial, functional, technical, cultural and legal aspects, which together decide the buildings technical, functional and economic lifespan. Mismatch between the functional and technical lifespan of office buildings results in structural vacancy and the end of the buildings economic lifespan, and by increasing a buildings functional lifespan or reducing its technical lifespan, the mismatch is cured and structural vacancy is prevented. Buildings with a long lifespan are durable buildings, and as such, durability is an aspect of sustainability. Buildings with a long lifespan contribute to lowering the construction industry's waste production, reducing construction related traffic, and reducing energy use for construction (Lichtenberg 2005). Depending on a buildings lifespan, the building materials are more or less important to the total environmental load of the building. Buildings constructed for a long lifespan should be built with focus on sustainable energy solutions, the type of building materials is less important, while if a building is built to last for less than 20 years, it should be built focusing on a sustainable use of building materials and recycling or re-use of the materials after demounting or deconstructing it. In the case of a building with an expected lifespan of 20 years, attention should be paid to both energy consumption and building materials (Van den Dobbelsteen 2004). Calculating the Life Cycle Costs of adaptation versus demolition and new construction, adaptation was found to be favourable (De Jonge 2005). Hence, prolonging a buildings lifespan is sustainable, and desired from a sustainability point of view. This logic is the base for the following theoretical framework that considers building lifespan and the means necessary to improve the correlation between the different types of building lifespan. Increasing a buildings functional lifespan is possible by extending the functional lifespan of the buildings original purpose, or by making several lifespans possible by enhancing the buildings transformation potential. Based on literature reviews, this chapter describes interventions and initiatives in order to develop a theoretical framework on limiting structural vacancy.

	Cause	Cope	Prevent
Market			Laws and regulations, willingness to invest
Location			Urban sustainability by mix-use locations and transformations
Building			Extended lifespan, functional, technical and economic life-span, adaptability, transformation potential

Table 29 Market, location and building are the 3 topics considered within the 3 themes of this research, Cause, Cope, Prevent. The topics comprise several aspects:

16.1 Market

All actors involved in the development of office buildings influence the development and the characteristics of its process and product. Developing office buildings for an extended functional lifespan or multiple lifespans is however complicated. Though there has been a focus on adaptability by architects and researchers since the 1960s, few developments were completed according to these ideas. For years, the development of office buildings has been driven by economic growth and high expectations for the future office market, and simultaneously real estate developers and investors took over the development and management of office buildings from the traditional owner-occupier. Real estate developers, with a short investment perspective, have played an important role in office developments. At the same time, architects were working on concepts of standardisation and minimisation of measurements, moving towards the cockpit architecture (tight fitting buildings and spaces for one use only) that was so common in office buildings from the 1970s and 1980s.

The focus on low costs and short development time spans from the same period led to malfunctioning buildings, and according to Brand, buildings constructed since the 1970s don't work (Brand 1994). The developer's typical behaviour and short time perspective of initiating, developing and selling is one reason for the focus on short development time and low cost. However, developers work for an investor or otherwise sell developments to investors, who should also be able to see the problems of a cost-focus instead of focussing on both costs and quality. Investing in adaptability or other measures to increase the building life span is only interesting to the developer if the investor is willing to pay a higher purchasing price (Arge 2005). Therefore, the market issue of developing office buildings with a longer lifespan boils down to two issues; the extra costs and benefits of such developments to the investors, and the investors' perceived benefit of buildings with a longer technical, functional and economic lifespan.

The value of (office) buildings

The value of office buildings is assessed according to the value of the office rents. Investors therefore relate investments in office buildings to the added fitness for use that investments in specific features add to an office building and the willingness to pay for these features by potential office users. Next to location characteristics, some characteristics of the office building influence the buildings fitness for use and thereby add to an increased rental income for the investor (Koppels et al. 2009).

Measures taken to increase the functional life span of office buildings by adaptability do not directly have consequences for the first user and their added value is therefore more difficult to calculate. The first user will not be willing to pay extra for these measures; the concept of the adaptable office building is that after the ended tenancy by the first user, new users will continue to be willing to pay for the use of the office building for a longer time period, so that structural vacancy will not occur. The investors' willingness to pay will depend on the perceived benefit over time, whereas the real benefit will depend on whether functional changes are needed or not.

Investors company profile and behaviour

Developing office buildings with an intended longer lifespan requires investors who are willing to invest for a longer timespan. Real estate investors typically consider investment periods of 10-15 years, basing NPV calculations on this investment perspective. In the housing market, housing associations typically consider long-term investments. The initiative of the Amsterdam housing association "Stadgenoot" to develop and invest in the "Solids", meant to have a technical lifespan of 200 years and serial functional lifespans is an example of such an investment (Bijdendijk 2006). Also, housing associations are known for investments in urban areas, accepting initial loss, focus on value increase in the long run and calculations focusing on a high exit yield.

Investors in the office market, though most in need of short-term results can be future potential investors in buildings with an expended lifespan, but need market evidence of higher exit yields to compensate for higher initial costs. Public investors, like the Government Buildings Agency, are parties that play a natural role as forerunner. An example of a pilot-project is the development of a new tax-office in Groningen, based on the idea that the building will function as offices for the first 20 years before it may be transformed into housing (Figure 70).

Figure 70 The new tax office in Groningen, developed by the Government Buildings Agency, designed by UN studio. (UN studio)

Investment scopes and sustainability

An expanded functional lifespan or multiple functional lifespans by adaptation or transformation can contribute to sustainable development. Although such contributions are not as easily recognised and accounted for as the more technical energy or water saving solutions. Buildings with climate facades, maximised thermal insulation and reduced CO_2 emissions are obviously sustainable interventions, and are accounted for in Life Cycle Assessment models (LCA), such as Green Calc, Greenstar or BREEAM (Eichholtz et al. 2008; dgbc 2009). However, all stay interventions that are not necessarily parts of the base building, and may be added to the building in a later phase. Moreover, the required performance of the office environment, including comfort increasing and emission reducing building characteristics, changes over time. Interventions reducing the energy use and emissions from office buildings should therefore be seen as part of an adaptable building concept (Kendall 1999). The model of Eco-costs/Value Ratio (EVR) allows comparing new construction to renovation and maintenance (De Jonge 2005). This kind of LCA models could also be used in the initiative phase of new developments, for calculating the possible benefits of office buildings with future adaptation- and transformation- possibilities, compared to the "traditional" standardised office buildings.

193

16.2 Location

In the development of office buildings, the office building as a "product" is first developed, before an actual location is defined, based on its physical characteristics and the specific geographical market conditions. This does not downplay the importance of the quality of the location for a sustainable development. The location to a great extent determines a buildings lifespan. Obsolescence takes place on both building and location level, preceding the end of a buildings lifespan. Different forms of obsolescence on the scale of the location are defined (Nutt 1988; Baum 1993):

- Environmental obsolescence: when the conditions in a neighbourhood render it increasingly unfit for its present use
- Location obsolescence: when the resources and image of the location are increasingly unfavourable to the organisations and the staffs preferences
- Site obsolescence: when the site value becomes higher than the facility asset

The lifespan of buildings can be subdivided in the functional, technical and economic lifespan. On the scale of the location or the building site, it makes sense to broaden the definition of the economic lifespan by adding social lifespan, as the public perception of the location is accordingly influencing its economic potential, as defined by Blakstad (2001). The functional lifespan of the location depends on its ability to adapt to changing preferences and needs of its users. Likewise, Giedion stated that the future of the city depended on its ability to transform (Giedion 1967). On a location scale, like on the building scale, the image of the location and the availability of "newer and better" locations may increase the relative functional obsolescence of the location in comparison to other locations: New areas drive out old areas! [sic] (Geraedts and Van der Voordt 2003, 2007).

Finally the technical lifespan of the location considers the physical obsolescence of the location and site itself (Brand 1994). Brand sees the site as eternal; a piece of the earth. However, the infrastructure and cultural landscape or cityscape of a certain site may become worn down and cause obsolescence of a property, though normally the functional lifespan of a location will be critical. Considering the lifespans of the location in an IFD (Industrial, flexible, demountable) perspective, ending the technical lifespan of the location to fit the functional or the economic lifespan seems extremely improbable. Regarding the IFD concept and the concept of robust buildings as the two possible concepts for sustainable development therefore makes developing locations with a long functional lifespan seem extra viable.

Regarding sustainability as one of the important issues in the development of new office buildings, also the use of land or space must be optimised. Sustainable development according to the World Commission on Environment and development (WCED 1987) means "a development that meets the needs of the present without compromising the ability of future generations to meet their own needs". In terms of urban development it means minimising the use of space and avoid sprawl by locating building sites within the existing urban fabric (van den Dobbelsteen and de Wilde 2004). Minimising the use of space has several aspects, considering both spatial efficiency and the diversity of functions and their use of space.

16.2.1 Single use

According to Giedion and his contemporaries, the future success of the city would depend on its ability to transform and enlarge to give room for the automobile and to "free" its inhabitants by separating functions (Giedion 1967). In Amsterdam, the freedom generated by functionalist urbanism impinged on new extensions, though it never had an effect on the city centre (Jolles et al. 2003). Again, the transformation potential of cities is appealed to, as obsolescence now occurs in none-places like the single use locations so desired by Giedion (Augé 2000; Florida 2004; Rodenburg 2005). The single use location is a phenomenon known throughout history and since the industrial revolution monofunctionality was the rule in urban planning. Though the locations technical lifespan at that moment was maybe not ended; making locations suited for a new functional lifespan normally requires a full renovation of the location, its infrastructure and arrangement - just think about the large scale transformations of inner city brownfield areas. Another and more modern example is the "F-buurt" in the Bijlmermeer, Amsterdam south-east. Its urban plan and architecture was based on the ideas of CIAM and was characterised by a strict zoning plan defining the use of the area and an equally tight functional scheme for the housing. The area was functionally obsolete already in 1990, 17 years after completion. Even in Amsterdam, the most competitive housing market of the Netherlands, a total renewal of the area was needed and was as expensive as redevelopment. In the final renewal scheme parts were redeveloped, parts were renovated (Maccreanor 2005). Intensifying the use of single use space enhanced the sustainability of urban areas only by reducing the use of space, but otherwise has none of the advantages of mixed use areas.

Monofunctional office locations in the Netherlands show the same tendencies of decay as the brownfields once did. A study on the monofunctional office location Amsterdam South-East (Schalekamp et al. 2009) shows that the location is obsolete and its economic lifespan is ended, though the development of the location was initiated in the 1980s. An average of 45% of the office space in this location is structurally vacant. Altogether, the development and decay of this location so far has taken 20 years. Though office buildings are still constructed in the location, the depreciation of the location is irreversible, and the problems were already signalled in the structure plans of 1996 and 2003 (Jolles et al. 2003). To speak again with Giedion, heroic operations are necessary (Giedion 1967). The study of Amsterdam South East may be seen as a single case study, and generalisation of the findings of single case studies is always disputed, though a single case study of a typical case or a critical case is seen as quite reliable (Miles and Huberman 1994; Patton 2002). Amsterdam South-East may be seen as a typical case, as more office locations like it are experiencing dilapidation and depreciation.

16.2.2 Mixed use

Mixed use areas are used 24 hours a day. Combining housing, work, retail and leisure functions in the same location, some functions, like industry or other functions that cause noise nuisance, air pollution or otherwise threaten the safety of people passing by, should not be part of the mix. The mixed use areas may comprise functions that are used simultaneously or sequentially, comparable to Hertzbergers idea of the polyvalent space (Hertzberger 1991). Functional diversity implies a pleasant and socially safe area as a result of 24 hour use and the social control employed by several user groups. The areas are also more economically viable, more culturally and aesthetically interesting and safer than monofunctional areas (Jacobs 1961). Mixed use areas are increasingly favoured to monofunctional areas by different user groups, specifically by the upcoming creative class (Florida 2003). 'Place' is essential to economic life; people put a high value on face-to-face meetings, and these meeting are increasingly taking place in dynamic urban locations, as the office employee spends less time in the office and more time working at home or somewhere else. Furthermore, mixed use areas as they are more intensively used than monofunctional areas allow for a better accessibility by public transport and higher investments in public space, something that is appreciated by its users and enhances the sustainability of the area (van den Dobbelsteen and de Wilde 2004; Rodenburg 2005). Better accessibility by public transport is one of the advantages of mixed use environments as it also helps fighting the low air quality (caused by i.e. traffic congestion) which correlates to urban areas and has a negative impact on the possibility for realising housing or other frail functions. Following, the main reason why multifunctional land use is not more popular, is the complexity of the spatial planning in technical and organisational way, and therefore is – traditionally – only applied in case of scarcity of space and high land prices. In cases where the spatial claims on a location are high, users are willing to pay the extra price for multifunctionality (Rodenburg and Nijkamp 2004). Though almost eradicated by the modern movement, multifunctionality has recently been reintroduced to many cities and locations as a solution to revitalise monofunctional downtowns, business districts and suburban office parks (Tiesdell et al. 1996; Beauregard 2005). While monofunctionality worked for a the predictable economy of growth, multifunctional locations will be much more fit to react to the future of an uncertain economy.

16.3 Building

Architects have traditionally been interested in the flexibility and adaptability of buildings and cities, and most research and studies concerning these themes were performed by architects. Since the dawn of times different activities claimed different building types although today we recognise far more types than for instance the Romans who used the basilica for trade, parliament and temple next to the urban housing and the villas. Or what to think of the Vikings who recognised one type only; depending on how the building was situated on its plot it had different uses…if in the middle: housing, next to it: accommodation for cattle and slaves, on the shore: a boathouse. Until the renaissance, theory hardly existed about the use of different building types. Exceptional buildings like temples, churches, hospitals and palaces were designed specifically as such within the otherwise vernacular architecture. From the renaissance on, following Palladio, architects started to become more interested in typological studies (Habraken and Teicher 1998). However, until the industrialisation architecture was still based much more on experience and not so much on developing or implementing new ideas. Inspired by the inventions of new machines, the functioning of factories and the new ideas on production introduced by Taylor. Studies were performed on i.e. how office work is executed and how daily activities in the home were performed. The different functions were all described and the space required for specific tasks, the minimal measurements, became standard measurements used in architectural design (Frampton 1992).

The spatial analysis of human functioning like established by Bauhaus (Whitford 1984) and translated into a design tool by Neufert in the 1930s (Neufert et al. 2006) marked a paradigmatic shift in architectural thinking. Until this shift, buildings were designed and developed according to tradition; traditional typologies, traditional materials and sizes of traditional materials. After the shift, functional analyses were always performed before starting a new design; architecture from now on was based on analysis, not on tradition. Experiments were applied especially to social housing projects, often focusing on space-use, minimal measurements and intensive use.

After the Second World War the implementation of the modernists ideas took off and 'functionalism' as an architectural style was affirmed. A product of the functionalist way of thinking, and up till today one of the aspects that got the most attention from architects, was the research on functional overlapping of spaces, inspired by the need to use time-sharing of space to deal with small budgets and little space. In the forties and fifties the social housing production was mainly aimed at accommodating people as efficient as possible to catch up with the high demand after years of low (or no) production.

Social housing was developed that could accommodate the 'typical family', consisting of one pair of parents and 2-6 children. However, the efficient housing machine knew only a couple of different dwelling types and sizes, requiring the architects to think about different possibilities for use of the same apartment. The flexibility concept was born, a concept exercised to the cream of the crop by van den Broek in his housing project in Rotterdam. These first ideas on flexibility concerned only the changeability of an apartment's interior between day- and night- use, solving the problems of the tightly accommodated family. However, the line of thought was set forth in international architectural discourse, discussing flexibility or adaptability with a longer time-span.

16.3.1 Adaptability, flexibility and solid buildings

Several architects and architectural researchers have been working on the theme of building adaptability. John Habraken presented his book "support, an alternative to mass housing" (Habraken 1972), first published in Dutch as "De dragers en de mensen", already in 1961. In this work he discusses housing as an act that is not completed by the developer or the constructor, but instead offers a system of supports and finishing elements, in which the inhabitants may choose the finishing elements. In this way, a compromise is made between desired small scale housing production and needed large scale production. In 1964 Habraken took initiative to start the Foundation for Architectural Research (Stichting Architecten Research, SAR), that focused on industrial manufacturing methods and the industrial production of the support structure. Habrakens work in this period was inspired

*Figure 71
Hertzbergers
concept of
polyvalence in
the Diagoon
houses.
(Hertzberger,
1991)*

both by Le Corbusier and the Japanese metabolism. Le Corbusier in many of his projects described the apartment as an infill in a larger structure, i.e. in plan Obus he suggested a structure consisting of floors supported by columns, stairs, electricity and sewerage, within which the inhabitants were free to build their own home on a "lot" inside the structure (Frampton 1992). Though inspired by Le Corbusiers ideas, Habraken did not agree with Le Corbusier on the structure that was offered. While Le Corbusier saw the structural elements floors and columns as necessary, Habraken had a structure in mind that was closer connected to architecture, including the dwellings outer walls.

Simultaneous to Habraken, Hertzberger was developing his architecture of polyvalence, regarding change to be the permanent factor of architecture (Hertzberger 1991). To allow for changes in the built environment, space must be described and not function. Polyvalence is created by describing variance and possible correct solutions, not saying that the perfect solution does not exist. In well-known projects such as the Diagoon houses in Delft and the office building for Centraal Beheer in Apeldoorn, Hertzberger displays his idea of the polyvalent developed from the idea that different activities can take place in the same space, overlapping or consecutively in time. To achieve this polyvalence, the Diagoon houses were designed to suit a variety of living patterns, as each unit consisted of a number of more or less identical rooms, situated around the main service areas. A comparison of the lay-out of the Diagoon houses with the Centraal Beheer offices show a different application of the same concept. Here, spaces are defined that overlap and to a certain extent can claim parts of the collective space, making it possible to work in different constellations. Adjustments to other functions than working are possible, though the scale of the scale of the structure is determinative.

Habrakens idea of adaptability was based on the idea that a dwelling is a product of its inhabitants. The ideas were a reaction to the "Neue Sachlihkeit" that opted for slum clearance and massive new construction, and defined a form of structuralism as also seen in the work of Hertzberger; structures that accommodate coincidence. Seeing mass-production of housing as inevitable, he sought to offer a freedom of choice within the frames of mass-construction. In this sense, Habraken has another point of view than the architects and researchers who have studied adaptability later on. While in later studies, adaptability has foremost been seen as an instrument for expanding a buildings life-span, to Habraken adaptability gave tenants the possibility to influence the design of their own dwelling. The SAR continued this line of research focusing on the manufacturing and assembly of mass-produced housing. The idea of "Open Building" was developed and the research group OBOM (Open Building Strategic Studies) at Delft University of Technology continued the work of the SAR, aiming at "co-ordination of dimensions, positions and interfaces of parts, searching to control gaps and tolerances and define the domains of disciplines and their tradesmen, their duties and liabilities" (Cuperus 2004). The research group is still working on ideas for a "capacity to change" index for buildings, using a technical approach and with keywords like "open" and "lean" construction (obom 2009). The initiative for the research group was given already in 1976 as Van Randen was appointed Professor at the university. In his inaugural speech he augmented the need to study the joints of the building components instead of the components and thereby opening the construction (Van Randen 1976).

Duffy (1990), considering mainly the office building, was interested in the buildings capacity to adapt to the changing requirements of its user, resulting in a robust building. He defined buildings as systems with several subsystems or layers and recognized shell, services and scenery, whereas scenery is everything that can be altered without influencing the functioning of the services or the shell. The services are including electricity, sewerage and ventilation, and servicing elements like elevators, while the shell includes both the buildings facade and its construction. His way of defining adaptability is based on refurbishments of office buildings and which elements or layers as he put it may be altered in order to renew the working environment without influencing the technical functioning of the office building itself. The distinction between different layers is related to the dissimilar lifespans of the layers. Though buildings in Europe and North America have a life expectancy of 50-70 years, the other elements or layers have far shorter lifespans: The servicing systems have a lifespan of 15-20 years, the spatial divisions and fittings 5-10 years, and the workstation equipment and furniture less than 5 years (Nutt 1988).

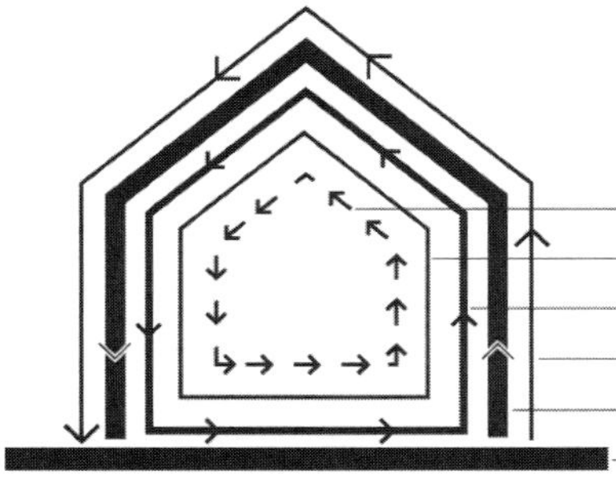

STUFF
SPACE PLAN
SERVICES
SKIN
STRUCTURE
SITE

Figure 72
Shearing layers
of change
(Brand 1994)

Duffy's approach was adapted by Brand who categorises the different parts of a building in six layers; site, structure, skin, services, space plan and stuff (Brand 1994). Stuff to Brand is simply furniture and other loose components within the building, while space plane corresponds to Duffy's scenery. They share the idea of services being a specific layer, while to Brand the structure and the skin are two different layers, building forth on the ideas of Le Corbusier and Habraken. He defined buildings as systems with several subsystems or layers and subordinate to the site; important is his work because he also considered alterations outside the original building.

Blakstads PhD-research from 2001 used the notions of layers like used by Brand and Duffy. Her research focused on office organisations and their space use, studying several organisations and the alterations made in their accommodation over a time span of several years. In her research, she chose to define flexibility and adaptability as separate though complementary concepts. Flexibility in Blakstads research considers alterations "from the bottom up"; change or possibilities for change within a limited set of alternatives, while adaptability approaches the problem "top down" and considers the capacity to answer to unexpected changes by interventions in the building (Blakstad 2001).

Van der Voordt and van Wegen (2005) studied the design techniques for incorporating flexibility. As in architectural research terminology is never treated consistently, a list of used terminology was also provided, defining flexibility as "easily adjusted to suit changing circumstances". Additionally, polyvalence is defined as predestined adjustability by movable walls or doors; neutral is defined as capability of being adjusted without influencing layers higher in the layer-hierarchy as defined by Brand; while variable is defined as the opposite of fixed and capable of being adjusted without exorbitantly high costs. The initial building costs entailed by the measures to achieve flexibility should be carefully weighed against benefits or savings on later adjustments. The measures vary from demountable building parts for future extensions or changes (division flexibility) to the use of sliding doors or partitions (polyvalent room boundaries).

Finally, Leupen (2006) also referred to Duffy, Brand and Habraken and built forth on their research. Leupen recognises five layers; structure, skin, scenery, services and access, which he further refers to as frames. To be a frame, the layer must be independent of and have the ability to free the layer that it frames. A high independency of the layers makes adaptations possible. Case studies are central in Leupens research and illustrate his theory. According to Leupen, buildings that consist of several frames are sustainable and are more likely to be adapted than buildings were the different layers are dependent on each other. Again, this is illustrated by two examples; a house from 1820, adapted several times to fit the users requirements, and a house from the post-war reconstruction era that is to be demolished because it cannot be adapted to fit contemporary functional requirements.

Figure 73 The IFD project XX-office by XX Architects (Post 1998).

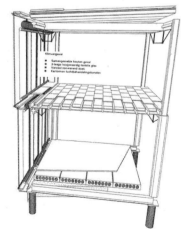

Beloved buildings

The above studies are opting for sustainable architecture in the form of durable architecture, all being academic approaches or based on experiences from the architectural practice. Frank Bijdendijk, CEO of the housing corporation "Stadgenoot", introduces the "solid" (Bijdendijk 2006). A solid is an urban building that is designed and developed to accommodate different functions. The only functions not allowed are functions that may hinder the use of the other parts of the building. According to de Jonge, the most important function of the design is its quality and ability to generate "love", because beloved buildings are always adapted and reused and are thereby sustainable (Kasteren 2002). This quality is difficult to describe but it is evident for instance in the old Venetian "palazzo" or the Amsterdam warehouses. The architecture of the solid is "absolute"; the form of the building is defined architecturally and not following function (Leupen et al. 2005). The solids are developed for a technical lifespan of 200 years, considering that several functional alterations and technical upgrades will be performed during the buildings life. The investment perspective is that of a normal development; for a housing corporation approximately 30 years, so that after 30 years the buildings may be technically or functionally upgraded.

16.3.2 IFD

Considering sustainability though not necessarily durability are buildings designed and developed according to the ideas of IFD: Industrial, flexible and demountable buildings. The idea behind IFD is industrial manufacturing of the building parts (building becomes assembly of building parts), flexible buildings in use (adapting becomes replacing), and demountable buildings (demolishing becomes disassembly). Industrial building aims at optimising the use of labour, materials and machines by industrial manufacturing methods and by processing all building material in factories. On the building site the building components are assembled. The method claims flexibility in the freedom of spatial flexibility for the first user, easy replacement of components to fit eventually new uses, flexibility in the compartmenting of the building and the possibility for adding or subtracting square metres according to the wishes of the user. At the end of the buildings economic and functional life-cycle, it can be disassembled and the parts may be re-used if they are not worn out (Groenendijk et al. 2000; Bouwmeester and SEV 2001; Bouwmeester and SEV 2003).

Figure 74
Nagakin capsule
tower by Kisho
Kurokawa

　　　　An example of an IFD-building, designed and built according to the ideas of IFD, is the XX office. The XX office building designed by XX architects was realised in Delft in 1998. The technical lifespan of the building was set to 20 years to match the economic lifespan of the building. After 20 years, the building can be dismantled and the building parts recycled. All the joints in the building are demountable and ensures the disassembly (Post 1998). IFD building as a concept was developed as a national Dutch innovation programme initiated and subsidised by the Dutch government and monitored by the SEV (The Steering Committee for Experiments in Public Housing). However, the three main themes; industrial, flexible and demountable are not new ideas and have been considered separately in earlier proposals for flexible or adaptable building methods (Groenendijk et al. 2000; Bouwmeester and SEV 2001; Bouwmeester and SEV 2003). The industrial component was considered also by Habraken and the SAR. Flexibility has been an issue in several projects by different architects, and disassembly of buildings was also an issue for the Japanese metabolists (Figure 74) and also for Habraken in his ideas for mass housing.

In her doctoral thesis, Durmisevic studies design for disassembly focussing on how buildings and their components must be designed and built for later disassembly. Following the theory of the building as separate layers, Durmisevic advocates for an approach to enhance transformation possibilities by deconstruction (Durmisevic 2006). Durmisevic's thesis and the IFD project are both interesting studies and experiments. However, these approaches are both systemic and require specific settings in order to work. Also, the idea of the recyclable building is questioned by new environmental research focusing on a cradle-to-cradle perspective of materials, claiming that recycling of building materials (because these themselves are always composite) is still a downcycling of the material since large amounts of energy is needed for the material to be transported, re-manufactured and reused (McDonough and Braungart 2002).

Though sharing the idea of the building as a series of layers, the IFD concept and buildings for disassembly are radically different from the "robust concepts" in their point of departure. The technical lifespan of the IFD buildings is designed to adapt to the functional and economic lifespan, while the idea of the different layer concepts is the quite opposite; buildings should be designed with a permanent part that will last for 100 years (Leupen 2006) or even 200 years (Bijdendijk 2006), and that makes these buildings sustainable.

17   Characteristics and conditions for low vacancy

In part 1, Cause, based on literature review, a Delphi Survey and the Office Scan, the building and location characteristics with an effect on structural vacancy were revealed, together with the market conditions causing structural vacancy. Structural vacancy is a result of a continuous quantitative and qualitative mismatch in the demand and supply of office space within a market, and the study concentrated on the relationship between the quality of the demand and supply. The preferences of office users for specific building and location characteristics were studied in a Delphi survey; a stated preferences inquiry asking a panel of real estate experts and advisors which characteristics are important to the office user (Remøy et al. 2007). Furthermore, 200 office buildings in Amsterdam were studied in The Office Scan, a revealed preferences study showing the relation between structurally vacant office buildings and specific building and location characteristics. The Office Scan revealed a relationship between the office user preferences for specific physical characteristics and the performance of office buildings and locations- from structurally vacant to high-end property. Based hereupon, this chapter presents a framework defined for the development of office buildings and location with low vacancy, within the context of the market conditions, focusing again on the case of Amsterdam.

17.1 Market conditions

In Amsterdam, like generally in the Netherlands, large-scale office plans were under construction in 2001 as the IT bubble burst. Immediately after this collapse, there was a reduction in the amount of office buildings constructed. Soon though, new developments again caught speed, partly as a result of the municipality's incentives to speed up the prestigious project of the Zuidas development and the revitalisation and intensification of the Arena location in Amsterdam South East, and supported by low interest rates. On the first of January 2009, the office building vacancy in Amsterdam had risen to 1.3 million lettable square metres, 18% of the total stock of 7.3 million (Dynamis 2009). The oversupply in the Amsterdam office market has grown slowly though steadily during the last years; the available supply in new constructions has been reduced, while the vacancy in existing office buildings increased, revealing the mechanism of a typical replacement market.

The municipality of Amsterdam is aware of the office market problems and has appointed a "city-pilot" to guide investors and potential users to existing, well-functioning office buildings next to an "office-pilot" who guides possible investors and developers to a transformation project (OGA 2008). However, the municipality helps maintaining the vacancy problem by offering new land leases and approving of new developments in stead of focusing on the existing supply. As van Gool puts it in a magazine interview (Reimerink 2008): the municipality, the real estate developers and investors – up front they all earn money by developing and investing in new land and new buildings, all blaming each other for the problems at the rear end of the market. As long as the production of offices continues without there being a quantitative need for more square metres, the vacancy and the structural vacancy will remain high.

17.1.1 Possible interventions and developments ex-ante by private actors

Investor: investment in existing buildings and locations

Investors typically see real estate as an asset; in the office market, office space is sold and bought, rented out and leased. Investors may be institutional, representing for instance a pension fund, a group of smaller private investors of various sizes and constellations, or single party private investors. The different groups of investors again comprise diverse investment profiles, some willing to take risk for possible high returns, others directed towards steady though lower returns. Finally, some investors active in the Dutch office market (partly) develop the office space in which they invest (Hordijk 2005; Gehner 2008).

Compared to investments in the stock market, investments in the office market are seen as relatively low-risk investments and in periods with a volatile stock exchange investments in real estate are popular. As a result, during the last 10 years investments in the office market still performed better than stocks, although since 2001 the vacancy of office buildings increased. Again, the mechanisms of the replacement market were of great importance. The vacancy in new developments was low with an available supply of 8% (Dynamis 2009). During the whole period the risk was low, the rents and profits high. For institutional investors with high cash-flows, this is an interesting market, and developers of new office buildings have little problems finding investors for their developments. High vacancy, no rent-incomes and low profits describe the down-side of the market, where profit is still realisable though with high risks. This part of the market is controlled by smaller, local investors (Schiltz 2006).

As office users increasingly prefer city centre locations or multifunctional locations, these should be interesting locations for smaller parties' investments, because of their scale and because of their future value. Focusing on renovation of these existing plots and buildings instead of purchasing second-hand properties on the city fringes may be a potential high profit investment that adds to slowing down the replacement market. Also, there is a demand for small office buildings in well accessible central locations with a high level of facilities. For large institutional investors, investments in high end new developments will stay interesting, as there is always demand for large, qualitatively supreme office space. Sustainable investments have already proven profitable (Eichholtz et al. 2008) and may steer the office market towards more sustainable developments, considering not only material use, but also location and lifespan issues. However, sustainability needs to be seen in a broader perspective, including life-cycle cost models that include adaptability as a means of increasing a buildings life span.

However, though all groups of investors have specific market knowledge; most investors seem to lack knowledge of the objects in which they invest (symposium Office Pilot 2009). Office buildings are bought like assets, focusing on the value of existing tenancies. However, some office users were convinced to rent office space in new office buildings and will leave for another new building once their lease contract ends. Office buildings with a bad external or internal appearance or strange lay-outs will be functionally outdated within a short time span and if the current tenant leaves, finding a new tenant is difficult. Knowledge about the office market, office buildings and user preferences would help investors to be more suspicious about new investments - Past Performance is no Guarantee of Future Results!

Finally, valuation assessments of structurally vacant office buildings have been too high for a long period of time (Hulsman and Knoop 1998) and should be devaluated. By rent-free periods for tenants, office rents have been kept on an artificially high level, thereby influencing the assessed market value. In 2008, devaluations of office buildings finally took place, with an average of 5%. For 2009, the average should be 15% or more, knowing that the real value of some structurally vacant office buildings might be set 50% higher than reasonable (symposium Office Pilot 2009).

Figure 75 actors in the office market do not take responsibility for the overproduction of office space; a circle of blame maintains the overproduction.

Developer: Redevelopment, costs and quality

The real estate developer often gets the blame for structural vacancy in the office market. In times with high structural vacancy, office developers do not initiate a development without a signed user-contract for the greater part of the development. Potential office users are therefore often approached by developers who can sell rented developments to an investor, and thereby convince the municipality to cooperate. Greenfield developments are less complex than brownfield or inner city (re)developments. Again, the possibilities are considered; the calculated risks and costs should be comparable to the estimated opportunities, quality and benefit (Gerritse 2005). However, in markets with high demands, costs and quality easily come out of sync, since office space is scarce. Offices developed in the 1980s are examples of such developments; buildings that now have a high level of structural vacancy. As office users get more professional in their accommodation strategies, developers are up to new challenges. The following was declared by a developer who was interviewed for the Delphi survey: "Studies of user preferences are really interesting. Maybe we should start doing something with it. Normally, we tell users what they want". That strategy may be possible in a sellers market, though in a buyers market with professional user organisations, costs and quality will need thorough calibration. If high benefit with no risk is not an option, then more complex projects, like redevelopments and renovations, will stand a chance.

User: New buildings or redevelopments in existing areas

The user (organisation) of office buildings of course plays an important role in the office market. Few developers take the risk of developing an office building without an already known user. However, few users are "new"; rather these users leave existing office buildings behind to move to a new building. As long as office users prefer new offices to existing offices, the replacement market will persist, and so, this "circle of blame" is completed (Figure 75). As user preferences are slowly changing towards a preference for inner city and mixed use locations, buildings in large office locations on the city fringes will have increasing problems competing (part 1, chapter 5). Typically, inner city locations are either existing office locations and comprise renovations of existing office buildings, or redevelopments of a site. Office users locating to inner city areas move in spite of the lack of new buildings, a compromise has been made. Office users locating to larger buildings on more remote locations do not accept compromises; as long as new developments are offered, these users will move.

17.1.2 Possible government interventions and regulations ex-ante

As municipalities play an important role in the development of new areas, governmental or municipal regulations also play an important role in preventing structural vacancy. While the municipality stimulates transformation of structurally vacant offices into housing, it also stimulates the development of new office space, and so it keeps beating the air. The office market is a cyclical market, and high levels of (structural) vacancy have been experienced before. However, since 2002 the vacancy levels have been more or less constantly high and rising, and in specific geographical markets, like Amsterdam, it seems that these vacancy levels will stay, unless actions are taken to reduce the oversupply. Former research has opted for several solutions, of which most are related to legal or fiscal measures (Hulsman and Knoop 1998; Decisio 2006):

- Tax on vacant office building
- Tax benefits for transformation
- Oblige developers to redevelop vacant office buildings for residential function when developing new offices
- Higher greenfields land cost, lower costs for "second-hand land"

The first two options were discussed with developers (13.4). The first option, tax on vacant office buildings, brought about strong reactions from developers and investors, as such a tax will be disadvantageous to investors who own structurally vacant office buildings – though these are not the same investors who invest in the new buildings that finally drive old buildings off the market. The second alternative did not augment the same intense reactions, but all interview groups (developers, investors and housing associations) doubted the impact of the measure. The lukewarm reactions were argued by the unpredictability of the government and municipality; also existing subsidies are not trusted and never calculated in an estimate.

The third measure, obliging developers to redevelop vacant office buildings, was brought up by housing associations during a couple of the interviews. The measure seems complicated, though probably effective. If low risk and high profit are the reasons for initiating a greenfield development, then these developments would all of a sudden be far less lucrative. The measure is a possible government regulation that needs further consideration.

The fourth and last proposed measure was brought up by one of the interviewed developers. This measure asks the municipality to react to vacancy within its borders. Municipalities earn large amounts of money on land sales, and the low purchasing price of undeveloped land compared to the high purchasing price of inner city locations or brownfields, seems to be a genuine cause of structural vacancy. As long as municipalities keep subsidising the development of new office buildings on Greenfields, the structural vacancy will stay high. Adjusting the price of land is an interesting possible government regulation.

17.2 Location characteristics

The results of the office scan revealed that the odds of structural vacancy of office buildings on mixed-use locations with high status are low. However, in an unbalanced office market where the supply is higher than the demand, vacancy and structural vacancy will occur. Still, in a mixed-use location, structural vacancy will have less impact than in a monofunctional location, as buildings or spaces for other functions like retail, leisure and housing are not necessarily also vacant, so the vacancy risk is spread over more sectors. Also, the vast character of the monofunctional office location, with street-side parking, unused green areas and monotonous streets and public space amplifies the experience of vacancy.

An interesting characteristic of monofunctional office locations is their intrinsic ability to generate superfluous construction: The production of office space in such locations is cheap, fast and simple and until recently with low risks and high profitability. Examples are seen in Amsterdam South East, where new office buildings are constructed next to buildings that were structurally vacant for years. This observation has led to the following conclusion on location characteristics: Putting an end to the development of monofunctional office locations would put an end to cheap, fast and simple developments, and possibly put an end to the overproduction of office space. Monofunctionality was not included as a characteristic in the studies on the cause of structural vacancy. A high amount of office space (clustering) and few facilities in the location are however characteristics that describe monofunctionality and that were found to correlate to structural vacancy. Office buildings in locations with a high level of facilities and low amount of office space have lower odds of structural vacancy. Likewise, the status of a location is defined by a set of variables: the amount of square metres dedicated to distribution and manufacturing, the occurrence of litter and graffiti in the location, the vicinity to parks and squares, and the design of public space. Office buildings in a high status location have lower odds of structural vacancy. Accessibility by car and public transport were not found to influence the odds of structural vacancy. Although the odds of structural vacancy correlate to the distance to a railway station, a substantial part of the office buildings in the sample that were located far from a railway station were not vacant. The location characteristics that were studied and which reduce the risk of structural vacancy are listed as following:

- Increasing the status of the location decreases the odds of structural vacancy
- Increasing the number of facilities in the location decreases the odds of structural vacancy

Figure 76
office location
and building
in Amsterdam
South East

17.3 Building characteristics

From the office scan it could be concluded that office buildings with a good external and internal appearance and a flexible lay-out are have low odds of structural vacancy. More parking places and built parking facilities were found to reduce the odds of structural vacancy at the 30% level. In the Delphi study on user preferences, the same four characteristics were also ranked high by the office accommodation expert panel, confirming the outcome of the office scan. In literature (Nutt et al. 1976; Salway 1987; Baum 1993; Blakstad 2001), functional obsolescence is described as obsolescence resulting from changes in the way of working and aesthetical obsolescence is described as obsolescence resulting from outdated appearance. In the Office Scan, these two forms of obsolescence were found to be closely related to structural vacancy. Hence, when developing new office buildings functional and aesthetic qualities should be focused on.

Studying the relationship between building characteristics and the office rent, Koppels et al. (2009) found no relationship between the flexibility of office space and the rent levels, whereas a strong relationship was found between the flexibility of office space and structural vacancy. This finding indicates that a lack of flexibility is a reject-characteristic; if the flexibility of the building is insufficient, office users will not consider the building suited for accommodation and it will be structurally vacant. Lowering the rent will have no direct influence, though it could attract new users to whom the rent was originally too high and whose organisation fit in the building. The building characteristics that were studied and which reduce the risk of structural vacancy are listed as following:

- Good external appearance of the office building decreases the odds of structural vacancy
- Good internal appearance of the office building decreases the odds of structural vacancy
- High flexibility of floor lay-out in office buildings decreases the odds of structural vacancy.
- Better parking facilities than surrounding properties reduces the odds of structural vacancy.

18 Characteristics and conditions for transformations

Part 2, Cope, presented an idea on how transformation into housing can be a way of coping with structurally vacancy of office buildings. Several transformations from offices into housing were studied ex-post (Remøy and Van der Voordt 2007) and the transformation potential of office buildings was linked to the characteristics of the office buildings that were again described typologically (Remøy and De Jonge 2007). The transformation potential of structurally vacant office buildings in Amsterdam was studied. Though this research shows that transformation in many cases is a feasible way of coping with structural vacancy, as yet few projects are completed. The reasons of the low transformation rate so far may be described by the characteristics of buildings and locations and by market conditions. Changes in market conditions or in the characteristics of new office building- and location-developments may enhance the transformation potential of future office buildings. This chapter describes the characteristics and conditions that influence the transformation potential of office buildings.

18.1 Market

The market conditions for transformation are described by the office market, the housing market and national and local laws, regulations and policies. Several actors operate within the office market and the housing market. Most are active in both fields, though one important actor, the investor, is normally restricted to one of the two markets. The most important actors involved in transformations are the local and national governments, real estate investors, owner-occupants and developers (including housing associations), architects, users and neighbours. Together, these actors are the real estate market and also decide the market conditions. Based on part 2, it is apparent that the Dutch market conditions until 2008 have not been optimal for transformation. Developments in this market that would further enhance transformation are possible.

18.1.1 Possible developments within the market

Investor: Focus on long-term investments

Investors in the office market to a great extent obstruct the possible transformation of structurally vacant office buildings by the valuation of property in their own portfolios. In the interviews with real estate developers, the purchasing price of office buildings was seen as one of the largest obstacles for transformation. Housing investors – also potential investors in transformation projects – share the view of the developers. Office investors on the other hand base their valuations on estimates by independent assessors and blame developers for too low or wrongful assessments of the buildings. Hence, the valuation problem is not one-sided and is boosted by the segmentation and the culture of blame within the real estate market.

Investors may be part of the solution to this problem. Investment in office buildings that are developed for extended life-spans by extended use or by enhancement of the transformation possibilities is a task for real estate investors.

Office buildings with extended life-span are sustainable as building materials, waste, energy and transport are saved. It is assumed that the value of buildings with extended or multiple functional lifespans will depreciate more slowly than traditional "cockpit offices", offices built after a strict functionalist scheme, fitting only one function. Additionally, recent research has shown higher profits of sustainable office buildings and investing in buildings with longer lifespan may increase the profit for investors.

Developer: Focus on redevelopment

On all levels of society, urban development is discussed, as it influences people's daily lives. Since the beginning of the industrial revolution, cities have grown rapidly. Sprawl is a phenomenon of low density cities with vast areas of highways, suburbs, malls and car dependency, first seen in American cities and strongly associated with cities like Los Angeles. In the Netherlands the situation is not as severe. However, if cities are allowed to sprawl, public transport will be less efficient, more roads are needed, congestion gets worse and suburbs will grow. Redeveloping inner city areas or transforming existing office buildings contribute to sustainable housing development as new land is not claimed, the infrastructure is already there and existing materials are re-used. Again, building materials, waste, energy and transport are saved.

Until the 1970s office buildings were developed in the city-centre, on small-scale office locations near the city centre or spread around housing areas. From 1980 onwards, the office market was booming, and especially there was a growth of rental offices. Office developments in the city centres or housing areas were time-consuming and small-scale; profit demanded less effort in the new, large scale office areas near the ring-roads or access-ways of the cities (Kohnstamm and Regterschot 1994). Developing office buildings on un-used land is less expensive than developments in inner city areas and for developers who, unlike investors, typically profit from a building project on a short term, this type of developments are financially more interesting than developments on reused land in the city centres. The land is less expensive, and the profit does not differ considerably. Next to lower benefits, the risks of developments in the inner city are higher than in new areas, and typically developers actively acquiring projects in the city centres are specialised in this kind of developments and are often combined developers and contractors. The developer typically works for an investor or an owner-user and reacts well to this market. As long as investments in monofunctional office areas are popular, these developments will take place.

However, some developers are successfully specialised in inner-city developments. These projects are often architecturally successful eye-catchers and financially successful projects as well: As city centres are again becoming popular and highly valued locations, the quality of the buildings developed in these areas also rises and so do the building costs and the developers turn-over.

18.1.2 Possible governmental and municipal regulations

Laws and policy to encourage transformations

Interference with the market by national or local governments is a possible way of influencing the market conditions for transformation. Several already existing instruments for interference have been discussed (Hulsman and Knoop 1998; Decisio 2006): dialogue with possible private actors, adapt zoning plans, soft interpretations of the building decree, use existing subsidies, vacancy-tax for owners of structurally vacant office buildings, subsidies by lower taxes, cooperating with private parties in PPP projects (Public-private partnerships or business ventures), and even a clean-up duty for developers: if developing new land for offices, then a structurally vacant office building must also be transformed, renovated or otherwise made fit for new use.

Spatial regulations – the Spatial Planning Act and the Zoning Plan

The Dutch spatial regulation and building regulations distinguish between different uses. In the spatial regulations, this is experienced in the zoning plans (Figure 77). Segregation between different functions and facilities is a product of the functionalist ideas that have influenced urban planning since the 1930's and that is still the most influential movement in urban planning. However, this functional zoning is no longer needed. Transformation of office buildings into housing is frustrated by zoning plans that acknowledge different areas for different functions. Of course, some activities like industrial production are dangerous or damaging to the public health or are a nuisance to nearby occupants. These functions also

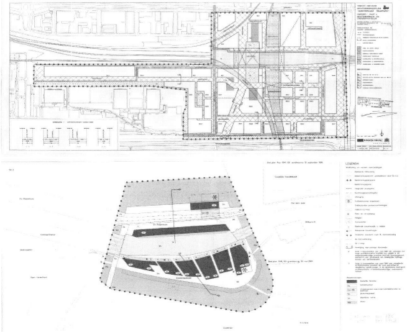

*Figure 77
Zoning plan
for Amsterdam
Teleport from
1996, an
example of a
monofunctional
location, defined
in the zoning
plan, and
Zoning plan
for Amsterdam
Oosterdoks-
eiland from
2001, ascribing
"urban
functions" to all
building plots
(DRO
Amsterdam)*

211

typically have a different scale and take place in different types of buildings and locations than offices and housing. To support transformation, municipalities should not initiate new zoning plans that distinguish between housing and offices, but rather distinguish between activities' effect on their surroundings. In recent zoning plans, "urban function" has been used as descriptions for plots that may accommodate both housing and offices. Examples of such zoning plans are seen for central urban areas.

Building regulations

The Dutch building decree also distinguishes between different uses. In general, the regulations for housing and functions for staying the night are stricter than for other functions. The regulations for other functions, like offices, are described according to the amount of occupants per square metre at the most busy hour of the day (VROM 2003). Some of the differences in the building regulations are of critical importance for transformation possibilities and are listed below (Table 4). The building decree additionally distinguishes between existing buildings and new buildings (van Zeeland 2007). Next to the building decree, specific municipal building regulations may also be of . One of the main discussions in the field of transformation is whether the rules for existing or new buildings should be achieved when transforming an office building into housing. For the design of a new office building with a high transformation potential the current rules for new office buildings must be accomplished, not knowing what the future requirements for offices or housing will be. The building decree comprises rules for several issues; i.e. safety, health, usability, energy, environment. All tend to be time-dependent; with every amendment more and safer fire-escapes are required, more ventilation, the required floor-height is increasing, buildings should be more energy-efficient and environmental requirements are new and not yet completely implemented. Most changes have lead to increasing building size, as ventilation, insulation, stair-wells and elevators claim more space (horizontally and vertically) and the free ceiling height itself is increasing as well.

Table 30 critical differences of the building regulations for housing and offices (VROM 2003).

Housing	Offices
The fire resistance of the main structure in minutes is 90 for buildings lower than 7m and 120 for buildings taller than 7m.	The fire resistance of the main structure in minutes is 90 for buildings taller than 5m. Only for buildings taller than 70m, 120 minutes is required.
One housing unit is a fire compartment (max 500 m^2). The walls between each compartment and the escape routes delay fire with at least 60 minutes.	A fire compartment is maximum 1000m^2.
The distance to the nearest exit should not exceed 15m. Two separate escape routes are required.	The distance to the nearest exit should not exceed 30m. Two separate escape routes are required.
Acoustic insulation between different units of at least 20dB are required	No requirements
The elevator car should be at least 1.05mx2.05m, and max distance to the elevator is 90m.	The elevator car should be at least 1.05mx1.35m

18.2 Location

Mix use locations; offices, housing, leisure and retail

The location is one of the most important aspects of a buildings transformation potential. Together with the purchasing costs and the intrinsic characteristics of the office building, the location is also seen as one of the three most important obstacles for a transformation project.

The ex-post studies of transformations (Remøy and Van der Voordt 2007), typically comprise office buildings with quite similar characteristics. Most are situated in or near city centres, 2 are located in housing areas, and one on the border between a housing area and an industrial area. Also studying 30 other transformation projects ex-post (Oudijk et al. 2007), only one project was situated in an office park, the rest were all located in city centres, housing areas or on the fringe of such areas. Developers, investors and housing associations are obviously reluctant to invest in transformation projects in monofunctional office areas and office and industrial locations. Geraedts and Van der Voordt concluded that monofunctional office areas are not suited for transformation into housing (Geraedts and Van der Voordt 2007).

Comparing the Dutch situation to international studies enhances this conclusion: Transformation from other functions into housing only – with a few exceptions - takes place in central urban areas and housing areas. Several studies reported on transformation of office buildings in London, Toronto and New York, all following after years of high vacancy levels in the office market. Though different in building- scale and type, the projects were all situated in central urban areas (Coupland and Marsh 1998; Heath 2001; Beauregard 2005; Hamnett and Whitelegg 2007).

The case of Amsterdam

Studying Amsterdam the same tendencies are visible. Transformation takes place in the city centre, while in the remote monofunctional office areas, no initiatives are found. Transformation of office buildings in monofunctional areas is only possible if more transformations are taking place. One option would be to first transform some buildings into shops, gyms, restaurants and other services, then in a second phase adding housing to the program, partly by transformation and partly by demolition and new construction. A second option is to start transformation of buildings adjacent to existing housing, facilities or public transport, applying the so-called "ink-stain method" to slowly improve the quality of the area. The ink-stain method departs from the idea that transformation of one office building into housing may inspire other actors to transform or redevelop buildings in the vicinity, and so a whole area can be transformed with small means (Post 2007). However, the risk is high that the redevelopment takes a long time and investors drop off along the way. The third option would imply an urban area development, considering the whole area as one development.

Schalekamp et al (2009) describe the possibilities for transformation of structurally vacant office buildings in monofunctional office areas by describing the case of Amsterdam South East. This research concludes that transformations of the office buildings in the area are only possible as part of a larger area development. However, such a development is complicated as the buildings in the area are owned by several different investors and the vacancy is spread over several buildings, of which most are partly still used. Though the vacancy in the area already reached 20-25%, the sense of urgency among the involved parties is not high enough to start an urban area development.

Transformation of structurally vacant office buildings in monofunctional office areas is a complex task. Still after several years of decline, increasing dilapidation and depreciation, the power needed to pull the area out of the accelerating degradation is not available. One by one, the buildings could have been sold for transformation into housing or other functions, but as part of a large monofunctional area with other structurally vacant office buildings surrounding it, no developers or investors are interested as they see no potential inhabitants.

New multifunctional developments or mixed-use locations are locations with an ascribed functional mix or without functional designation. Like traditional city centres, these locations have a functional mix of working, housing, leisure and retail. Within these locations the functional requirements for transformations are met and transformations of individual buildings can take place, presuming that the functional mix of the location also makes it financially, technically and legally suited for transformation.

18.3 Building

Geraedts and van der Voordt's "Transformation Meter" (2007) described several building and location characteristics that decrease the buildings transformation potential, and other building and location characteristics were described as "risk-factors". Studying 14 completed transformations ex-post (Remøy and Van der Voordt 2007) the brakes and triggers, risks and opportunities for transformations were revealed, also testing the results of the Transformation Meter. Using the results from this study and from a series of interviews with developers and investors, a reverse SWOT-model was developed, describing which characteristics would increase the transformation potential of new office buildings and locations, enhancing strengths and reducing weaknesses. The SWOT-model considers market conditions as external opportunities and threats (Table 31).

The base building

Whether the building characteristics or the building costs influence the transformation potential of an office building becomes a theoretical discussion. Most brakes and risks that were found in the ex-post study of transformations (12.2) and that apply to the building can be eliminated, albeit influencing the building costs. However, discussing the building from the layered building concept, the base building equals the structure (Brand 1994), the part of the building that cannot be altered without being demolished. Other building characteristics that describe the adaptable layers of skin, services, space plan and stuff are more easily altered and therefore have a larger effect on the transformation building costs, though these characteristics are not as such technical obstacles for transformation.

Building costs

In a study of transformation building costs (Mackay et al. 2009) the building costs were defined by relating costs to building elements as described in the elements method NL/SfB. The study revealed that in 95% of the cases, the highest costs were linked to the facade, the interior walls or the contractor costs. Though the contractor costs are not related to one physical characteristic, they are influenced by the buildings characteristics. The costs of the interior walls are more or less stable – when transforming office buildings into housing, partitioning walls have to be built between apartments. Hence, these costs are not as interesting as they are quite predictable. More interesting are the on average highest costs of transformation projects: The costs related to the facade. Though a large variation in the costs is seen across the cases studied, peculiarly enough the costs relating to the facade in most cases add up to 20-25% of the total building costs.

A logical conclusion would be to develop a functionally robust facade with a long technical lifespan that will not need to be altered - or even demolished - to accommodate a transformation. However, in the interviews with developers the comment was frequently made that a facade remake in most of the cases is needed to create a new image for the transformed building and not because of the technical state of the facade. Hence, the results of the case studies are inconclusive as to whether or not the facade of office buildings should be developed to be dismantled or whether it should be developed to accommodate both offices and housing. The characteristics influencing the building costs are however accounted for and can be studied as such.

Concluding upon the adaptability of the location, the base building and the building costs, the transformation potential of adaptable office buildings can be described using a SWOT analysis. In this case the SWOT advices on the Strength and Weaknesses for the development of adaptable office buildings for future transformations. Market conditions are seen as external influences and represent Opportunities and Threats.

Strengths	Weaknesses
Structure: columns with large span > 5.4m Structural grid that fits typical apartment grids Robust structure: Extensions / balconies possible Depth/Width: living space 5m < 10m one-side lit, or living space 5m < 20m two-side lit Height: living space > 2.6m Floors: steel structure or monolithic flat slab concrete floor, sufficient acoustic insulation Shafts (services): decentralised or distributed throughout the floor Entrance: central with access to main staircase and elevators Façade: grid suits apartments, enough daylight, adequate thermal insulation, demountable or adaptable Independent building layers The x-factor (specific image)! Hire a famous architect! Luxurious, oversized public space (French) balconies or floor to ceiling windows Mixed-use locations, including facilities for housing Accessibility by car and public transport	Structure: Cantilevered floors Load bearing internal walls Depth/Width: Structural grid that thwarts subdivision into apartments Height: living space 2.60 < 5.50 Floors: Hollow beam floors, deficient acoustic insulation Shafts (services): Combined with central elevators and staircases Entrance: Not central, no central staircase or elevators Façade: strip-windows, daylight access too low, not adaptable, not demountable Combined structure and services Focus on costs instead of quality, low-quality materials All elevator cars too small for stretchers, shafts not adaptable Fire resistance demands for housing is different than for offices Monofunctional (office) locations Noise or air pollution Locations not accessible by public transport
Opportunities	Threats
High demand for housing, resulting in high prices Governmental subsidies or policies to enable transformations Zoning plans that allow functional transformations Changes in building legislation, making requirements for offices and housing more similar Changes in the Spatial Planning Act , making requirements for offices and housing more similar Changes in the Spatial Planning Act, making functional transformations easier	High office prices, low housing prices, resulting in high purchasing prices Governmental ignorance, policies that disable transformations Monofunctional zoning plans Changes in building legislation, making requirements for offices and housing more different The Spatial Planning Act, existing differences in requirements for offices and housing Changes in The Spatial Planning Act, making functional transformation more problematic

19 Towards adaptability of building and location

Based on the two preceding chapters and the total of this research, this chapter presents a framework for office buildings and locations that will contribute to lower levels of structural vacancy. Furthermore, this framework considers buildings and locations that enhance the transformation potential of office buildings into housing. The framework is developed based on studies of structural vacancy and transformations of office buildings, and logical ex-ante argumentation on the effect of adaptable buildings and locations on transformation possibilities. Measures that prevent structural vacancy of office buildings are measures that prolong the use of office buildings or enable new use by increasing the buildings adaptability.

19.1 Market conditions

Market (private parties)	Focus on sustainability, quality and adaptability of new developments	*Table 32 Market conditions that reduce structural vacancy and enhance adaptability and transformation possibilities of the building stock*
	Focus on indirect yield (future value) instead of direct yield (rent income)	
	More knowledge about building characteristics and user preferences	
	Realistic value assessment of office buildings	
	Multi-disciplinary or joint-venture organisations	
Market (public parties)	Develop mixed-use zoning plans	
	Reduce building decree differences between offices and housing	
	Facilitate and stimulate urban redevelopment and transformation	
	Stop urban expansion to increase income from land exploitation	
	Subsidise redevelopment by more expensive greenfield developments	

Market conditions define the context within which office building and locations are used, adapted, transformed, redeveloped and reused. The market conditions are determined by several external forces, like macroeconomic changes, demographic developments and happenings that cause sudden changes. These market conditions have an effect on the use, the design and development, and all actors involved in use and development of office buildings. Accordingly, market conditions influence the quantitative demand and supply of office space and possible mismatches in the demand and supply. As qualitative mismatches in demand and supply cause overproduction of office space, the quantitative mismatch will further increase. Adaptation or renovation, transformation or demolishment are possible ways of coping with these mismatches, and inventions in building and location characteristics are ways of limiting or preventing these mismatches.

However, public or private actors who are involved in the development of office buildings and locations may also influence the market conditions. Governments at different levels may influence the market conditions for developing office buildings and locations, and for transformation. Likewise, private parties such as developers, investors and housing associations may shape the future market conditions for their own business by looking further than their current interests.

19.2 Location characteristics

Table 33 location characteristics that reduce structural vacancy and enhance adaptability and transformation possibilities

Site	
	Develop mixed-use locations with functions that do not have negative influences on the use of other functions
	Do not develop mixed-use locations near sources of nuisances for any of the possible functions
	Develop locations with facilities for offices and housing
	Develop locations that are accessible by public transport
	Develop locations that have good quality public space
	Redevelop central locations to enhance accessibility

Brand defined the site as the base layer in an adaptable building. The results from the Office Scan and the studies on the transformation potential of office buildings sustain this idea. If the building is located on a site that is only suited for one function, it makes little sense to adapt the building to a new function. Some functions are not adaptable and may also cause nuisances to other functions. These functions, like manufacturing and distribution, may better be located on locations that are not combined with other functions. However, because of the association between office work and factory work that was developed by the modernist, office buildings tend to be located in or near manufacturing and distribution locations, rather than in locations that mix offices with housing, retail and leisure.

Existing locations that experience location or functional obsolescence should be redeveloped into locations that sustain the adaptation of office buildings. Likewise, if new locations are developed, these should be developed as locations that after 20 years may accommodate different functions than the functions that are considered at the moment of planning. To sustain the adaptability of office buildings, office locations should be accessible by public transport, have a functional mix with some housing, facilities for office workers and facilities for residential accommodation, and the location characteristics should furthermore append to a safe location without hindrances and nuisances for functions that are possible within a mixed-use location. Additionally, the functions and facilities in the office location should add to the required level of status of the office location, and to the required level of safety and social security for offices and other functions. The measures that reduce the odds of structural vacancy are also measures that increase the possibilities for adaptation and transformation. Finally, a check list sums up the location characteristics that have the highest influence on the adaptability and transformation potential of office buildings.

19.3 Building characteristics

Structure	Design the structure as columns and free floors
	Sizes that allow changes in the space plan, large distance between columns and ceiling height that allows horizontal transportation of installations
	Structural system that allows alterations in the services (placing or refitting shafts)
	Over-dimension to last one century: ceiling height 0.2 metres, distance between columns 0.9 metres
	Over-dimension to allow for balconies or other horizontal extensions, thereby placing columns in the façade
Skin	Make the façade grid as small as possible as it enhances adaptability of the space plan
	Make alterations in the façade possible: possibilities for changing or enlarging windows
	Make extra insulation possible as the requirements for offices and housing increase
	Make removal of the façade feasible
	Use materials that can be maintained, and maintain the façade

Table 34 building characteristics that reduce structural vacancy and enhance adaptability and transformation possibilities

Office buildings that are designed from the idea of different layers or components are more adaptable and flexible than office buildings with installations incorporated in the structure. These buildings are not only more easily transformed, but are also more easily demounted, hence adaptation or transformation are not the only possible future redevelopments of these buildings, but also open perspectives for IFD developments or developments from a cradle to cradle perspective. It may be argued that historic buildings on central urban locations are easily adapted as well. However, these are adapted because of their rich history and monumental appearance. The transformation of historic buildings has been revealed to comprise high risks of hidden flaws and long procedures, and eventually the transformation building costs of these buildings is high. Developing and designing new buildings in the same way will not append the qualities of historic buildings to new buildings, though some lessons may be learned.

Modern office buildings are designed from the functionalistic point of view – form follows function. In the eagerness of fitting form as specifically possible to the function, a small change in function causes mismatch between form and function. Office buildings built from this principle are difficult to adapt, because of their specific structure that has been tailored to fit, both in strength and size. A specific characteristic is the situation of columns away from the facade, as in this way the moment-forces or the floor can be reduced and therewith the complete construction can be minimised. However, this specific characteristic of the structure again decreases its adaptability.

To design new adaptable office buildings, the structure should not be fit too specifically to a current function. The Office Scan revealed that even office buildings that are 15 years old are functionally outdated. Accordingly, departing from the concept of the building as layers, all layers that change less frequently than every 15 years should be adaptable, or make functional adaptation or transformation possible. According to Brand (1994) the site and the structure are then the two most important factors; the site is "eternal" while the lifespan of the structure differs from 30 to 300 years. The facade or, as Brand writes, the skin, changes every 20 years to keep up with fashion or technology, or it needs a large scale renovation. Changes in the facade are one of the major cost generators of transformation projects. Preferably, the facade should be designed and developed as adaptable and demountable, to allow for flexibility in future adaptations or transformation.

As structural vacancy is a result of a qualitative mismatch in demand and supply of office buildings, and as this mismatch is again related to the buildings functional obsolescence, few measures can prevent structural vacancy, except for measures that increase the possibility for adaptation and transformation of office buildings, enhancing the possibility for coping with structural vacancy and thereby limiting structural vacancy. As mentioned in the study by Geraedts and van der Voordt (2003, 2007), maintenance of the building and the quality and appearance of its exterior are measures that reduce the odds of structural vacancy. Finally, a check list sums up the building characteristics that reduce the odds of structural vacancy and enhance the adaptability and transformation possibilities of office buildings.

CONCLUSIONS

20　Overall conclusions and reflections

This research started with the idea that transformation is a way of coping with structural vacancy in office buildings; hence research questions were formulated about the possibility and feasibility of transformations. Building transformation is a well known phenomenon; inner city buildings loose their function and adapt to new use. In the Netherlands, a large amount of office buildings loose their function and remain structurally vacant; transformation does not take place. From this point of departure, three main research questions were formulated, asking what are the causes of structural vacancy; which role do market conditions play and which part can be ascribed to location and building characteristics? Can building transformation be used to cope with structural vacancy? Compared to other alternatives, such as consolidation, adaptation or demolishment and new construction; to which extent is building transformation a feasible way of coping with structural vacancy? To which extent can structural vacancy in new developments be prevented, and can structural vacancy be limited through the development of adaptable or transformable office buildings?

20.1 Research findings

The research was defined as three subjects, considering the cause of structural vacancy, how to cope with, and how to prevent structural vacancy from occurring. The three parts were studied separately, using literature reviews and quantitative and qualitative empiric research methods. The research findings are concluded and reflected upon in the following subchapters and are summarised in a matrix that also explains the structure of this research, considering cause, cope and prevent, and within each research part studying the aspects of the market, location and building.

20.1.1 Cause

Market: Mismatch of demand and supply is qualitative

Though the office market and conditions were not the main topic of this research, market characteristics and conditions are important to explain structural vacancy. A very simple explanation to structural vacancy of office buildings is that the supply of office space is higher than the demand; the market is unbalanced with a quantitative mismatch between demand and supply. The quantitative demand is determined by the number of employees and the square metres office space per employee. Office buildings are developed to achieve a future match in demand and supply, hence they are developed based on future market potentials, albeit developments in future demands are difficult to predict. These developments are based on macro-economic, technical, cultural and social changes that again influence the employment market and the use of square metre per employee. Studying the Amsterdam office market, by the end of 2007 the office stock counted 5.7 million square metres, whereas 1.2 million square metres were vacant – meaning that the vacancy in Amsterdam was 21% by the end of 2007 (Bak 2008). 450000 square metres were structurally vacant, equalling 38% of the available supply and 8% of the total stock. Why are offices still developed in a market that has such an oversupply of office space?

The answer to this seemingly quantitative question is qualitative. Office organisations search their offices within a specific geographical market and market segment. Within this market context, accommodation is chosen based on location and building characteristics. Office accommodations with certain characteristics are preferred to others. Therefore, office users' preferences for office space with specific location and building characteristics were studied, first by a stated preferences study by means of a Delphi approach and then by studying the influence of location and building characteristics on the odds of structural vacancy in a statistic revealed preferences study, the Office Scan.

Location: Monofunctionaity increases odds of structural vacancy

Structural vacancy concentrates in specific locations. Like a former study focussing on structural vacancy in Dutch national context (Sprakel and Vink 2007) the study of Amsterdam showed concentration of structural vacancy in monofunctional office locations and office location with a mix of distribution and industrial functions. Though the Delphi study concluded that accessibility by car, status and accessibility by public transport to be more important for the preference of office users, the Office Scan showed that status and the level of facilities in the location are more important characteristics for explaining structural vacancy. It is therefore curious that most office developments still take place in (monofunctional) office locations (Bak 2008).

However, using logistic regressions to study the effect of physical characteristics on the odds of structural vacancy, location characteristics were found to have less effect than building characteristics. This outcome is at a first glance quite surprising, though it has a logical explanation. The parallel PhD-research of Koppels (Koppels et al. 2007; Koppels et al. 2009) studies the influence of location and building characteristics on the rent level. This research reveals that location characteristics have the highest influence on the rent level. Hence, as location characteristics to a great extent explain the rent level, after selecting a market segment and location, office organisations select a building based on which building characteristics are found to be best suitable for the organisation. In summary, location characteristics that increase the odds of structural vacancy are:

- Monofunctionality
- Lack of status
- Lack of facilities

Building: Inflexible floor plans increase the odds of structural vacancy

There's a general picture of what a redundant, obsolete or structurally vacant office building probably looks like. "Vacant buildings are ugly and have too few parking places", was a statement by one of the Delphi study panellists. Exterior appearance was the second most important characteristic in the Delphi study. However, measuring ugliness is difficult, so in the Office Scan the technical state of facades was measured, together with the buildings facade material. The Office Scan revealed that office buildings with certain facade materials have higher odds of structural vacancy. The uni-variable analyses showed a relationship between structural vacancy and glass or natural stone facades of low technical state. The association between facade materials and structural vacancy was found independent of the construction year of the building though combinations of certain materials with construction periods were revealed to increase the odds of structural vacancy.

Car parking was found to be the most important characteristics in the Delphi study, whereas the Office Scan gave ambiguous results of the association between structural vacancy and parking. This phenomenon is explained by the relationship between the amount of parking places and the type of location where the office is situated. Offices near highways have more parking places than office buildings in central urban areas, but offices in central urban areas are located nearer to facilities and in locations with more status, and the location characteristics overrule the importance of parking.

Space efficiency and layout flexibility were the third and fourth most important characteristics defined by the Delphi study. These characteristics may be described partly by the same variables, though the Office Scan focused on layout flexibility, measured by the variables structural grid size and facade grid size. The two variables were collinear and were found to have an effect on the odds of structural vacancy; when the size of the structural grid increases, the flexibility increases and the odds of structural vacancy decreases, and if the size of the facade grid increases, the flexibility decreases and the odds of structural vacancy increases. In summary, building characteristics that increase the odds of structural vacancy are:

- Less car parking than surrounding buildings
- Glass facades of low technical state
- Bad internal appearance
- Low layout flexibility

20.1.2 Cope

Market: High purchasing price reduces transformation potential

Market aspects of coping with structural vacancy were defined as conditions that influence the possibility and feasibility of residential transformations - from offices into housing, considering the office market and the housing market and seeing the transformation market as a product of the two. The influence of market conditions on transformation potential was studied by interviews, first explorative, and then in a later stage of the research interviews with real estate developers and housing associations were held, discussing the relationship between market conditions and the actor's interest for getting involved in a transformation project. One of the biggest experienced obstacles to residential transformation is the financial value of structurally vacant office buildings, as the purchasing price is one of the largest items in a transformation cost estimate. Influencing the purchasing price was not a topic in this research. However, the value assessment of structurally vacant office buildings is found to be inadequate and reconsidering this method could be part of further studies.

Location: Monofunctional locations require transformation

Just like office organisations choose accommodation hierarchically by first selecting geographical market and market segment, then location, then building, people looking for a new place to live make the same considerations. Studying completed residential transformations, these were all located in central urban areas with a mix of functions or in locations where the main function is housing. A single transformation project was located on the edge between a light-industrial zone and a housing area and one was located in a monofunctional office location. From a behaviouristic point of view this finding would be considered a fact and further studies would concentrate on the location choices that were revealed. However, knowing why transformations do not take place in monofunctional office locations applies better to this research as it already concluded that most structurally vacant office buildings are located on monofunctional office locations.

Office buildings in monofunctional office locations have no potential for residential transformation unless the locations monofunctionality is also dealt with. That was the outcome of a study based on interviews with developers and housing associations that also discussed the transformation potential of locations. A study on transformation of monofunctional office locations discussed different approaches for location transformations (Schalekamp et al. 2009), considering "the ink stain method"; starting with the transformation of one building and expecting it to trigger other transformations, a stepwise method; starting with the implementation of housing from an edge of the location or by adding facilities, and finally a transformation scheme for the whole location. The last method was advised. Though rigorous, time consuming and complicated, other approaches were found to have too little impact on the location and would not trigger new transformations. An exception was transformations of buildings of considerable size, large enough and with character to determine the identity to the whole location.

Other location characteristics that reduce the residential transformation potential consider air pollution, noise and stench, as the legal requirements for housing are stricter than for offices. Some office locations are located near industrial sites, and some locations even have a mix of offices and industry. In such locations, transformation is impossible because of air pollution, noise or stench nuisances.

Building: Structure and facade decide office buildings transformation potential

To study the transformation potential of office buildings the financial, functional, technical, legal and cultural, architectural and historic issues were distinguished. These issues were found to be associated with the different characteristics of the building that were defined typologically. Different partial studies – a cross case analysis of 14 completed residential transformations (Remøy and Van der Voordt 2007), 31 interviews with developers and housing associations (Remøy and van der Voordt 2009) and a transformation cost study (Mackay et al. 2009) – came to the same conclusion; building structure and facade were found to be the two characteristics of a building that have the most influence on the buildings transformation potential.

The cross case analysis and the cost analysis showed the impact of adaptations of the facade on the financial feasibility of transformations. Due to functional, technical, legal, architectural or historic issues, the building costs related to the transformation of the facade are substantial. Specifically, the requirements for thermal and acoustic insulation are increasing and are also stricter for housing than for offices, and so the facades in most studied cases needed a technical upgrading. In other cases, transformation of monumental buildings led to higher building costs as elements were manufactured specially for that project in order to keep the appearance of the original building.

Neither the cross case analysis nor the cost analysis showed the importance of the main structure for the transformation potential of office buildings. However, the structure was mentioned by actors involved in the 14 completed transformations, and was referred to as important for deciding the new function for the building, the layout and the sizes of apartments. In the 31 interviews with developers and housing associations, the structure was mentioned frequently, and was seen as the biggest obstacle and opportunity of the building. If the structure is not technically and functionally adequate for transformation into housing, the building will not be transformed. That is also the reason that the importance of the structure was marginalised in the cross case analysis and in the cost analysis. If the floor height of a building is too low, if the columns are situated too close to each other, or if the technical quality of the structure is dilapidated, the building cannot be transformed.

Concluding, the size and condition of the building structure is critical to its transformation potential. All other characteristics may be altered, though all alterations have an effect on the functional, technical, legal, cultural, architectural and historic feasibility of the transformation, and eventually the financial feasibility. In summary, primary aspects enhancing the residential transformation potential of structurally vacant office buildings are:

- High demand for housing, housing prices that compete with office prices
- Realistic value assessment leading to lower purchasing prices
- Mixed-use locations
- Large scale structural grid and adaptable or removable facade
- Limited interventions to reduce building costs

20.1.3 Prevent

Market: Knowledge of user preferences can limit structural vacancy

Structural vacancy can be prevented by simply developing less office space. However, renewals or new developments will always be needed as office organisations look for high quality accommodation to fit their business activities. Taking old buildings off the market is another way of preventing structural vacancy, and by developing adaptable or transformable office building, a longer lifespan or multiple lifespans can be anticipated, contributing to the sustainability of the built environment.

On different levels, measures can be taken to stop superfluous development of office buildings and to stimulate adaptation, transformation and redevelopment of buildings and locations. Local governments have important incomes from developing and selling or leasing out land. Developing new office locations is therefore an interesting activity for municipalities, though by doing so they stimulate the development and oversupply of offices. Developing offices on "new" land requires less initial investments than redevelopment of central urban areas, as former investments in the location will have to be compensated and the purchasing price of existing buildings is high.

Though office organisations increasingly prefer mixed-use locations or locations with a high level of facilities, developers keep developing offices in monofunctional office locations. These developments are highly unsustainable. Users are found for a first lease period, after which the odds of structural vacancy increase. Investors have little knowledge about the relationship between building characteristics and user preferences and investments are based on current cash flow, though after a few years the tenant leaves and new tenants cannot be found. Time for investors to wake up and question the future value of their purchase!

Location: Developing mixed-use locations can limit structural vacancy

Mixed use locations have less structural vacancy, are preferred by both office employees and organisations, and offices in mixed-use locations are more easily adapted or transformed than offices in monofunctional locations. Then why are most offices still developed in monofunctional locations? Cheap land, simple developments and low architectural ambitions make these developments far less expensive than developments in central urban areas. Redevelopments of locations in the city centres are often complicated because of existing infrastructure and buildings, the land is expensive, and high architectural ambitions are often demanded. Again, the blame is on all actors in the real estate market, who all take part in a circle of blame by claiming its somebody else's fault.

Building: Adaptability can limit structural vacancy

Building costs add up to half the costs of residential office transformations. Hence, developing adaptable office buildings that are more easily transformed into housing can enhance office buildings transformation potential. To a large extent, adaptability can be achieved by design. Large measurements and high technical quality of the structure and a flexible layout of the floors increase buildings adaptability. Moreover, facades should be adaptable or replaceable. Designs involving replaceable and adaptable facades would be best suited, as the final choice of replacing or adapting can be taken at the moment of transforming the building. Adaptation-schemes that can be realised by design are preferable, since these are almost cost-neutral compared to standard office buildings.

Other measures, like over dimensioning office buildings are also interesting as such schemes are probable to enhance future adaptability and renovation potential. Schemes that include built-in facilities for anticipated future use are not interesting; the future is not possible to predict, and so the possibility is high that costly built in measures will never be used. Though over dimensioning may be interesting for future adaptability, possible future costs and benefits need to be compared to initial costs. In the 31 interviews with developers and housing associations, schemes based on over dimensioning were found interesting. However, the willingness to invest by office building investors was doubted. Investors' interests and willingness to invest is an issue that could be focussed on in future studies.

Conditions and characteristics that reduce the odds of structural vacancy and enhance adaptability and transformation potential

Table 35
Conditions and
characteristics
that reduce
the odds of
structural
vacancy and
enhance
adaptability and
transformation
potential

Market	Focus on sustainability and adaptability of new developments	
	Focus on capital growth instead of rent income	
	More knowledge about user preferences and building characteristics	
	Realistic value assessment of office buildings	
	Multi-disciplinary or joint venture development and investment organisations	
	Develop mixed-use zoning plans	
	Reduce building decree differences between offices and housing	
	Facilitate and stimulate urban redevelopment and transformation	
	Stop urban expansion by more expensive Greenfield developments	
Location	Mixed-use locations with facilities for offices and housing	
	Develop and redevelop locations well accessible by public transport	
	Develop locations with good quality public space	
Building	Design building structure as columns and free floors	
	Large size structural grid, small size facade grid	
	Adaptable structure and facade	
	Over dimensioned structure to fit several life spans	
	Replaceable facade	
	Maintainable facade and maintenance of the facade	

20.2 Answers to the main research questions

In the beginning of this research, three main research questions were formulated, asking what are the causes of structural vacancy; which role do market conditions play and which part can be ascribed to location and building characteristics? Can building transformation be used to cope with structural vacancy? Compared to other alternatives, such as consolidation, adaptation or demolition and new construction; to which extent is building transformation a feasible way of coping with structural vacancy? To which extent can structural vacancy in new developments be prevented, and can structural vacancy be limited through the development of adaptable or transformable office buildings?

This research considers a topic with a broad outline and comprises three parts, based on several partial studies. Each of the three parts has been described separately and could be seen as a comprised research, again including three topics. This 3x3 structure was apparent in an early stage of this research and describes

	Cause	Cope	Prevent
Market	Quantitative: Too many square metres office space in the market	Realistic valuation of structurally vacant offices / purchasing price	No development of new office locations, raise costs for land lease in new developed locations
	Qualitative: The oversupply is caused by a qualitative misfit of demand and supply	Redundant / obsolete / structurally vacant office space is recognised as such	Regional cooperation on urban development and office developments
	Superfluous new developments lead to fast functional ageing and functional obsolescence	Demand for housing can be realised in transformed buildings	Invest in durability: long lifespan or multiple lifespans
	Mismatch between functional and technical lifespan		Anticipate adaptability
Location	Low status, No or few facilities	Mixed-use locations, Central urban locations, Locations with housing	Mixed-use locations: Mix of offices, housing and facilities reduces vacancy and enhance transformation potential
	Monofunctional office locations and locations with a mix of offices and industry or distribution activities	Redevelop monofunctional locations to become mixed-use	No mix of offices and industry or offices in industrial sites
		Air quality and noise levels permit housing	
Building	Bad external appearance, bad internal appearance, low flexibility, large buildings	Iconic buildings, monuments, specific architecture, buildings that provide identity to the location	Anticipate architectural quality to reduce odds for structural vacancy and enhance transformation potential
	Buildings from 1980-1995	Main building structure determines functional transformation potential	Anticipate adaptability in design of office buildings Technical adaptability of structure Adaptable or replaceable facade
	Less parking than surrounding buildings	Facade determines financial feasibility, influenced by technical, legal, architectural, cultural and historic aspects	

Table 36
Research matrix
answering the
main research
questions

its structure as a matrix of related studies. The research as a whole was built up as a multiple phased research design; the partial studies were defined separately and chronologically had an effect on the next partial study. The 3 main research questions have been answered in the three parts of this book and are shortly summarised in Table 36.

20.3 Implications for practice

This research concludes the influence of building and location characteristics on structural vacancy and on the transformation potential of office buildings. Moreover, based on this research advice is given for how to prevent structural vacancy in the future by developing office buildings for longer or multiple life spans. The following discusses this research's implications for practice, recognising the different groups and actors involved in office developments and residential transformations.

Real estate developers

Real estate developers develop projects for an owner, an investor, or take the initiative to develop for tenants or even without a known user or buyer. In some cases, real estate developers act like hitmen; developing new office buildings, offering incentives for new tenants, and when the tenants are found the building is sold to a real estate investor. Towards the end of the lease contract, the tenant is offered a new property with new incentives, and the first developed building is left vacant…Of course, this picture describes a small part of the real estate development branch and of course it is also exaggerated. However, these cases are known to occur (Reimerink 2008) and this kind of developments contributes to an increase of vacancy in the office market and increases the speed of ageing of the existing building stock.

Like other development types, residential transformation of structurally vacant offices into housing is often taken on by specialised developers, and expertise on transformations is found within this group, which also is often engaged in other central urban area developments. Next to transformations, these developers are often specialists in housing developments, and some work solely for housing associations. 31 interviews with developers and housing associations revealed that developers with transformation experience have a different view on the opportunities and obstacles for transformation projects. Interestingly, developers with experience find the building location the most important opportunity and the purchasing price the biggest obstacle. Correspondingly, although non experienced developers also see the importance of the location, the building is also found to be important for the opportunities of the transformation, while it is also seen as the biggest obstacle. Developers with transformation experience recognise few risks put forth by the building itself, and actually this deserves to be called a mythbuster: the technical risks of transformations are much lower than conceived.

Housing associations, or developers working for housing associations, have a different view on opportunities and obstacles of transformations than commercial developers. As housing associations often work for specific target groups, the potential of the building and location to accommodate specific groups of inhabitants is seen as important, together with the possibility of strategic possessions in central urban areas. The interest of housing associations in strategic possessions is noteworthy, and reveals the opportunities of this actor in transformation projects: as housing associations invest for longevity, they are able to make strategic use of their development. Investing in a location and upgrading it costs money and time, and the opportunities are seen as future profit and capital growth from improved quality, not only of the building but of the location as well.

Real estate investors

As owners are in most cases not occupiers, real estate investors are an important actor in the office market. Investors stay involved in a property for a longer time. However, investors are often accused of being the responsible actor for structural vacancy. Investors also have a reputation problem after various reports of murky real estate transactions where structurally vacant office buildings were sold as part of larger portfolios, showing that structural vacancy is a real problem to real estate investors. Investors who invest in new office buildings are typically larger private or institutional investors, while older, obsolete offices are often owned by small private investors, real estate limited partnerships or niche firms specialised in high risk investments. This "layered" characteristic of the group is one of the most obvious explanations of the fact that investors don't seem to see that vacancy will occur in relatively new developments, together with the fact that investors assess a property by the characteristics of its tenants, not by the property's physical characteristics.

Though structural vacancy is a problem for real estate investors, they do not seem to feel the urgency of doing something about it. Again, properties are assessed and valued based on their future potential tenancy value, but if there are no future tenants, then the assessed value should be zero! This fact is not recognised, investors keep waiting for new tenants and hesitate to devaluate their properties, and hence the purchasing price for structurally vacant office buildings is often too high to make transformation or other use possible.

Real estate investors have the key to limiting structural vacancy. By investing only in durable office buildings; meaning existing or new office buildings with long or multiple lifespans, and by assessing developments by their characteristics, not only by their tenants, real estate investors may limit the development of structural vacancy. After all, developers will not develop office buildings which no-one is buying… Furthermore, by assessing structurally vacant office buildings, facing that there are no future tenants, real estate investors should devalue these properties. Sunk costs should not determine future decisions.

Architects

This research has shown that the architectural design of office buildings influence the risk of structural vacancy as well as the buildings transformation potential. The appearance of an office building is one of the building characteristics the most associated with structural vacancy. The odds of structural vacancy are higher in buildings with architectural characteristics. The facade material combined with the year of construction of the building is of significant influence on the buildings

Figure 78

The circle of blame. Actors in the office market do not take responsibility for the overproduction of office space; a circle of blame maintains the overproduction: A developer finds a user for a potential development, a development with a user finds an investor, the municipality is happy with a new user and new investments, the municipality blames the developer for the high vacancy in the municipality.

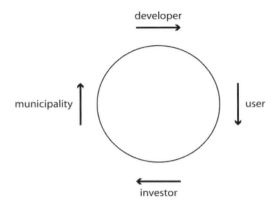

vacancy risk. Facades of natural stone are associated with low structural vacancy, while glass facades from before 1995 are associated with a higher level of structural vacancy. Also, the odds of structural vacancy are higher for buildings with low daylight admittance than buildings with high daylight admittance. The flexibility of the layout as measured by the structural grid and the facade grid was also found to influence the odds of structural vacancy, together with the appearance of the buildings entrance.

All these characteristics of the office building define the architectural quality of the building and are part of the architects design. Though van Meel noticed that some characteristics of the office building, like building height, floor plan and workplace design are determined long before the architect gets involved in a project (Van Meel 2000), the characteristics that describe the buildings appearance and flexibility are designed by the architect. Equally, the transformation potential of an office building is to a large extent decided by its architectural design. Though the size of the structural grid and the floor height are normally decided by the developer, again before the architect gets involved, architects can still have their saying in the decision making. The location of stairs and elevators is another important characteristic that defines the transformation potential of an office building. By thinking of possible future reuse for housing or offices when designing, large mistakes can be prevented.

Planners

Structural vacancy concentrates in monofunctional office locations. Additionally, the transformation potential of office buildings located in monofunctional office locations is much lower than for office buildings in mixed use locations. To transform office buildings in monofunctional locations, a strategy for redevelopment of the whole location would be needed, raising the complexity of the transformation. This research is not the first to praise mixed-use locations but adds evidence to the polemics on this theme. The evidence is obviously needed, since large scale monofunctional developments are still initiated on the city fringes and in locations near important highways. These developments are argued for by local governments as necessary for the office market and for the competition with other municipalities.

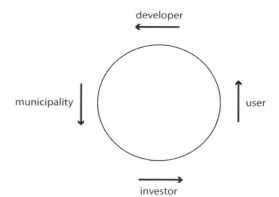

developer

municipality

user

investor

Figure 79
The circle of ambition. Actors in the office market can turn the circle of blame into a circle of ambition: developers start urban redevelopments and trigger municipalities to invest, municipalities form an alliance with investors with properties in the area, investors contribute to redevelopment, new users make cash flow possible and trigger developers to transformation or urban redevelopment.

Municipality

Though the largest municipalities are taking actions to limit structural vacancy, they also help producing it. While the municipality of Amsterdam has introduced an office pilot to help facilitate transformation processes, it also keeps developing new monofunctional office locations, stimulating the development of new offices. The municipalities are in a difficult position. As developers and office organisations threaten to move to neighbouring municipalities if new developments are not allowed, municipalities feel forced to give in. But new developments are also very profitable for the municipality as they generate land -lease or –sale incomes and so it is clear that the municipality has more than one interest. Together with real estate investors, the municipality should play a key role in limiting structural vacancy by being more critical towards which developments are accepted, focusing more on urban management than development, focusing as well on the durability of new developments. Making regional agreements or agreements with neighbouring municipalities would make is possible to stop "blackmail-developments". The municipality may also consider policies that demand redevelopment of structurally vacant office buildings into housing (by transformation or demolition with new construction) in exchange of land for new developments, or policies to increase the price of new land so that redevelopment of existing locations becomes more lucrative.

National government

The national government has an important role in stimulating the development of a sustainable built environment and part of such a development are adaptable buildings with long or multiple lifespans. This research has shortly discussed the role of the national government in limiting structural vacancy by introducing taxes on structurally vacant office buildings or tax benefits for transformations, but concludes that this kind of measures are not desirable. Rather, the government should support municipalities in making regional agreements to limit the expansion of monofunctional office locations and to increase the quality of the existing built environment.

20.4 Further research

This research was broad in its setup as it aimed at connecting and expanding knowledge about structural vacancy of office buildings and transformation as a way of coping with it. The research goes in depth on the specific issues of building and location characteristics that influence the odds of structural vacancy, and on building and location characteristics that influence the buildings transformation potential. Other issues, such as the possibility to limit or prevent structural vacancy by market interventions have been studied less intensively and could be expanded. Furthermore, this research provides ideas for how to limit or prevent structural vacancy by developing adaptable or transformable buildings. As this part may be seen as a proposal for new developments, further validation of the research findings would be interesting. Finally, it would be interesting to test the specific results from the Amsterdam office market on other Dutch or international markets.

Generalisation on the cause of structural vacancy

Though market mechanisms are similar throughout the world, the combination of a specific city with its history, culture, urban fabric and geographic limits makes each market different. This research focused on the office market in Amsterdam, the main market in the Netherlands and city of headquarters and multinationals. Would the findings be different if another city and market were studied? A study of other Dutch cities could validate the findings from Amsterdam for other Dutch cities. Another option would be to compare the results from Amsterdam to other international main markets, such as London, Toronto and New York. The study of Amsterdam was performed using a large number of variables that describe building and location characteristics. Some of these were found not to influence the odds of structural vacancy. By ruling out these variables and thereby limiting the amount of variables, the studies could be conducted more efficiently.

New assessment methods could increase transformation potential

This research focused on residential transformation for coping with structural vacancy. Of course, it can be coped with in other ways as well; by consolidation, demolishment and possibly new construction, renovation or by other functional transformations. The financial benefits of the different strategies were compared to each other in a specific study (Muller et al. 2009), revealing that transformation is a good way of coping with structurally vacant office buildings. However, how to value structurally vacant office buildings is still a problem and the methods used by real estate assessors do not make sense. These methods all base the buildings value on the rent income, which is fiction if the building is structurally vacant. New assessment methods would be helpful for deciding which alternative for coping is the best in different situations.

Longer or multiple life spans

The possibilities for preventing or limiting structural vacancy by developing adaptable or transformable office buildings were studied. Based on the empirical studies of the cause of structural vacancy and transformation as a way of coping with it, transformable buildings are presented as a possibility for limiting structural vacancy in future developments. The ability of adaptable or transformable office buildings to react to changing needs and thereby preventing or limiting structural vacancy will be revealed as the buildings succeed several lifespans. However, stated preferences studies could be conducted by using qualitative or quantitative interviewing or vignettes, or by developing strategies for transformation and testing these for different scenarios.

Increased adaptability of office buildings contributes to longer or multiple lifespans, by continuation or alteration of the office building function or as transformation into housing or other functions. Hereby, increased adaptability contributes to a sustainable built environment. Though the effect of longer or multiple lifespans on sustainability is apparent, the specific effect of adaptability on sustainability could be studied by Life Cycle Assessment models, making it possible to calculate the sustainability benefits of different developments, just like it is possible to calculate the financial benefits.

Sources

Amsterdam, M. (2003) Een veilig Amsterdam. Retrieved 03.07.2009, from www.eenveiligamsterdam.nl.

Arge, K. (2005) Adaptable office buildings: theory and practice. *Facilities,* 23(3/4): 119-27.

Atelier V and Motivaction (2005) Office Styles. Atelier V.

Augé, M. (2000) *Non-places introduction to an anthropology of supermodernity.* London, Verso.

Avidar, P., K. Havik, et al. (2007) Gentrification: stromen en tegenstromen. *Oase,* 73: 9.

Baarda, D. B. and M.P.M. de Goede (2001) *Basisboek methoden en technieken handleiding voor het opzetten en uitvoeren van onderzoek.* Groningen, Stenfert Kroese.

Back, A.d., J. Coenen, et al. (2004) *Gesloopt, gered, bedreigd omgaan met naoorlogse bouwkunst.* Rotterdam, Episode.

Bak, R.L. (2006) *Offices in figures 2005.* Zeist, CB Richard Ellis.

Bak, R.L. (2008) *Offices in figures 2007.* Zeist, CB Richard Ellis.

Bakker, M.M. (2002) *Architectuur en stedebouw in Amsterdam 1850-1940.* Zwolle, Waanders.

Barlow, J. and D. Gann (1993) *Offices into flats.* York, Joseph Rowntree Foundation.

Barlow, J. and D. Gann (1995) Flexible Planning And Flexible Buildings: Reusing Redundant Office Space. *Journal of Urban Affairs,* 17(3): 263-276.

Bastianello, M. (1995) *Progetto Bicocca, un contributo per Milano policentrica.* Milano, Electa.

Baum, A. (1991) *Property investment depreciation and obsolescence.* London, Routledge.

Baum, A. (1993) Quality, Depreciation, and Property Performance. *The Journal of Real Estate Research,* 8(4): 541-565.

Baum, A. and A. McElhinney (1997) *The Causes and Effects of Depreciation in Office Buildings: a Ten Year Update,* working paper of the Department of Land Management and Development, University of Reading.

Beauregard, R.A. (2005) The Textures of Property Markets: Downtown Housing and Office conversions in New York City. *Urban Studies,* 42: 2431-2445.

Benraad, K. and H. Remøy (2007) Belevingswaarde. In: T. Van der Voordt, R. Geraedts, H. Remøy and C. Oudijk (Eds.) *Transformatie van kantoorgebouwen thema's, actoren, instrumenten en projecten.* Rotterdam, Uitgeverij 010: 480 blz.

Benraad, K. (1994) *Van werkplek naar woonstek, herbestemming van kantoorpanden.* Stuurgroep Experimenten Volkshuisvesting. Rotterdam, SEV.

BHH (2008) WE're Amsterdam. Amsterdam, Boer Hartog Hooft.

Bijdendijk, F. (2006) *Met andere ogen.* Amsterdam, Het Oosten Woningcorporatie.

Blakstad, S.H. (2001) *A strategic approach to adaptability in office buildings.* Trondheim, Norwegian University of Science and Technology, Faculty of Architecture, Planning and Fine Arts, Department of Building Technology.

Bluestone, D. (1991) *Constructing Chicago.* New Haven, Yale University Press.

Bottom, C., S. McGreal, et al. (1998) The suitability of premises for business use: an evaluation of supply/demand variations. *Property Management,* 16(3): 134-144.

Bouwmeester, H. (2001) *Demonstratieprojecten IFD-bouwen 2000 een omslag in bouwen een omslag in denken.* Rotterdam, Stuurgroep Experimenten Volkshuisvesting.

Bouwmeester, H. (2003) *Demonstratieprojecten IFD-bouwen op de drempel van 2002 een doorbraak 23 voorbeelden van industrieel, flexibel en demontabel bouwen.* Rotterdam, Stuurgroep Experimenten Volkshuisvesting.

Brand, S. (1994) *How buildings learn; what happens after they're built.* New York, Viking.

Brounen, D. and P. Eichholtz (2004) Demographics and the Global Office Market-Consequences for Property Portfolios. *Journal of Real Estate Portfolio Management,* 10(3): 231-242.

CBS (2006) Bouwen en wonen. yearly, Centraal Bureau voor de statistiek.

Coenen, J. (2007) Transformatie als architectonische opgave. In: T. Van der Voordt, R. Geraedts, H. Remøy and C. Oudijk (Eds.) *Transformatie van kantoorgebouwen thema's, actoren, instrumenten en projecten.* Rotterdam, Uitgeverij 010: 480 blz.

Colwell, P.F., H.J. Munneke, et al. (1998) Chicago's Office Market: Price Indices, Location and Time. *Real Estate Economics,* 26(1): 83-106.

Coupland, A. and C. Marsh (1998) *The Cutting Edge 1998; The conversion of redundant office space to residential use.* R. Research, University of Westminster.

Coxe, W., N.F. Hartung, et al. (1987) *Success strategies for design professionals; superpositioning for architecture and engineering firms.* New York, McGraw-Hill.

Cuperus, Y. (2004) Open Building. Retrieved 22.02.2009, 2009, from www.obom. org.

Davidson, P., M. Merritt-Gray, et al. (1997) Voices from practice: mental health nurses identify research priorities. *Archives of Psychiatric Nursing,* XI(6): 340-345.

De Jong, F. (1997) *Woonvoorkeurenonderzoek: theorie, empirie en relevantie voor de praktijk.* Delft, Publikatieburo Bouwkunde.

De Jonge, H. (1990) The Philosophy and Practice of Maintenance and Modernisation. *Property Maintenace Management and Modernisation,* Singapore, Longman.

De Jonge, H., M.H. Arkesteijn, et al. (2008) *Corporate real estate management designing an accommodation strategy.* Delft, TU Delft.

De Jonge, T. (2005) *Cost effectiveness of sustainable housing investments Online resource.* Delft, DUP Science.

Decisio (2006) *Stimuleren hergebruik en herbestemming lang leegstaand commercieel vastgoed - een handreiking voor gemeenten*. Amsterdam, Decisio.

Delbecq, A.L., A.H. van der Ven, et al. (1975) *Group Techniques For Program Planning*. Glenview, Scott Foresman.

Den Heijer, A.C. (2003) *Inleiding vastgoedmanagement*. Delft, Publikatieburo Bouwkunde. Dewulf, G. and H. de Jonge (1994) *Toekomst van de kantorenmarkt 1994-2015*. Delft, TU Delft.

Dgbc (2009) Dutch Green Building Council. Retrieved 03.07.2009, 2009, from www.dgbc.nl.

DiPasquale, D., and W.C. Wheaton (1996) *Urban Economics and Real Estate Markets*. Upper Saddle River, New Jersey, Prentice-Hall.

Douglas, J. (2006) *Building adaptation*. Oxford, Butterworth-Heinemann.

DTZ (2006) Cijfers in perspectief 2006. Utrecht, DTZ Zadelhoff v.o.f.

DTZ (2007) Nederland Compleet 2007. Nederland Compleet. D. Z. v.o.f. Amsterdam, DTZ Zadelhoff v.o.f. 2009: 80.

DTZ (2009) Nederland Compleet 2009. Nederland Compleet. D. Z. v.o.f. Amsterdam, DTZ Zadelhoff v.o.f. 2009: 80.

Duffy, F. (1990) Measuring building performance. *Facilities,* 8(5): 17-21.

Duffy, F. (1998) *Design for change the architecture of DEGW*. Basel, Birkhäuser.

Duffy, F. and K. Powell (1997) *The new office*. London, Conran Octopus.

Dunse, N. and C. Jones (1998) A hedonic price model of office rents. *Journal of Property Valuation and Investment*, 16: 297-312.

Dunse, N., Leishman. C. and C. Watkins (2001) Classifying office submarkets. *Journal of Property Investment & Finance*, 19(3): 236-250.

Durmisevic, E. (2006) *Transformable building structures. Design for dissassembly as a way to introduce sustainable engineering to building design & construction*. Delft, TU Delft.

Dynamis (2006) Sprekende cijfers kantorenmarkten 2006. Amersfoort, Dynamis.

Dynamis (2007) Sprekende cijfers kantorenmarkten 2007. Amersfoort, Dynamis.

Dynamis (2009) Sprekende cijfers kantorenmarkten 2009. Amersfoort, Dynamis.

Edwards, B. (1992) *London Docklands: urban design in an age of deregulation*. Oxford, Butterworth.

Eichholtz, P., N. Kok, et al. (2008) Doing Well by Doing Good? Green Office Buildings. *Berkeley Program on Housing and Urban Policy*: W08.

Elkington, J. (1994) Towards the sustainable Corporation: Win-win-win business strategies for sustainable development. *California Management review*.

Field, A. (2005) *Discovering statistics using SPSS*. London, Sage.

Fink, A., J. Kosecoff, et al. (1991) *Consensus Methods: Characteristics and Guidelines for Use RAND*. Santa Monica, RAND corporation.

Florida, R. (2003) "Cities and the Creative Class." *City & Community*, 2(1): 3-19.

Florida, R. (2004) *The rise of the creative class ... and how it's transforming work, leisure, community and everyday life*. New York, Basic Books.

Flyvbjerg, B. (2006) Five misunderstandings about case-study research. *Qualitative Inquiry*, 12(2): 219-245.

Frampton, K. (1992) *Modern architecture; a critical history*. London, Thames and Hudson.

Fuerst, F. (2007) Office Rent Determinants: A Hedonic Panel Analysis.

Gehner, E. (2008) *Knowingly taking risk investment decision making in real estate development.* Online resource. Delft, Eburon.

Geraedts, R. and N. De Vrij (2004) Transformation meter revisited. In: Kendall S. (Ed.) *CIB w104 Open Building Implementation.* Ball State University.

Geraedts, R. and T. van der Voordt (2003) Offices for living in: An instrument for measuring the potential for transforming offices into homes. *Open House International*, 28(3): 80-90.

Geraedts, R. and T. van der Voordt (2003, 2007) Good buildings drive out bad buildings. In: Jia, B. (Ed.) *International Conference on Open Building*, Hong Kong, The University of Hong Kong.

Geraedts, R. and T. van der Voordt (2007) A Tool to measure opportunities and risks of converting empty offices into dwellings. *ENHR ; Sustainable Urban Areas*, Rotterdam, TU Delft.

Gerritse, C. (2005) *Kosten-kwaliteitsturing in de vroege fasen van het huisvestingsproces.* Delft, DUP Science.

Giedion, S. (1967) *Space, time and architecture the growth of a new tradition.* Cambridge, Mass., Harvard University Press.

Gillen, N. (2008) Demand profiles of Organisations and the Associated Implications for Real Estate and Location. In: Vande Putte, H. (Ed.) *Corporations and Cities*, Brussels, Publikatieburo Bouwkunde.

Goodman, C.M. (1987) The Delphi technique: a critique. *Journal of Advanced Nursing*, 12: 729-734.

Green, A. and I. Price (2000) Whither FM? A Delphi study of the profession and industry. *Facilities*, 18(7/8): 281-292.

Green, B., Jones, M., et al. (1999) Applying the Delphi technique in a study of GPs information requirement. *Health and Social Care in the Community*, 7(3): 198-205.

Greene, J.C. and V.J. Caracelli (1997) Defining and describing the paradigm issue in mixed-method evaluation. *New Directions for Program Evaluation*, 1997(74): 5-17.

Groat, L. and D. Wang (2002) *Architectural research methods.* Hoboken, Wiley.

Groenendijk, P., P. Vollaard, et al. (2000) *Industrieel, flexibel en demontabel bouwen demonstratieprojecten IFD-bouwen 1999 : zien is geloven.* Rotterdam, Stuurgroep Experimenten Volkshuisvesting.

Gunst, D.D. and T. de Jong (1989) *Typologie van gebouwen; planning en ontwerp van kantoorgebouwen.* Delft, DUP.

Habraken, N.J. (1972) *Supports: An alternative to mass housing.* London, Architectural Press.

Habraken, N.J. and J. Teicher (1998) *The structure of the ordinary form and control in the built environment.* Cambridge, Mass., MIT Press.

Hall, P. (1999) The future of cities. *Computers, Environment and Urban Systems*, 23(3): 173-185.

Hamnett, C. and D. Whitelegg (2007) Loft conversion and gentrification in London: from industrial to postindustrial land use. *Environment and planning 39,* (1): 106-124.

Hanson, W.E., J.W. Creswell, et al. (2005) Mixed methods research designs in counseling psychology. *Journal of Counseling Psychology*, 52(2): 224-235.

Harmsen, H. and G. van der Waal (2008) *De oude kaart van Nederland leegstand en herbestemming.* Den Haag, Atelier Rijksbouwmeester.

Harvey, D. (1989) *The condition of postmodernity an enquiry into the origins of cultural change.* Oxford, Blackwell.

Hasson, F., S. Keeney, et al. (2000) Research guidelines for the Delphi survey technique. *Journal of Advanced Nursing*, 32(4): 1008-1015.

Healey and Baker (1987) National Office Design Survey. National Office Design Survey. London, Healey and Baker.

Heath, T. (2001) Adaptive re-use of offices for residential use The experiences of London and Toronto. *Cities*, 18(3): 173-184.

Heim, M., S. Hoogstraten, et al. (2006) Plan Amsterdam. Amsterdam, DRO. 4: 32.

Hek, M., J. Kamstra, et al. (2004) *Herbestemmingswijzer herbestemming van bestaand vastgoed.* Delft, Publikatieburo Bouwkunde.

Hendershott, P.H. (1996) Valuing properties when comparable sales do not exist and the market is in disequilibrium. *Journal of Property Research*, 13(1): 57-66.

Hendershott, P.H., C.M. Lizieri, et al. (1999) The Workings of the London Office Market. *Real Estate Economics*, 27(2): 365-387.

Hertzberger, H. (1991) *Lessons for students in architecture.* Rotterdam, Uitgeverij 010.

Hessels, M. (1992) *Locational dynamics of business services; an intrametropolitan study on the Randstad Holland.* Utrecht, Koninklijk Nederlands Aardrijkskundig Genootschap.

Het Oosten. (2004) Solids, retrieved 03.07.2009, from www.solids.nl.

Hofmans, F., M. Schopmeijer, et al. (2007) ABT-Quickscan. In: T. Van der Voordt, R. Geraedts, H. Remøy and C. Oudijk (Eds.) *Transformatie van kantoorgebouwen thema's, actoren, instrumenten en projecten.* Rotterdam, Uitgeverij 010: 480 blz.

Hordijk, A. (2005) *Valuation and construction issues in real estate indices.* The Hague, Europe Real Estate Publishers.

Hordijk, A. and W. van de Ridder (2005) Valuation model uniformity and consistency in real estate indices: The case of The Netherlands. *Journal of Property Investment & Finance,* 23(2): 165-81.

Hosmer, D.W. and S. Lemeshow (2000) *Applied logistic regression.* New York, Wiley.

Hulsman, C.L. and F.A.M. Knoop (1998) *Transformatie van kantoorgebouwen sturingsmiddelen om herbestemming van kantoorpanden te bevorderen.* Delft, Delft University Press.

Ibelings, H. (1999) *Nederlandse stedenbouw van de 20ste eeuw.* Rotterdam, NAi Uitgevers.

Jacobs, J. (1961) *The death and life of great American cities.* New York, Random House.

Jairath, N. and J. Weinstein (1994) The Delphi methodology: a useful administrative approach. *Canadian Journal of Nursing Administration*, 7: 29–42.

Jameson, F. (1999) *Postmodernism, or, The cultural logic of late capitalism.* Durham, Duke University Press.

Jennen, M. and D. Brounen (2006) Clustering Effects on office rents; herding in the Amsterdam market. *ERES.* Annual European Real Estate Society Conference, Weimar, Germany, Bauhaus-Universität Weimar.

Johnson, R.B. and A.J. Onwuegbuzie (2004) Mixed Methods Research: A Research Paradigm Whose Time Has Come. *Educational Researcher,* 33(7): 14.

Jolles, A., E. Klusman, et al. (2003) *Planning Amsterdam scenarios for urban development 1928-2003.* Rotterdam, NAi Publishers.

Kamerling, J.W., M. Bonebakker, et al. (1997) *Hogere bouwkunde Jellema. Dl. 9. Utiliteitsbouw; bouwmethoden.* Leiden, SMD/Waltman.

Keeris, W. (2007) Gelaagdheid in leegstand. In: T. Van der Voordt, R. Geraedts, H. Remøy and C. Oudijk (Eds.) *Transformatie van kantoorgebouwen thema's, actoren, instrumenten en projecten.* Rotterdam, Uitgeverij 010: 480 blz.

Keeris, W. and P.W. Koppels (2006) Uncertainty about the vacancy rate in the Dutch office market due to the different vacancy types and stratified structure. *ERES.* Annual European Real Estate Society Conference, Weimar, Germany, Bauhaus-Universität Weimar.

Kendall, S. (1999) Open building: an approach to sustainable architecture. *Journal of Urban Technology,* 6(3): 1-16.

Kohn, A.E. and P. Katz (2002) *Building type basics for office buildings.* New York, Wiley.

Kohnstamm, P.P. and L. J. Regterschot (1994) *De manager als bouwheer de rol van de bestuurder bij de realisatie van nieuwe huisvesting.* Den Haag, Ten Hagen en Stam.

Koppels, P., H. Remøy, et al. (2009) The added value of image: a hedonic office rent analysis. *ERES 2009,* Stockholm.

Koppels, P., H. Remøy, et al. (2009) Economic value of image, location and building. *Real Estate Research Quarterly,* 8(3): 6.

Koppels, P., H. Remøy, et al. (2007) Office users willingness to pay; a Delphi approach. *ERES 2007,* London.

Korteweg, P.J. (2002) *Veroudering van kantoorgebouwen probleem of uitdaging?* Utrecht, KNAG.

Latham, D. (2000) *Creative re-use of buildings. Vol. 2. Building types.* Shaftesbury, Donhead.

Le Corbusier (1986) *Towards a new architecture.* New York, Dover.

Lemmer, B. (1998) Successive surveys of an expert panel: research in decision making with health visitors. *Journal of Advanced Nursing,* 27: 538-545.

Leupen, B. (2006) *Frame and generic space.* Rotterdam, 010 Publishers.

Leupen, B., R. Heijne, et al. (2005) *Time-based architecture.* Rotterdam, Uitgeverij 010.

Lichtenberg, J. (2005) *Slimbouwen.* Eindhoven, Aenas.

Linstone, H.A. and M. Turoff (1975) T*he Delphi method; techniques and applications.* Reading, Addison-Wesley.

Louw, E. (1996) *Kantoorgebouw en vestigingsplaats een geografisch onderzoek naar de rol van huisvesting bij locatiebeslissingen van kantoorhoudende organisaties*. Delft, Delftse Universitaire Pers.

Lynch, K. (1960) *The image of the city*. Cambridge, Mass., MIT Press.

Maccreanor (2005) The sustainable city is the adaptable city. In: B. Leupen, R. Heijne and J. v. Zwol (Eds.). *Time-based architecture*. Rotterdam, 010 Publishers.

Mackay, R., P. De Jong and H. Remøy (2009) Transformation building costs; understanding building costs by modelling. *Changing Roles*, Wijk aan Zee, Delft University of Technology.

Mason, J. (1996) *Qualitative researching*. London, Sage.

McDonough, W. and M. Braungart (2002) *Cradle to cradle remaking the way we make things*. New York, North Point Press.

McKenna, H.P. (1994) The Delphi technique: a worthwhile approach for nursing? *Journal of Advanced Nursing,* 19: 1221-1225.

Miles, M.B. and A.M. Huberman (1994) *Qualitative data analysis an expanded sourcebook*. Thousand Oaks, Sage.

Minami, K. (2007) A study of the Urban Tissue Design for Reorganizing Urban Environments. *BSA 2007,* Tokyo, Tokyo Metropolitan University.

Mouzakis, F. and J. Henneberry (2008) Geographical externalities of local real estate markets: An empirical examination of UK data. *Journal of European Real Estate Research*.

Muller, R., H. Remøy and J. Soeter (2009) De Amsterdamse Transformatiemarkt - structurele leegstand 4% lager. *Real Estate Research Quarterly*, 8(1):3.

Neufert, E., P. Neufert, et al. (2006) *Architects' data Neufert*. London, Blackwell Science.

Norberg-Schulz, C. (1980) *Genius loci; towards a phenomenology of architecture*. London, Academy.

Nutt, B. (1988) *The strategic design of buildings*. Long Range Planning 21(4): 130-140.

Nutt, B., D. sears, et al. (1976) *theory and applications obsolescence in housing*. Westmead, saxon.

NVB (2006) Kantoorgebruikers in profiel. Voorburg, N.v.v.o.e. bouwondernemers.

obom. (2009) obom strategic studies. Retrieved 22.04.2009, from www.obom.nl.

OGA. (2006) Grondbezit en erfpachtcontracten. Retrieved 12.06.2009, from www.oga.nl.

OGA. (2008) Kantorenloods. Retrieved 06.06.2008, from www.oga.nl.

Ogawa, H., K. Kobayashi, et al. (2007) A study on the architectural conversion from office to residential facilities through three case studies in Tokyo. *BSA 2007*, Tokyo, Tokyo Metropolitan University.

Okoli, C. and S.D. Pawlowski (2004) The Delphi method as a research tool: an example, design considerations and applications. *Information & Management,* 42(1): 15-29.

Oudijk, C.P.A., H. Remøy, et al. (2007) Projectanalyses. In: T. Van der Voordt, R. Geraedts, H. Remøy and C. Oudijk (Eds.) *Transformatie van kantoorgebouwen thema's, actoren, instrumenten en projecten*. Rotterdam, Uitgeverij 010: 480 blz.

Pallasmaa, J., S. Holl, et al. (1994) *Questions of perception; phenomenology of architecture.* Tokyo, A and U.

Patton, M.Q. (2002) *Qualitative research and evaluation methods.* Thousand Oaks, Sage.

Pevsner, N. (1976) *A history of building types.* London, Thames and Hudson.

Post, J. (1998) xx building. Retrieved 23.02.2009, from www.xxarchitecten.nl.

Post, J. (2007) Verpoppen van de Plaspoelpolder. In: T. Van der Voordt, R. Geraedts, H. Remøy and C. Oudijk (Eds.) *Transformatie van kantoorgebouwen thema's, actoren, instrumenten en projecten.* Rotterdam, Uitgeverij 010: 480 blz.

Powell (2003) The Delphi technique: myths and realities. *Journal of Advanced Nursing,* 41(4): 376-382.

Property.nl. (2008) Stabiele markt in 2008 voor beleggingen in Nederlandse kantoren. Retrieved 24.01.2008, from www.propertynl.com.

Quigley, J.M. (1999) Real Estate Prices and Economic Cycles. *International Real Estate Review,* 2(1): 1-20.

Reid, N. (1988) The Delphi technique: its contribution to the evaluation of professional practice. *Professional Competence and Quality Assurance in the Caring Professions.* R. Ellis. London, Chapman & Hall.

Reimerink, L. (2008) Kantorenmarkt vraagt om sturing. *Building Business,* maart 2008: 68-69.

Remøy, H. (2007) De markt voor transformatie van kantoren tot woningen In: T. Van der Voordt, R. Geraedts, H. Remøy and C. Oudijk (Eds.) *Transformatie van kantoorgebouwen thema's, actoren, instrumenten en projecten.* Rotterdam, Uitgeverij 010: 480 blz.

Remøy, H. and H. de Jonge (2007) Transformation and typology; Vacancy, characteristics and conversion capacity. *BSA 2007,* Tokyo, Tokyo Metropolitan University.

Remøy, H., P. Koppels, et al. (2008) The Legacy of the Modern Movement: Appreciation of Office Locations in the Context of the Contemporary City. In: Vande Putte, H. (Ed.) *Corporations and Cities,* Brussels, Publikatieburo Bouwkunde.

Remøy, H., P. Koppels, et al. (2009) Keeping up Appearance. *Real Estate Research Quarterly,* 8(3): 6.

Remøy, H., P. Koppels, et al. (2009) Structural vacancy of office buildings; the influence of building and location. *ERES 2009,* Stockholm.

Remøy, H., P. Koppels, et al. (2007) Characteristics of vacant offices: A Delphi-approach. *ENHR Rotterdam 2007,* Rotterdam, TU Delft.

Remøy, H. and T. van der Voordt (2007) Conversion of office buildings; a cross-case analysis. *BSA 2007,* Tokyo, Tokyo Metropolitan University.

Remøy, H. and T. van der Voordt (2007) A new life - conversion of vacant office buildings into housing. *Facilities,* 25(3/4): 88-103.

Remøy, H. and T. van der Voordt (2009) Sustainability by adaptable and functionally neutral buildings. In: M. Verhoeven, M. Fremouw (Eds.). *SASBE '09; 3rd CIB International Conference on Smart and Sustainable Built Environments,* June 15-19, 2009, Delft, The Netherlands: 150 blz.

Reuser, B., E. van Dongen, et al. (2005) *What's in a box*. B. Reuser. Delft, Delft University of Technology.

Rietdijk, N. and NVB (2005) *Thermometer koopwoningen : najaar 2005*. Voorburg, NVB.

Rodenburg, C.A. (2005) *Measuring Benefits of Multifunctional Land Use; Stated Preferences Studies on the Amsterdam Zuidas*. Economic and Business Faculty. Amsterdam, Vrije Universiteit Amsterdam.

Rodenburg, C.A. (2006) Quantification of economic benefits of multifunctional land use–An empirical analysis among employees. *Journal of Housing and the Built Environment*, 21(1): 69-81.

Rodenburg, C.A. and P. Nijkamp (2004) Multifunctional land use in the city: a typological overview. *Built environment*, 30(4): 274-288.

Rossi, A. and P. Eisenman (1985) *The architecture of the city*. Cambridge, Mass., MIT Press.

Rowe, E. (1994) *Enhancing judgement and decision making: a critical and emperical investigation of the Delphi technique*. Bristol, University of Western England.

Rust, W.N.J., Management Studiecentrum, et al. (1997) *Vastgoed financieel theorie en toepassing van de financiële rekenkunde in de vastgoedpraktijk*. Delft, Delftse Universitaire Pers.

Salway, F. (1987) Building depreciation and property appraisal techniques. *Journal of Property Valuation and Investment*, 5.

Sandelowski, M. (2000) Combining qualitative and quantitative sampling, data collection, and analysis techniques in mixed-method studies. *Res Nurs Health*, 23(3): 246-55.

Sassen, S. (2002) *Global networks, linked cities*. New York, Routledge.

Schalekamp, M., H. Remøy and F. Hobma (2009) Transformatie van kantoorterreinen. *Real Estate Research Quarterly*, 1(4): 6.

Schiltz, S. (2006) *Valuation of vacant properties*. Amsterdam, Amsterdam School of Real Estate

Schmidt, R.C. (1997) Managing Delphi Surveys Using Nonparametric Statistical Techniques. *Decision Sciences*, 28(3): 763-774.

Schoonenberg, W. (2006) ABN-AMRO-gebouw van Duintjer in de Vijzelstraat op de monumentenlijst? *Binnenstad*, 218: 1.

Simon, H.A. (1996) *The sciences of the artificial*. Cambridge, Mass., MIT Press.

Smit, A J. (2007) Transformatie van verouderde bedrijventerreinen. In: T. Van der Voordt, R. Geraedts, H. Remøy and C. Oudijk (Eds.) *Transformatie van kantoorgebouwen thema's, actoren, instrumenten en projecten*. Rotterdam, Uitgeverij 010: 480 blz.

Soeter, J. and P. Koppels (2006) The unbalanced office market. *ERES*. 13th annual European Real Estate Society Conference, Weimar, Germany.

Spierings, T.G.M., R.P. van Amerongen, et al. (2004) *Jellema hogere bouwkunde. Dl. 3. Bouwtechniek, draagstructuur*. Utrecht, ThiemeMeulenhoff.

Sprakel, E. and B. Vink (2007) Transformatie vanuit beleggersperspectief. In: T. Van der Voordt, R. Geraedts, H. Remøy and C. Oudijk (Eds.) *Transformatie van kantoorgebouwen thema's, actoren, instrumenten en projecten*. Rotterdam, Uitgeverij 010: 480 blz.

Stadswonen (2008) Stadswonen. Retrieved 06.06.2008, from www.stadswonen.nl.

Stake, R.E. (1995) *The art of case study research.* Thousand Oaks, Sage.

Stevenson, S. (2007) Exploring the Intra-Metropolitan Dynamics of the London Office Market. *Journal of Real Estate Portfolio Management,* 13(2): 93.

Stichting REN (1992) Real Estate Norm (REN-norm). Nieuwegein, Stichting REN Nederland.

Ten Have, G.G.M. (1992, 2002) *Taxatieleer onroerende zaken.* Leiden, Stenfert Kroese.

Tiesdell, S., T. Oc, et al. (1996) *Revitalizing historic urban quarters.* Oxford, Architectural Press.

Tse, R.Y.C. and J.R. Webb (2003) Models of office market Dynamics. *Urban Studies,* 40(1): 71-89.

Van den Dobbelsteen, A. and S. de Wilde (2004) Space use optimisation and sustainability—environmental assessment of space use concepts. *Journal of Environmental Management,* 73(2): 81-89.

Van den Dobbelsteen, A.A.J.F. (2004) *The sustainable office an exploration of the potential for factor 20 environmental improvement of office accommodation* Online resource. TU Delft.

Van den Hoek, J., P. van Wesemael, et al. (2007) *Leegstaande kantoren als stedelijke opgave.* Amsterdam, Architekten CIE Van der Voordt, T., R.P. Geraedts, H. Remøy, C. Oudijk, Eds. (2007) *Transformatie van kantoorgebouwen thema's, actoren, instrumenten en projecten.* Rotterdam, Uitgeverij 010.

Van der Voordt, T., H.B.R. van Wegen, et al. (2005). *Architecture in use an introduction to the programming, design and evaluation of buildings.* Oxford, Architectural Press.

Van der Werf, F. (1993) *Open ontwerpen.* Rotterdam, Uitgeverij 010.

Van Dinteren, J.H.J. (1989) *Zakelijke diensten en middelgrote steden een vergelijkend onderzoek naar de vestigingsplaatskeuze en het functioneren van zakelijke dienstverleningsbedrijven in Noord-Brabant, Gelderland en Overijssel; een wetenschappelijke proeve op het gebied van de beleidswetenschappen.* Amsterdam, Koninklijk Nederlands Aardrijkskundig Genootschap. Van Meel, J. J. (2000) *The European office; office design and national context.* Rotterdam, 010 Publishers.

Van Kasteren, J. (2002) *Buildings that last: guidelines for strategic thinking.* Rotterdam, NAi Uitgevers. Van Randen, A. (1976) *Nodes and noodles.* TU Delft, Delft University Press: 24.

van Zeeland, H. (2007) Transformeren volgens het Bouwbesluit. In: T. Van der Voordt, R. Geraedts, H. Remøy and C. Oudijk (Eds.) *Transformatie van kantoorgebouwen thema's, actoren, instrumenten en projecten.* Rotterdam, Uitgeverij 010: 480 blz.

Veldhoen, E. (1998) *Kantoren bestaan niet meer / versie 2.0 een vitale organisatie in een digitale werkomgeving door Erik Veldhoen.* Rotterdam, Uitgeverij 010.

Venema, P. and Twijnstra Gudde (2004) *Het nationale kantorenmarktonderzoek 2004 resultaten en visies.* Amersfoort, Twijnstra Gudde.

Vijverberg, G. (2001) *Renovatie van kantoorgebouwen literatuurverkenning en enquête-onderzoek opdrachtgevers, ontwikkelaars en architecten*. Delft, DUP Science.

Vijverberg, G. (1995) *Huisvestingsbeleid basis voor bouwkundig onderhoud; kantoorgebouwen in eigendom*. Delft, Delftse Universitaire Pers.

VROM (2003) Bouwbesluit, VROM.

Walen, J.D. (1988) *Voor- en achterdeureffekten van kantoornieuwbouw; ruimtelijke effekten van verhuisketens in kantoorpanden in Den Haag als gevolg van nieuwbouw*. Amsterdam, Universiteit van Amsterdam.

WCED (1987) *Our common future*. Oxford, Oxford University Press.

Wheaton, W., Torto, R. and P. Evans (1997) The Cyclic Behaviour of the Greater London Office Market. *Journal of Real Estate Finance and Economics*, 15: 77-92.

Wheaton, W. (1999) Real Estate "Cyclus": Some Fundamentals. *Real Estate Economics*, 27(2): 209-230.

Whitford, F. (1984) *Bauhaus*. London, Thames and Hudson.

Worthington, J. (1998) *Reinventing the workplace*. Oxford, Architectural Press.

Yin, R.K. (1989) *Case study research; design and methods*. London, Sage.

Zijlstra, H. (2006) *Building construction in the Netherlands 1940 - 1970 Continuity + changeability = durability*. Delft, TU Delft.

Zijlstra, H. (2007) Bouwtechnologisch onderzoek: ontstaan, bestaan en ver(der) gaan van gebouwen. In: T. Van der Voordt, R. Geraedts, H. Remøy and C. Oudijk (Eds.) *Transformatie van kantoorgebouwen thema's, actoren, instrumenten en projecten*. Rotterdam, Uitgeverij 010: 480 blz.

Sources of images are incorporated in the image captions. Where no mention is made, the image is produced or owned by the author.

Appendix 1: Persons and companies that have contributed to the research

Initial interviews on real estate markets generally and the transformation market specifically, February 2006

1. Eddy Halter, CEO, DTZ Valuation Advisory Services
2. Alfred van't Hof, Real Estate Analyst, DTZ Valuation Advisory Services
3. Maarten Donkers, Head of Research, FGH
4. Vincent Gruis, Associate Professor Housing management, Delft University of Technology
5. Peter Boelhouwer, Scientific Director and Professor Housing Systems, OTB, University of Technology

Interviews on 14 ex-post case studies of transformation projects, August 2005-August 2006

6. Cor Mooy, CEO, Giesbers-Maasdijken Development
7. Ed Lensink, Wim Oosterwold, architects, Bureau voor Architektuur& Ruimtelijke ordening Martini BV
8. Marcia Mulder, Architect, Harmonische Architectuur
9. Marc van Rooij, Senior Real Estate Developer, BAM Vastgoed BV
10. Anke Colijn, Architect, Feekes & Colijn Architects
11. Erik den Breejen, CEO, ABB Development
12. Karina Benraad, Architect, Karina Benraad Architecten
13. Smeulder, Developer, DUWO
14. Harm van Papenrecht, Architect, Soizo Architecten
15. Hennie Schipperijn, Real Estate Developer, Van Hoogevest Development
16. Wim Stijger, Architect, Op Ten Noort Blijdenstein
17. Ton Raven, Real Estate Developer, BAM Vastgoed BV
18. Michiel van Rennes, Real Estate Developer, Rabo Vastgoed
19. Bert Klinkenberg, Project Manager, Stichting In
20. Ton Kandelaars, Architect, Ton Kandelaars Architecten
21. Frank de Garde, CEO, Van Straten Bouw en vastgoed
22. Paul Dahlmans, Project Manager, Vesteda
23. Germt Stuve, Owner, WEN Vastgoed
24. Jan Jacobs, Architect, A12 Architecten
25. Theo Oving, Owner, Architectenbureau Oving
26. De Jong, Owner, De Jong Bokstijn Architecten
27. Panel members, Delphi study on office organisations preferences for building and location characteristics when searching for accommodation, February – April 2007
28. Herman Vande Putte, Assistant Professor Real Estate Management, Delft University of Technology
29. Cor Brandsema, Office Pilot, the Municipality of Amsterdam
30. Cees Van der Spek, Corporate Accountmanager, OVG Property Development

31. Vincent Taapken, Commercial Manager, OVG Property Development
32. Ruben Langbroek, Researcher, KFN Research and Strategy
33. Aart Hordijk, Director ROZ Netherlands, Professor Real Estate, Nyenrode University
34. René Buck, CEO Buck Consultants International
35. Frits Tonnaer, Senior Asset Manager at Fortis Real Estate
36. Jacques Boeve, Real Estate Consultant and Owner, DTZ Zadelhoff vof
37. Bart VInk, Head of Research, DTZ Zadelhoff
38. Leo Hendriks, Senior Researcher, Rijksgebouwendienst
39. Juriaan Van Meel, Owner, ICOP Real Estate Consultants
40. Dennis Meulenhorst, Head of Research, Boer Hartog Hooft Real Estate Advisors
41. Barbara Westrik, Real Estate Agent, Boer Hartog Hooft Real Estate Advisors
42. Wim Pullen, Director, Centre for People and Buildings, TU Delft
43. Piet Korteweg, Assistant Professor, Economic Geography at Utrecht University
44. Jeroen Simons, Architect and Partner, Inbo Architects
45. Rob Mans, Managing Director, CBRE Real Estate Advisors
46. Erik Louw, Senior Researcher, TU Delft, OTB Research Institute

Interviews on market conditions, location and building characteristics that influence a buildings transformation potential, April 2008 – October 2008

47. Gerard Streng, CEO, BAM/Office Up
48. Hennie Schipperijn, developer, Van Hoogevest Development
49. Frank de Garde, CEO, Van Straten Real Estate
50. Cor Mooy, CEO, Panagro
51. Erik den Breejen, CEO, ABB
52. Aad Bouwhuis, region executive, Rabo Vastgoed
53. Cees Busscher, CEO, Dura Vermeer
54. Rudy Stroink, CEO, TCN
55. Arjen Mulder, developer, Vesteda
56. Emil van der Maten, developer, In de Stad Development
57. Ton Boon, developer, Maarsen Groep
58. Mariet Schoenmakers, executive, AM
59. Willem Gaymans, CEO, Kondor Wessels
60. Cees van Oort, developer, Fortis vastgoed
61. Karel Sant, executive, Bavon de Vor, developer, Ballast Nedam
62. Celine Lonis, developer, Heijmans
63. Scief Houben, CEO, Blauwhoed Eurowoningen
64. Kiewiet, developer, Smits bouwbedrijf
65. Henri van Dam, developer, Synchroon
66. Edwin van de Woestijne, managing director, Wereldhave
67. Richard Kaagman, CEO, NOVA development
68. Jean Baptiste Benraad, CEO, Stadswonen
69. Andre Smeulders, developer, Duwo

70. Frank Bijdendijk, CEO, Het Oosten
71. Sylvia Lisapaly, project manager, Vestia
72. Bob Stolker, CEO, Vereniging Zaanse Volkshuisvesting
73. Jaap Krommendijk, project manager, Wooncorporatie de Woonplaats
74. Thom Aussems, CEO, Trudo
75. Ton Jochems, CEO, SSH Utrecht
76. Rene Brouwer, head of real estate development, Far West
77. Wijnand Looise, head of area development, Anneke Haringa, developer, Delta Forte

Companies and contacting persons contributing to the Office Scan by providing data of office buildings in their portfolio

78. Altera: Cyril van den Hoogen, Kees van der Meulen, Jeroen de Koning
79. Annexum: Mariette Bosch, Peter Horsman
80. KFN (bought up by ING): Ruben Langbroek
81. MN Services: Philip Bisschop, Martijn Scholten
82. SPF: Roel Nienhuis, Henk Honing
83. Uni-Invest: Fleur Abas, Lucas Duijndam
84. Maarsen Groep: Gerard Kohsiek, Maarten Muijsson

Appendix 2: List of variables studied in the Office Scan

	Variables	Indicators	Data collection method
	ID		
I-1	Address		
		Street	Database
		House number	Database
		Postal code	Database
I-2	Building size		
		Building size (Lettable Floor Area)	Database/ Archive Drawings
		Building size (Gross Floor Area)	Database/ Archive Drawings
I-3	Building period		
		Year of construction	Database/ Archive Drawings
		Year of renovation	Database/ Archive Drawings
	Building		
B-1	Flexibility		
		Standard floor size	Archive Drawings
		Standard unit size, compartmenting possible	Archive Drawings
		Distance between columns (parallel to the longest facade)	Archive Drawings
		Distance between columns (parallel to the shortest facade)	Archive Drawings
		Façade grid	Archive Drawings
		Flexibility of interior walls	Archive Drawings
		Free floor height	Archive Drawings
		ICT infrastructure	Archive Drawings/on site
B-2	Recognisability of the organisation		
		Company name on the facade	On site
		Single tenant / multi tenant	On site
		Private Entrance	On site
B-3	Exterior appearance		
		Tall building, landmark, monumental, otherwise specific architecture	On site
		Visibility of entrance from streets	On site
		Façade material	On site
		Technical state of the facade	On site
B-4	Interior specifications		
		Spatiality of the entrance; Floor space/height	Archive Drawings
		Entrance size: >50m2	Archive Drawings
		Reception available in entrance space	On site
		Waiting area in entrance space	On site
		Quality of finishing	On site
		Technical state of interior	On site
B-5	Comfort		
		Type of heating/cooling installations	On site
		Operability of heating/cooling installations	On site
		Operability of windows	On site
		Operability of lights	On site
		Exterior sun shading	On site
		Daylight admittance as % of the facade	Archive Drawings

	Variables	Indicators	Data collection method
B-6	Facilities		
		Pantries (size, availability per m2 and unit)	Archive Drawings/On site
		Restaurant	On site
		Conference room and meeting spaces	Archive Drawings/On site
		Shops	Archive Drawings/On site
		Bank	Archive Drawings/On site
B-7	Routing		
		Central staircase	Archive Drawings
		Emergency staircases to be used daily	Archive Drawings
B-8	Parking		
		M2 office space assigned to 1 parking place	On site
		Type of parking facilities	On site
		Bike parking	On site
	Location		
L-1	Image		
		Housing within 500 metres (land use grids, 10 x 10m)	ARCviewmaps / CBS
		Employment in industry within 500 metres	ARCviewmaps / LISA
		Employment in distribution within 500 metres	ARCviewmaps / LISA
		Safety index (objective, police database)	Database
L-2	Access-ibility by public transport		
		Distance to nearest railway station and InterCity station	ARCviewmaps / National Road Database
		Distance to nearest tram, metro, bus stop	ARCviewmaps / National Road Database
L-3	Access-ibility by car		
		Travel time to highway, travel time to airport	ARCviewmaps / NAVTEQ
L-4	Facilities		
		Shops within 50 metres, shops within 500 metres	ARCviewmaps / Locatus
		Shops for daily necessities within 50 metres, shops for daily necessities within 500 metres	ARCviewmaps / Locatus
		Restaurants and cafés within 50 metres, restaurants and cafés within 500 metres	ARCviewmaps / Locatus
L-5	Clustering		
		M2 office space within 500 metres	ARCviewmaps / Bak
		Office employment within 500 metres	ARCviewmaps / LISA
L-6	Public space		
		Presence and type of street furniture (lampposts, garbage cans, benches)	On site
		Type of paving	On site
		Presence and type of green (trees, bushes, flowers, grass)	On site
		Street type (highway, main road, local street, dead end street)	On site
		Public squares land use measured in grids of 10 m x 10m in a 500 meter radius	ARCviewmaps / CBS
		Water land use measured in grids of 10 m x 10m in a 500 meter radius	ARCviewmaps / CBS
		Public park land use measured in grids of 10 m x 10m in a 500 meter radius	ARCviewmaps / CBS

Summary

Office building vacancy is becoming an increasingly visible part of the cityscape. Billboards shout "for rent" and office locations look abandoned even in the middle of the day. Still, new office buildings and locations are being developed, adding up to the built environment. As hardly any office buildings are demolished, adapted or transformed, the vacancy increases. Office buildings are developed though there is no demand for new office buildings. Or…is there? New office buildings seem to be preferred by office users, who leave existing buildings behind, buildings that do not attract new users but remain vacant and become redundant and obsolete. "Throwawayism" is threatening the built environment, representing the unsustainable attitude of all actors involved in the design, construction and use of commercial real estate. This book starts with an inquiry into the cause of long term vacancy, followed by a study of how to cope with vacancy by means of residential transformation. The book is concluded by recommendations for how to prevent or limit long term vacancy in future office developments. This research focuses on Amsterdam, the largest city of the Netherlands, with the largest office market and the highest vacancy rates. The problem of long term vacancy is international though, and cities like London, Chicago, New York, Toronto and Tokyo struggle with it.

Causes of structural vacancy

Structural vacancy is defined as vacancy of the same space for three years or longer. Of course; the cause of structural vacancy is that there are too much office space within a certain market, city or location. Within a geographically limited market, office users move from one building to another, leaving certain buildings vacant. If these buildings are not rented out again they become structurally vacant. Structural vacancy is a problem for the owners of the buildings as it causes value loss, and is also a societal problem as it causes income loss for the government, depreciation of properties and a downwards spiralling development of whole areas.

Studying the preferences of office users, a panel of experts on office user preferences was asked to define a set of building and location characteristics important to office users looking for new office space. Subsequently, the relationship between physical characteristics and structural vacancy of 200 office buildings in Amsterdam was studied. 106 buildings had some level of structural vacancy, showing which characteristics increase the risk of structural vacancy. While former studies found hard factors like accessibility, parking possibilities and flexibility of the building to be the most important success factors for office buildings, this study revealed the importance of soft factors like image and status, visual quality and spatiality. Interestingly, even new buildings were found to be obsolete if the visual and functional qualities are low!

Transformation

Building transformation is a well known phenomenon; inner city buildings now loose their function and adapt to new use. However, the scale on which office buildings loose their function is unprecedented. Transformation is a sustainable way of coping with structural vacancy, as the buildings lifespan is extended. Case studies of transformed buildings ex post were conducted, pointing out important opportunities and obstacles for transformations, concerning market, location and building factors. With this knowledge, the transformation potential of structurally vacant office buildings in Amsterdam was studied. The possibilities for transformation, focusing on building and location characteristics, were discussed with 30 public and private developing companies. The financial value of office buildings was found to be one of the biggest obstacles for transformations. This value is based on potential tenancy income; thus the valuation method should not be used for structurally vacant buildings. The location of office buildings was a second obstacle. A substantial part of structurally vacant office buildings are located on monofunctional office locations, unsuited for residential transformations unless the location is transformed into a mixed-use location. Office buildings' characteristics were found to have less effect on the transformation potential, though having a large effect on the transformation building costs.

Preventing future vacancy

The cause of structural vacancy, quantitatively and qualitatively, and the physical characteristics that increase the odds of structural vacancy were revealed. Based hereupon, recommendations are given for how to develop future office buildings and locations with less risk of structural vacancy. Several studies have shown successful examples of residential office transformations. But why then is transformation not taking place on a larger scale? Based on the study of residential transformation as a means of coping with structural vacancy, recommendations are given for how to develop office buildings in order to increase the residential transformation potential and hence reduce vacancy risk.

Target audience

Though the office market is quantitatively saturated, high quality office buildings are still demanded. To reduce vacancy risk and increase residential transformation potential, office buildings should be developed in mixed-use locations. Architectural quality – meaning lay-out of floor plans, spatiality of the entrance and quality of the facade – should be focused on! For a sustainable development, governments and private parties need to focus on redevelopment of central urban areas. To increase the buildings transformation potential as well as its functional life span for office use, building components should be removable or transformable. The buildings installations should not be integrated in the buildings structure.

As recommendations are given for how to create office buildings with a longer functional, technical and economic lifespan, the book is applicable to the practice of real estate developers and investors, public and private planners, municipalities and architects. As the research topic can be generalised, the book is also of interest to scholars and researchers internationally. The Research establishes a connection between the two worlds of architectural discourse and statistic research. Furthermore, this research is extensive in its description of building and location characteristics, combining qualitative and quantitative research methods and giving new insights in the importance of architecture for the preferences of office users.

Samenvatting

Leegstand van kantoorgebouwen wordt steeds zichtbaarder in het straatbeeld. Billboards schreeuwen "te huur" en kantoorlocaties liggen er verlaten bij zelfs midden op de dag. Toch worden nieuwe kantoorgebouwen en locaties ontwikkeld, en wordt de gebouwde omgeving vergroot. Omdat er bijna geen kantoorgebouwen worden gesloopt, aangepast of getransformeerd, neemt de leegstand toe. Kantoorgebouwen worden ontwikkeld terwijl er geen vraag is naar nieuwe kantoorgebouwen. Of... toch wel? Kantoorgebruikers verlaten bestaande gebouwen die geen nieuwe gebruikers aantrekken, maar die leeg komen te staan, verouderen en overbodig worden. De wegwerpmentaliteit bedreigt de gebouwde omgeving, en representeert de weinig duurzame houding van alle actoren die betrokken zijn bij het ontwerp, de bouw en het gebruik van commercieel vastgoed.

Dit boek begint met een studie naar de oorzaken van structurele leegstand, gevolgd door een studie naar transformatie om de leegstand te beperken. Het boek wordt afgesloten met aanbevelingen voor hoe structurele leegstand in toekomstige kantoorontwikkelingen kan worden voorkomen of beperkt. Dit boek focust op Amsterdam, in Nederland de grootste kantorenmarkt met de hoogste leegstand. Structurele leegstand is echter een internationaal probleem, en steden zoals Londen, Chicago, New York, Toronto en Tokyo kampen hiermee.

Oorzaken van structurele leegstand

Structurele leegstand wordt gedefinieerd als leegstand van dezelfde ruimte voor drie jaar of langer. Natuurlijk is de oorzaak van structurele leegstand simpelweg dat er te veel kantoorruimte is binnen een bepaalde markt, stad of locatie. Binnen een geografisch beperkte markt verhuizen kantoorgebruikers en komen bepaalde gebouwen leeg te staan. Indien deze gebouwen niet meer verhuurd worden, komen ze structureel leeg te staan. Structurele leegstand is een probleem voor de eigenaren van deze kantoorgebouwen omdat het waardeverlies veroorzaakt, en is ook een maatschappelijk probleem omdat het tot inkomensverlies voor de overheid leidt en tot verloedering van panden, waardoor uiteindelijk hele gebieden zich volgens een neerwaartse spiraal ontwikkelen.

De voorkeuren van kantoorgebruikers zijn bestudeerd door een expertpanel een reeks van gebouw- en locatiekenmerken te laten rangschikken op volgorde van belang voor kantoorgebruikers op zoek naar nieuwe kantoorruimte. Vervolgens werd de relatie tussen fysieke karakteristieken en structurele leegstand van 200 kantoren in Amsterdam bestudeerd. Hiervan vertoonden 106 gebouwen structurele leegstand en blijkt welke kenmerken het risico op structurele leegstand verhogen. Terwijl eerdere studies harde factoren onderkende, zoals bereikbaarheid met auto of openbaar vervoer, parkeermogelijkheden en flexibiliteit van gebouwen, bleek uit deze studie het belang van zachte factoren zoals imago en status, visuele kwaliteit en ruimtelijkheid. Een interessante bevinding is dat zelfs nieuwe gebouwen een hoog leegstandspercentage hebben als de visuele en functionele kwaliteit laag is!

Transformatie

Transformatie is een bekend verschijnsel; gebouwen in de binnenstad verliezen hun functie en worden aangepast voor nieuw gebruik. Maar de schaal waarop kantoorgebouwen hun functie verliezen is niet eerder vertoond. Transformatie is een duurzame manier van omgaan met structurele leegstand, omdat hiermee de levensduur van gebouwen wordt verlengd. Case studies van getransformeerde gebouwen werden ex-post uitgevoerd, en wijzen op de belangrijkste kansen en belemmeringen voor transformaties, met betrekking tot de markt, locatie en gebouwfactoren. Met de kennis uit de ex-post case studies werden de transformatiemogelijkheden van leegstaande kantoorgebouwen in Amsterdam onderzocht ex-ante. Vervolgens werden in interviews de mogelijkheden voor transformatie besproken met 30 ontwikkelaars en woningcorporaties.

De financiële waarde van kantoorgebouwen bleek één van de grootste obstakels te zijn voor transformatie. De waardebepaling is gebaseerd op potentiële huurinkomsten, dus zou deze taxatiemethode niet voor structureel leegstaande gebouwen gebruikt moeten worden. Kantoorlocaties werden gezien als een tweede obstakel. Een aanzienlijk deel van de structureel leegstaande kantoorgebouwen zijn gelegen op monofunctionele kantoorlocaties die ongeschikt zijn voor transformatie naar woningen, tenzij de locatie wordt getransformeerd naar een multifunctionele locatie. De kenmerken van kantoorgebouwen bleken minder invloed te hebben op de transformatiepotentie, terwijl deze veel invloed hebben op de transformatie bouwkosten.

Voorkomen van toekomstige leegstand

De fysieke kenmerken die van invloed zijn op het risico van structurele leegstand zijn geinventariseerd. Hierop gebaseerd worden aanbevelingen gegeven voor hoe kantoorgebouwen en locaties met een lagere risico op structurele leegstand ontwikkeld kunnen worden. Verschillende studies hebben succesvolle voorbeelden van transformatie van kantoren naar woningen laten zien. Maar waarom vindt transformatie niet plaats op een grotere schaal? Gebaseerd op de studie van getransformeerde gebouwen ex-post worden aanbevelingen gegeven voor hoe kantoorgebouwen ontwikkeld kunnen worden om de transformatiepotentie te verhogen en daarmee het risico op structurele leegstand verlagen!

Doelgroep

Hoewel de kantorenmarkt kwantitatief verzadigd is, zijn nieuwe hoogwaardige kantoorgebouwen nog steeds gewenst. Om het leegstandsrisico te verlagen en de mogelijkheden voor transformatie naar woningen te verhogen, moeten kantoorgebouwen in de toekomst worden ontwikkeld op multifunctionele locaties. Focus op architectonische kwaliteit - waaronder lay-out, ruimtelijkheid, uitstraling en gevelkwaliteit - is cruciaal. Voor een duurzame ontwikkeling moeten overheden en private partijen zich concentreren op de herontwikkeling van centrale stedelijke gebieden. Om de transformatiepotentie en de functionele levensduur voor het gebruik als kantoorgebouw te verhogen moeten gebouwonderdelen vervangbaar of aanpasbaar zijn. De gebouwinstallaties moeten niet worden geïntegreerd in de gebouwstructuur.

Omdat aanbevelingen worden gegeven voor hoe kantoorgebouwen met een langere functionele, technische en economische levensduur kunnen worden ontwikkeld, is dit boek van belang voor zowel projectontwikkelaars en investeerders, publieke en private planners, als gemeenten en architecten. Het boek is interessant voor wetenschappers en onderzoekers op internationaal niveau, omdat de problematiek die bestudeerd wordt algemeen is. Het onderzoek legt verbanden tussen de twee werelden van het architectonisch discours en statistisch onderzoek. Bovendien is deze studie uitgebreid in haar beschrijving van gebouw- en locatiekenmerken, waarbij kwantitatieve en kwalitatieve onderzoeksmethoden gecombineerd worden en nieuwe inzichten geven in het belang van architectuur voor de voorkeuren van kantoorgebruikers.

Samandrag

Tome kontorbygg blir ein stadig synlegare del av bybiletet. Reklameskilt roper "til leige" og kontorområde ligg forletne sjølv midt på dagen. Likevel vert nye kontorbygg og nye kontorområde utvikla, som utbreiing på eksisterande bymiljø. Fordi knapt nokon kontorbygg vert rivne, tilpassa ny bruk eller transformerte, aukar mengda ledige kontor. Kontorbygg vert bygde sjølv om det ikkje er behov for nybygg. Eller ... er det? Organisasjonar forlet eksisterande bygg som ikkje verkar tiltrekkjande på nye brukarar, men som vert ståande ledige i lang tid for så å bli utdaterte og overflødige. Bruk-og-kast mentaliteten trugar landskap og bymiljø og representerer dei lite bærekraftige haldningane til alle aktørar som er involverte i prosjektering, bygg og bruk av kommersielle eigedommar. Denne boka startar med å granske årsakene til langvarig ledige kontorbygg, etterfulgt av eit studie av korleis transformasjon til bustader kan løyse overskotsproblemet. Boka avsluttast med tilrådingar for korleis å unngå eller minske mengda langvarig ledige kontorutbyggingar. Dette studiet legg fokus på Amsterdam, den største byen i Nederland, med det største kontormarkedet og den høgste lediheitsprosenten i Nederland. Sjølv om denne avhandlinga fokuserer på Nederland og Amsterdam, er problemet med langsiktig ledige kontorareal internasjonalt, og byar som London, Chicago, New York, Toronto og Tokyo slit med liknande problem.

Årsaker til strukturell ledige kontor

Strukturell ledige kontor er areal som har stått tome i tre år eller lengre. Sjølvsagt kan vi seie at årsaken til strukturelt ledige kontor rett og slett er at det er for mykje kontorareal innanfor eit bestemt marked, ein by eller stad. Men innanfor eit geografisk avgrensa marked, flyttar kontorbrukarar frå eit bygg til eit anna, slik at enkelte bygg blir ståande tome og etterkvart blir strukturelt ledige. Ledige kontor er eit problem for eigarane ettersom det fører til verditap, og det er også eit samfunnsmessig problem fordi det fører til inntekttap for kommunene i form av skatt, økonomisk svakare eigedommar og utvikling av heile områder i form av ein nedadgåande spiral. For å kunne studere preferansane til kontorbrukarar, vart eit panel av ekspertar på kontorbruk bedt om å definere eit sett av bygg og område eigenskap som er viktige for kontorbrukarar på jakt etter nye kontorlokaler. Deretter vart 200 kontorbygg i Amsterdam studert, der 106 i større eller mindre grad står strukturelt ledige. Studiet viser kva slag bygg og områdeeigenskapar som påvirkar preferansane til kontorbrukarar, og kva slag eigenskapar som aukar risikoen for at kontorareal vert ståande strukturelt ledige. Statusen til bygg og område og den visuelle kvaliteten til bygga vart funne å ha stor innflytelse på kontorbrukarar. Mens tidlegare studier har funne at harde faktorar som tilgang, parkeringsmulegheiter og fleksibilitet er dei viktigaste suksessfaktorene for kontorbygg, viste dette studiet betydninga av mjuke faktorar som image og status, visuell kvalitet og romkjensle. Interessant var det også at sjølv nye bygg vart funne å vere utdaterte dersom den visuelle og funksjonelle kvaliteten er lav!

Transformasjon

Transformasjon er eit velkjent fenomen; bygg i bysentra mister sin funksjon og tilpassast ny bruk. Men kontorbygg mistar no sin funksjon i eit raskt tempo.

Transformasjon er ein bærekraftig måte å takle strukturelt ledige kontorbygg på, ettersom livsløpet til bygga forlengast. Case-studier av transformerte bygg blei gjennomført ex-post, og peiker på viktige mulegheiter og hinder for transformasjon med tanke på marked, område og byggfaktorar. Basert på desse resultata vart transformasjonspotensialet til ledige kontor i Amsterdam studerte. Mulegheitene for transformasjon, med fokus på område og byggfaktorar, vart diskuterte med 30 offentlige og private eigendomsutviklarar. Den finansielle verdien av kontorbygg vart funnen å vere eit av dei største hindra for transformasjonar. Den finansielle verdien er basert på potensielle leigeinntekter, og skulle dermed ikkje vore brukt for strukturelt ledige bygg. Eit anna hinder er staden der kontorbygga står. Ein vesentleg del av strukturelt ledige kontorbygg ligg i monofunksjonelle kontorområde som er uskikka for transformasjonar, med mindre området også transformerast og fleire funksjonar leggast til. Byggfaktorar vart funne å ha mindre innverknad på transformasjonpotensialet enn områdefaktorar, men har likevel stor innverknad på byggekostnadane til transformasjonar.

Hindre tome kontor i framtida

Årsakene til strukturelt ledige kontor, kvantitativt og kvalitativt, samt fysiske eigenskap som påvirkar risikoen for at kontorbygg vert ståande ledige vart funne. Basert på dette er det gitt tilrådingar for korleis denne risikoen kan hindrast eller kontrollerast i utviklinga av framtidige kontorbygg og områder. Fleire studie har vist vellykka eksempel på transformasjon frå kontor til bustader. Men kvifor foregår da ikkje slike transformasjonar i større grad? Basert på studia av transformasjon til bustader som ein måte å hanskast med strukturelt ledige kontorbygg på er det gitt tilrådingar for utvikling av kontorbygg med auka transformasjonspotensiale og med redusert risiko for at kontor vert ståande strukturelt tome.

Målgruppe

Sjølv om kontormarkedet er kvantitativt metta, er kontorbygg med høg kvalitet fortsatt etterspurte. For å redusere risikoen for ledige kontorareal, bør kontorbygg utviklast i multifunksjonelle område. Arkitektonisk kvalitet - som planløysingar, romkjensle, utstråling og fasadekvalitet - må fokuserast på! For å forbetre potensialet for transformasjon til bustader, bør kontorbygg utviklast i multifunksjonelle område, og myndigheiter og private selskap må fokusere på utbygging i sentrale byområde for å oppnå ei bærekraftig utvikling. For å auke transformasjonspotensialet og den funksjonelle levetida til kontorbygg, må bygnadsdelar kunne endrast eller demonterast. Installasjonar bør ikkje vere del av bygnadskonstruksjonen.

Ettersom denne boka gir tilrådingar på korleis kontorbygg med lengre funksjonell, teknisk og økonomisk levetid kan utviklast, er boka aktuell for eigendomsutviklarar og investorar, offentlege og private planleggarar, kommuner og arkitektar. Boka kan også vere av interesse i forsking, ettersom problemet med strukturelt ledige kontorbygg er eit verdsomspennande fenomen. Studiet vil etablere eit samband mellom arkitektonisk diskurs og forsking som er basert på statistikk. Vidare er dette studiet omfattande i framstillinga av bygg og områdeeigenskapar, og kvalitative og kvantitative forskingsmetoder vert kombinerte for å gi ny innsikt i innverknaden av arkitektur på preferansane til kontorbrukarar.

Acknowledgements

…And then the only thing left to do is to thank all the people who contributed to this book. For a long time, I thought it unnecessary, since I wrote it and not them. However, at the end of writing this book it occurred to me that though writing a PhD thesis is a kind of lonely process, the process would not have been successful without the contributions of many. Therefore, I am really thankful to everyone who contributed to this research and this book!

Before even starting a research like this, some people already did a great job writing a research proposal and funding the research. I am very grateful to Hans de Jonge, who took the risk of hiring an architect to do this research, and whose visionary ideas and critical comments have helped me to stay focussed, and to Theo van der Voordt who was my daily supervisor and who sustained my efforts of becoming a researcher, and who has read and commented all my texts several times and never stopped trying to make me write shorter sentences.

The research for this book was started by writing another book; "Transformation of Office Buildings", a book in Dutch with the original title "Transformatie van kantoorgebouwen", together with Theo van der Voordt (again), Rob Geraedts and Collin Oudijk. When the book was published in January 2007, I had valuable case material for further research, interesting contacts who I was happy to confer with several times. A special thank to all of you!

Also, I would like to thank all the people who contributed professionally to my work; all the people I interviewed and the companies who were willing to share their data with me. Their names are listed in appendix 1. Next to answering all my questions with patience, they also revealed to me the worlds of real estate developers, investors, brokers, advisors and housing associations.

Next, I would like to thank all the MSc students who studied different aspects of transformation related to my thesis, and thereby helped me focus my research. I would especially like to thank Roderick Mackay and Marianne Schalekamp, and of course Wiechert Schenk and Ralph Muller who played two roles in my research; next to writing their own MSc theses on transformation they also worked as student assistants for this project.

I also owe my thanks to my colleagues at the Faculty of Architecture and at Real Estate & Housing for discussing, being critical and for being so inspiring through all their different backgrounds, research interests and personal interests. Thanks to John and Peter for important comments, thanks to Clarine for invaluable help with statistics, and thanks the most to Philip Koppels, with whom I shared data, database, and chemical candies, and who shared with me his knowledge of regressions and finance.

Marjolein, thanks for great help with the lay-out of this book!

And finally, to Jelle; Thanks for supporting me in my decision of quitting a good job in architecture and starting this research, for sustaining me through the whole process of research and writing and for actually reading my thesis. Also a special thanks for being a workaholic – I never have to apologise for late hours.

Curriculum Vitae

Hilde Remøy graduated as an architect from the Norwegian University of Science and Technology in 1997, after studying architecture for six years at the same university and at the Politecnico di Milano. During her study, she took part in several international research seminars and workshops.

From 1998 to 2005 she worked as an architect at different Dutch architecture offices, of which 4 years at Hoogstad Architecten. As an architect, she worked on different kinds of projects, from master planning to transformations and interior designs. During the same period, she incidentally lectured at international seminars for architecture students.

In 2005 she joined the department of Real Estate and Housing at the Faculty of Architecture of the Delft University of Technology to start a PhD research. She currently holds a position within the same department as Assistant Professor of Real Estate Management. While working on her PhD Research she wrote several conference papers, journal articles and book parts. She also contributed to the book "Transformatie van kantoorgebouwen" (Transformation of Office Buildings) published by 010 Publishers in 2007.